BEST BOOK OF
TRUE AVIATION STORIES

BEST BOOK OF
TRUE AVIATION
STORIES

Edited by

ROBERT A. ROSENBAUM

Illustrated by

KIYOAKI KOMODA

Doubleday and Company, Inc., Garden City, New York

For Diane and Ruth
whose father flew with the 13th Air Force

Grateful acknowledgment is made for the use of the following copyrighted material:

"Courier" from *Stranger to the Ground* by Richard Bach. Copyright © 1963 by Richard Bach. Reprinted by permission of Harper & Row, Publishers.

"To the South Pole" from *Come North with Me: An Autobiography* by Bernt Balchen. Copyright © 1958 by E. P. Dutton & Co., Inc. Reprinted by permission of the publisher.

"Skyrocket" from *The Lonely Sky* by William Bridgeman. Copyright 1955 by Holt, Rinehart and Winston, Inc. Reprinted by permission of the publisher.

"Escape" from *Beyond Horizons* by Lincoln Ellsworth. Copyright 1937, 1938 by Doubleday & Company, Inc. Reprinted by permission of the publisher.

"The Search" from *Fate is the Hunter* by Ernest K. Gann. Copyright © 1961 by Ernest K. Gann. Reprinted by permission of Simon & Schuster, Inc.

"The Flight of Friendship 7" by John H. Glenn, Jr., from *We Seven* by the Astronauts. Copyright © 1962 by Simon & Schuster, Inc. Reprinted by permission of the publisher.

"Thunderbolt" from *Thunderbolt!* by Robert S. Johnson with Martin Caidin. Copyright © 1958 by Martin Caidin and Robert S. Johnson. Reprinted by permission of Holt, Rinehart and Winston, Inc.

"Racer" from *Pilot* by Tony Levier as told to John Guenther. Copyright 1954 by Anthony W. LeVier and John L. Guenther. Reprinted by permission of Harper & Row, Publishers.

"Take Off" from *The Spirit of St. Louis* by Charles Lindbergh. Copyright 1953 by Charles Scribner's Sons. Reprinted by permission of the publisher.

"Two Weeks in the Air" from *The Flying Years* by Lou Reichers. Copyright © 1956 by Lou Reichers. Reprinted by permission of Holt, Rinehart and Winston, Inc.

"Down in Flames" from *Fighting the Flying Circus* by Captain Eddie V. Rickenbacker, edited and with a foreword by Arch Whitehouse. Copyright © 1965 by Doubleday & Company, Inc. Copyright 1919 by David Edward Rickenbacker and William Frost Rickenbacker. Reprinted by permission of Doubleday & Company, Inc.

"Pacific Air Lift" from *Under My Wings* by Basil L. Rowe. Copyright © 1956 by Basil L. Rowe. Reprinted by permission of The Bobbs-Merrill Company, Inc.

"Flying Tiger" from *Boring a Hole in the Sky* by Robert Lee Scott, Jr. Copyright © 1961 by Robert Lee Scott, Jr. Reprinted by permission of Random House, Inc.

"Flying the Mail" from *By the Seat of My Pants* by Dean C. Smith. Copyright © 1961 by Dean C. Smith. Reprinted by permission of Atlantic-Little, Brown and Co.

"The Elements" from *Wind, Sand and Stars* by Antoine de Saint Exupéry, translated by Lewis Galantière. Copyright 1939 by Antoine de Saint Exupéry; renewed 1967 by Lewis Galantière. Reprinted by permission of Harcourt, Brace & World, Inc.

"First Mission" from *Serenade to the Big Bird* by Bert Stiles. Copyright 1947 by Mrs. Bert W. Stiles. First published in the United States of America in 1952. Reprinted by permission of W. W. Norton & Company, Inc.

"Jubilee Mail" from *The Sky Beyond* by Sir Gordon Taylor. Reprinted by permission of Houghton Mifflin Company.

Library of Congress Catalog Card Number—67-15372
Copyright © 1967 by Robert A. Rosenbaum

All rights reserved, including the right to reproduce this
book or any portion thereof, in any form, except
for the inclusion of brief quotations in a review.

Printed in the United States of America

First Edition

Introduction

Some experiences are peculiarly difficult for the initiated to communicate to the uninitiated. He may describe the events of such an experience in correct sequence, he may describe his own feelings insofar as words permit—perhaps he will seek analogies or be moved to poetry or song—but the essence of the experience must remain forever incommunicable, to be shared fully only with other initiates.

Thus it is with flying. For a million years, all human experience was confined to the surface of the earth and its waters. Even today, relatively few people know at first hand the special thrill of flight. The passenger in an airliner may begin to understand part of what the pilot feels as he looks down on the familiar earth from the startling perspective of the skies, as he passes rapidly and effortlessly above natural barriers—rivers, oceans, mountains, deserts—over which other men once toiled for weeks or months. But the passenger's experience is always of a different order from the pilot's. Not until one has held the controls of a plane in his hands, has made the plane respond to his will, has felt himself and his machine become one, does he know the experience of flight.

The stories gathered in this volume were written by flyers, each of whom, in his own way, has tried to communicate to others who are not flyers what the experience of flight was like for him, whether in a wood-and-linen plane of forty years ago, a multi-engined commercial airliner, a jet fighter, an experimental rocket plane, or a spacecraft. Until the reader himself has "slipped the surly bonds of earth," he will not come closer to flight than he will in the company of these adventurers of the air.

R.A.R.

The Best Book Series

Contents

FROM

Fighting
the Flying Circus

EDWARD V. RICKENBACKER

While mass armies grappled on the Western Front during World War I, in the skies above them small numbers of daredevil pilots dueled in individual combat like knights of old. Their high spirits and gallantry, the fame of their doughty ships—Nieuports and Spads, Camels and Fokkers—have created a highly romanticized legend of the first air war. The leading American ace in World War I was Captain Eddie Rickenbacker. A famous racing driver, Rickenbacker enlisted in the Army shortly after the United States entered the war and was soon sent overseas as chauffeur to General Pershing. In August 1917, he succeeded in transferring to the Air Service. Trained in France, in 1918 he joined and later commanded the 94th Aero Pursuit ("Hat-in-the-Ring") Squadron, personally downing twenty-six German planes before the war ended. Here is one episode of air combat in World War I as recalled by Captain Rickenbacker.

Down in Flames

THE 94th Squadron had been at the front about one month when there arrived Lieutenant Kurtz, one of my companions of the training school days. On completion of his course at the flying school Kurtz had been selected to make a special study of aerial gunnery, in order to become an instructor to the thousands of young men who were now being drafted into Uncle Sam's aerial fleet. For this purpose he had been sent to England, and on returning to France Kurtz had received orders to report to the 94th Squadron at the front in order to secure actual war experience and to make trips over the enemy's lines.

After the newcomer had asked thousands of questions and received answers to them to the best of our ability, he suggested that he should proceed to the more advanced stage of an actual combat with the enemy. As I was second in command of the squadron, being Flight Commander of the 1st Flight at that time, it was my duty to arrange for him to accompany a patrol into enemy territory. No matter how much natural ability a man may possess, or how carefully he has been trained, his first experiences over the enemy lines, his first contact with enemy machines are rather trying to him. A moment's forgetfulness, a trifling foolhardiness, a slight miscalculation, and even a man who has been carefully and expensively trained and who possesses all the characteristics of a successful pilot, may fall before the skill of a more experienced enemy flier.

For this reason I always made it a practice to accompany new pilots on their first trip over the enemy's lines, and by my advice and by actual protection when aloft, assist them over that delicate period between the theory of the school and the hard practice of battle.

We were still flying the well-known Baby Nieuport single-seater "chasse" or fighting machine, equipped with a Gnome Monosoupape motor. It was, we believed, the best machine of its kind in service, although it had some faults. Having just arrived from the rear, Kurtz was not acquainted with the peculiarities of this machine. I therefore arranged for him to make a few short flights from our field and to practice frequent landings, so that if he ever should have sudden engine trouble he would be able to come down on any ground he found available. After a few days of this practice, he felt capable of handling the machine under all circumstances and ready for that greatest adventure of the young pilot: that first trip over enemy's lines.

We agreed that Lieutenant Kurtz should accompany Lieutenant Chambers and myself on what is familiarly known as a voluntary patrol. Chambers and I were in the habit of undertaking these extra patrols when the regular day's work was over, provided we were still, to use an aviator's slang expression, "Mad at the Boche." It was a beautiful summer morning, bright, clear and still—just such a morning as the Hun observation pilots would select to come over our lines and take photographs.

Our plan of action was carefully explained to our new comrade. We were to fly in V formation; I was to lead, Chambers on my left, and Kurtz one hundred meters behind and above us. He was not to engage in a combat, should we meet with any Boche airmen, unless the odds were with us. I have always made it a point to avoid a fight unless I can maneuver to get the best advantage. He was at all times to maintain his position behind and above us, playing the rôle of a spectator. He was instructed to try out his machine gun occasionally with a few short bursts if he had his plane pointing toward Germany. Finally, if we became scattered and he was unable to find us, he was to remember that the sun rose in the east, and, keeping it on his left, was to fly south until he felt certain that he was over French territory before making a landing.

It was decided that we should start promptly at eight o'clock, meet over the field at fifteen hundred feet, get our full altitude between Nancy and Toul, and cross over the lines at fifteen thousand feet. Before starting I noticed that Lieutenant Kurtz appeared rather nervous, but this was not a matter for concern under the circumstances. Little did I understand the reason for this nervousness then, or suspect in what a tragic manner it would later be revealed to me.

Lieutenant Kurtz's machine was climbing badly, so we got up to an altitude of 14,500 feet rather slowly; at that height I decided to pass from the comparative safety of our own side of the line to the hazard and adventure of the German positions. Mr. Hun was abroad, for I caught sight of the shimmer of what I believed to be a photo plane six miles inside our lines and very high up—probably nineteen thousand feet. As this enemy was certainly beyond our reach, I decided to keep the nose of my machine headed toward Germany and to continue to gain altitude as steadily as possible, at the same time keeping an eye on this nearby enemy, for there was just a chance that we might be able to reach his altitude and head him off before his work was done.

Suddenly, little fleecy white puffs appeared in the clear atmosphere ahead and above us. This antiaircraft activity of ours meant that more Huns were abroad in our vicinity. A few minutes more and we had spotted them; three powerful single-seaters of the Albatros type, fifteen hundred feet above us, and about half a mile ahead. As a signal to the others I wigwagged my wings, which is the aviator's way of saying, "Look out, and keep your eye on the leader." I had time to look back and see that Lieutenant Kurtz was well in the rear, and a little higher than the enemy then appeared to be. There was then no reason to fear for him. It was not necessary to give any thought to an experienced fighter like Lieutenant Chambers. I had been out enough with Reed to know that he was the equal to any two Huns. Doubtless Reed had seen the Boches before I had, for he was keeping close by me, probably wondering what my plan was going to be.

Keeping a close watch on our opponents, I rapidly analyzed the situation. The enemy had the advantage in height; they were three, probably all experienced men, while we were two fighters and one novice, who was seeing a German plane for the first time in his life. But the enemy pilots were inside our lines. Down below, several hundreds of men in the trenches were watching what to them was to be an equal fight—three Americans against three Germans. With their field glasses the French officers had picked out the black German crosses, and noted the red, blue, and white rings of the U.S. machines. Doubtless at that very moment they were discussing the outcome of the impending fight. They had the right to expect a fight, since we were three to three. So a fight it should be.

In the minds of the Germans there appeared to be no element of doubt or hesitation. Having the advantage of height, they suddenly, all three, swooped down on us; first one, then the second and third dived down and sprayed us with bullets from their machine guns. I had time to notice that Lieutenant Cham-

bers banked up on a wingtip and dived down; I did a half *vrille*, and in less time than it takes to tell, we were both out of range. The Germans in their diving attack had not only failed to get any of us, but had also lost their advantage of height. The tables were turned, or at any rate the conditions were equal, and retreat was evidently the uppermost thought in the minds of the Huns.

We gave chase, and in a few minutes I had succeeded in separating one of the planes from the formation. It was then either his life or mine! Perhaps I should get in the fatal shot; or maybe luck would be on his side; in either case, I was determined that it should be a fight to the death. Occupied as I was with my own enemy, I did have time to notice that Lieutenant Kurtz was doing well. He and Lieutenant Chambers were in full cry after the two remaining Albatros planes; the whole show was proceeding in the direction of Saint-Mihiel.

Mine was a running fight until we arrived over Thiaucourt, the little city about six miles inside the German lines. Here my enemy decided that conditions were in his favor, for he swung around and headed straight for me. But I was satisfied to accept the challenge, for I was one hundred yards behind and about two hundred yards above my opponent, and this gave me a not to be despised advantage. Nearer and nearer he came, heading toward me in a climbing turn, and working both his machine guns furiously. It is a sensation which almost defies description: there we were, only a few yards apart, sparring around one another like two prize fighters in a celestial ring. His incendiary explosive bullets were cracking all around me, and any one of them, if it touched a vital spot, was capable of putting an end to the fight. But my feelings were not personal; indeed, in those few critical moments which constitute the turning point of a fight the aviator usually has all thoughts of self driven away. With a quick half-turn of a *vrille* I secured a position on the tail of my enemy. I was then in such a position that he was unable to turn his gun on me. It was my chance, a chance which probably would be lost in the next fraction of a second. But I had no intention of losing it. With a pull on both triggers, a hail of bullets swept toward the German plane.

Down he swooped. Apparently he was out of control. Would he crash, or would he be able after that giddy dive to pull out and make a safe landing? That I could not tell, for while the spinning nose dive of an enemy always looks like certain destruction, it is often, in the hands of an artful pilot, the only highway to safety. Had I been over our own lines, I might have followed him down, and made certain of his crash. If I saw that he had regained control I could then immediately renew the fight at a lower altitude.

But I was well inside enemy territory and only ten thousand feet above ground. It was quite possible that while I had been occupied in this fight other enemy planes had gathered overhead and were preparing to wreak vengeance. Personal safety and the elementary rules of aerial fighting require the pilot in such circumstances to "regain altitude, or get back to the lines as soon as possible."

Thus I had to leave the issue of my fight in doubt. I had a faint hope that some other observer might be able to confirm the enemy's crash, and so allow me to place one more Hun to my credit. A few minutes later I realized that my recent instinctive fears were only too true. High above, but fortunately a considerable distance away from me, approached two German planes, which I rapidly concluded were the two machines which had succeeded in escaping from Kurtz and Chambers and were now determined to punish me when they discovered me so remotely isolated from my formation.

My only hope of safety lay in speed. Often on the race track, with wide open throttle, every nerve taut, every pent-up ounce of energy concentrated in my arms, have I wished that I could infuse just a little more power into my engine, could give just a little more speed to my car, in order to draw away from the man whose car was creeping up to and overhauling mine inch by inch.

But this case was even more crucial. Speed now meant safety, speed here meant life. My engine was throttled wide open, the nose of my machine was turned down, and I raced as I had never raced before, for the prize was life itself. But do what I could, it was impossible to shake off one of my opponents. Now I was directly over the lines; a few minutes more and I should be in our own territory and in a position either to land or get away from my persistent rival. However, the advantage the other fellow had in height was too much for me, and I realized that it was best for me to turn around and fight. In a flash I had kicked my tail around and was heading toward my opponent. He swooped down, reserving his fire, while I kept my fingers on the triggers of my guns. I had him in range, but I hesitated; the thought had flashed through my brain that perhaps in three seconds more I should be able to shoot with more deadly effect.

Now I had my sights on him; now was the time to release both guns. At that very moment his machine banked up on one wingtip, and there under the lower wing I saw the concentric red, blue, and white wings of the United States Air Service. The supposed Hun was friend Chambers, who was returning from chasing the enemy, and the second plane was that of Lieutenant Kurtz back from his first aerial scrap. God only knows why I held my fire for that brief fraction of a second. In talking it over later, Chambers said, "When I saw Rick swing round in that wild fashion I realized that he was still 'mad at the Boche,' and thought the time had come to let him see my colors."

It is not often that a man rises to the degree of joy I felt as we headed for home, the fight over, and all three safe. I had every reason to believe my German was down, possibly Chambers had got another, and Kurtz for his first time over had deported himself wonderfully.

I searched around for the pilot Kurtz, whom I regarded as being in my care, but to my surprise was unable to find him. I cruised around for a few minutes, searching in every direction, but not one plane could I see in the sky. I argued to myself that he must have gone home, and in consequence I turned my machine toward our aerodrome, hoping to pick him up at any moment. Just as I got sight of our landing ground my anxiety was relieved, for there, ahead of and below us was Lieutenant Kurtz making rings above our field, exactly as I had advised him to do.

Lieutenant Kurtz was evidently on his last turn over an adjoining field prior to landing when to my unspeakable horror I saw his Nieuport drop into a tail spin and crash straight to earth, after which bursts of angry flame shot up all around him. What could possibly have happened?

If help could be got to him without a moment's delay he might be pulled out of that wreckage before the flames consumed him. But I could not get to him, for the place where his machine had crashed was among barbed-wire entanglements and trench works so thick that a safe landing was impossible. Below was a road, only fifty yards from the burning machine, and on the road was a French *camion*. I speeded down, shut off my engine, and by signs and voice urged the driver to go to the rescue. The man stood still and watched. I realized later that he understood it was a hopeless task, for all the ammunition in the wrecked plane was exploding, and for any man to approach meant almost certain death.

Unable to land close by, I sped on to our own field, jumped out of my plane almost before it had stopped rolling; vaulted into the saddle of a motorcycle and raced toward the scene of the disaster with a vague wild hope that I might yet be able to do some good. Could I live for a million years I should not forget that awful sight of the charred remains of the man who had been my companion in the schools, and who only one brief hour before had set out with me full of life and hope.

A few hours later the mystery of that crash was revealed. As has already been mentioned, I had noticed before starting that Lieutenant Kurtz appeared nervous, but had not given the matter any great consideration. The explanation was given by a brother officer who had come with Lieutenant Kurtz to the squadron. Before starting on his last flight, Lieutenant Kurtz had confided to him that he was subject to fainting spells when exposed to high altitudes, and the only thing he was afraid of was that he might be seized with such a fit while in the air. Alas, his fear had been only too well founded. But what a pity it was he had not confided this fear to me, his Flight Commander!

The next morning a simple funeral procession wound its way down the leafy lanes, the while shells passed overhead with an incongruous whine. Awaiting me at the camp on my return from this sad ceremony was an official notice from the French commander. It stated, briefly, that an infantry officer, on outpost duty in No Man's Land, had observed that the German I had fought with had crashed to the ground a total wreck. I had got my Boche; but I had lost a friend, and he had perished in the manner most dreaded of all aviators, for he had gone down in flames.

FROM

By the Seat
of My Pants

DEAN C. SMITH

---

*After World War I, former army pilot Dean Smith tried every-
thing to keep flying—barnstorming, stunt flying, teaching. Nothing worked. In desperation, he turned in 1920 to a "last resort"
job—flying the mail. In this selection he recalls those early days
in the hazardous, haphazard "Pony Express of air transporta-
tion."*

Flying the Mail

BACK at the American Flying Club I found members still talking of the future and living in the past. For my part, I knew I
had to get an eating job but quick.

I asked around about a flying job, any flying job at all. If you
were really desperate, I learned, there were two "last resort"
jobs. You could get on as test pilot for Doctor Christmas, flying
the Christmas Bullet. Doctor Christmas had had three test pilots, his Bullets had made three flights, and the boys had chipped
in for three wreaths. But Doctor Christmas paid a hundred a
week—not bad while it lasted. Or you could join the Air Mail.

What was so dangerous anyway, I demanded, about flying the
mail? True, the Air Mail was all cross-country flying, much of it
over hilly, rough terrain. True, too, the planes, mostly DH-4's
and a few Curtiss R's, all war surplus, had to go in and out of

small and unimproved fields instead of military airdromes. Worse, there were only a few mechanics who knew a spark plug from an aileron, and it was about even money that the pilot would have an engine failure on any given flight. But worst of all there was the attitude of the Post Office Department. A pilot had to try to get through, regardless of the consequences; he couldn't cancel without giving it a try. Three or four of their pilots, it seemed, had learned to fly some pretty bad weather; and if those pilots could get through, the P.O. brass figured that the others should do the same. This was not a callous attitude on the part of the Department. It was necessary if effective flying carriers were to be developed, but it did make for short-lived air mail pilots.

I turned to Pop Anglin, who had led the mail pilots' strike a few months back, when they had rebelled against orders to take off regardless of weather. Although the pilots had won the strike, Pop shook his head solemnly. But he gave me the telephone number of D. B. Colyer, manager of the Post Office Air Mail Service, which had its headquarters at College Park, outside Washington.

Colyer seemed delighted at the prospect of hiring a pilot. He asked if I could fly a De Havilland. I said I'd never had any trouble with the plane. That was true enough, since I had never flown one. He told me to hustle down and he would pay the fare.

Even though everyone considered the Air Mail the next thing to suicide, you could at least be comfortable while life lasted. A mail pilot started at $2400 a year; he would get a $200 raise after he logged each fifty hours, until he was making $3600. If assigned to multi-engined planes like the Martin Bomber, he would get still another $100 a month. This added up to good money. This was my rationalization. Besides, what choice did I have?

College Park seemed a most unpretentious show to be the headquarters of the Air Mail Service. There were three or four shacklike wooden hangars, a hut for an office, and an exceedingly small, badly rolling, sod field. I was yet to learn that this was a sumptuous airdrome as compared with the typical Air Mail field.

I located D. B. Colyer. As soon as the southbound got in, he told me, the pilot would check me out in a Jenny. If he gave me an O.K., they would put me in a DH, and see what I could do. And if I then got down in one piece, I would be in business. A mechanic showed me the layout, as I quizzed him anxiously about the switches and valves on the DH.

The incoming pilot took little time to check me out. He hustled me into the front seat of the Curtiss trainer, had me take off, make a quick circle of the field, and land. That was all. He gave Colyer a breezy O.K. and was off.

The De Havilland was a challenge, more psychological than actual, but enough to make me nervous as I climbed in for my first flight. When I was introduced to the JN-4 I had been impressed with the throb of its 90-horsepower engine. The DH had a Liberty engine of 400 horsepower; its roar made the ground shake. But the mechanic's lesson proved invaluable, and I carefully followed his instructions. Once clear, I taxied to the corner, pointed the plane the long way of the field, and gave her the gun before I had time to change my mind. The plane took off easily. After a few maneuvers I knew I was flying the plane instead of the plane flying me, and I started getting a boot out of it.

There was an exhilaration to flying an airplane in those days: their slow speed and light wing-loadings allowed short turns, sharp dives, and quick pull-outs that are impossible in faster

planes. We did not rely on gauges and indicators; we flew by feel, noting the control pressures on our hands and feet, the shifting weight of our bodies, and the pitch of the singing wires. I was careful with my first few landings, bringing the DH in flat, with a bit of power until I got over the fence. After a dozen landings I taxied in to find I had become a mail pilot. This was in April 1920.

The Air Mail operation, initially flying from Washington to New York, had been extended by a route from New York to Chicago and very recently as far as Omaha. After several days at College Park, I was given a permanent assignment based at Bellefonte, Pennsylvania, whence I was to fly to Cleveland. Bellefonte lies at the heart of the Allegheny Mountains, in central Pennsylvania. I checked in with a Mr. Tanner, the field manager, and asked him what I was to do. So far as he knew, he said, I had only to fly back and forth to Cleveland. Never having been to Cleveland, I asked him for maps. He smiled. There were no maps. Sometimes on his first trip a pilot would fly behind someone who knew the run.

When Max Miller, the senior pilot of the whole Air Mail Service, showed up, I asked him how to get started. Rand McNally road maps, he explained, were useful, but they didn't show the landmarks I would use most in flying the run, such as the shape and layout of the towns, the distinctive appearance of the hills and valleys, where the low places were that let you work your way through weather, and the location of possible landing fields. After I came to know my run, Miller said, I'd fly to Cleveland the way I'd walk to the drugstore; I'd know the way.

Miller and I picked up maps of Pennsylvania and Ohio. Then he began to talk. He kept on talking for a long time. From the field here at Bellefonte you head west through the gap in the ridge. Climb as you veer a bit north, passing over the center of this railroad switchback up the side of Rattlesnake Mountain, then due west again to clear the top of the ridge at, say, 2200 feet. After about ten miles you hit the railroad again at Snow Shoe—look sharp, it's only four or five houses—then follow the railroad on down the other side of Rattlesnake to the valley where you pick up the West Branch of the Susquehanna River, winding along to the town of Clearfield, which you will know by three round water reservoirs just south of town. Next, you have to get over about thirty miles of plateau to Du Bois. This is pretty high, about 2200 feet, but it is fairly smooth on top and there is a white gravel road cut through the trees straight to Du Bois. As you come into town you will see the railroad to your right and just south of the railroad a piece of flat pasture you can land on in a pinch. Then the highway leads you for fifty miles through Brookville to Clarion. Each of these towns has a half-mile race track. The one at Clarion is half full of trees, but the one at Brookville is clean and hard, and it's the best emergency field from here to Cleveland: as soon as you land you will be met by a girl named Alice Henderson, driving a big Cadillac, who will be pleased to look after you. After Clarion, the country gradually gets lower until you cross the Allegheny at Greenville, which you can identify by a big S bend in the river. From then on it's clear sailing.

And so he went on, naming towns, hills, rivers, roads, factories, race tracks, all the way to Cleveland. The airfield was in East Cleveland, at the Glenn L. Martin plant. It was easy to find, just a quarter of a mile from the lake shore—or so Miller assured me.

I had expected to make my first trip escorted by one of the Cleveland pilots. But within a few days the westbound came in, and there was no pilot except me available to take it on to Cleveland. The weather was far from promising; it had been raining off and on all day, and low clouds were barely clearing the ridges. However, no one seemed concerned as they transferred the mail to my DH and warmed up the Liberty, so I took off and headed west through the gap in the first ridge. Max's instructions proved a great help. I made it over Rattlesnake Mountain and followed the river to Clearfield without much trouble. Opaque veils of cloud forced me to twist and dodge my way between them as the squalls grew heavier. By the time I reached the slope leading up to the plateau, the clouds were so solid that I had to circle back. I hated to give up. Over Clearfield again the sky looked brighter to the north, so I blithely headed that way, happily ignorant that I was flying over some of the wildest country in

Pennsylvania, high and rugged, with few houses and no fields for fifty miles around.

I was able to work my way west by heading for openings between the clouds, zigzagging from one to another. I knew I was north of the course, but not how far north; I knew I was working west, but I couldn't guess at what rate. I was amazed to find I was barely clearing the trees, although the altimeter showed close to 3000 feet above sea level. The terrain was rushing at me with relentless speed. After a long half hour, the rain eased a bit and the clouds rose. I relaxed a little. I was showing them that a rookie could get through.

Just then, the engine stopped cold. As a rule when an engine fails, it will give some warning. The water temperature will rise, or the oil pressure will drop, or there's a knocking or clanking. Even if it is only a minute or two, it gives the pilot a chance to look around and head for a field or open place. However, when the timing gear in a Liberty engine fails, one second it is roaring along even and strong, and the next there is a tremendous, loud silence. I quickly twisted all the knobs and gadgets in the cockpit, but there was no response and the engine stayed dead. While my hands were trying to restart the engine, my neck was stretching and my eyes searching for some sort of field to land in. I was surrounded by heavily forested, sharply rolling hills. To my left was a cuplike basin with a small clearing. It was down-wind, but my gliding radius didn't allow much choice. I went for it.

To reach the clearing required a sharp, almost vertical S turn, first left, then right, while killing just enough speed and altitude to land, down-wind, and still miss a nearby cliff. I can even now feel the rain slanting in my face and see that open space rocking and swinging in front of me as I pulled out of the turn. One thing I could not know: the clearing was choked with brush and weeds, hiding a three-foot ledge of rock directly in front of my landing spot. The ledge slammed into the undercarriage as I hit. The plane snapped like a popper on the end of a bull whip. I was catapulted into a long head-first dive, like a man shot from a circus cannon. Fortunately, I landed in the brush and rolled to a stop in a sitting position. The padded leather ring that rimmed the cockpit hung from my neck like a lei. I was still holding the

rubber grip pulled loose from the control stick. My seat belt lay across my lap. I felt around to determine that I had no broken bones. The wreckage of the plane was piled in a heap, like crumpled wastepaper.

Except for this lone field, the place appeared to be a wilderness of trees. After some exploration I located a little-used path and started to follow it. It meandered along for about half a mile and turned onto a dirt road that I followed downhill for perhaps another mile before I came to a small cabin. Sitting on a bench before the cabin were an elderly man and woman, barefooted and dressed in work clothes. They smiled and waved. My first impression was astonishment at how clean they were, their scrubbed faces glowing above the faded calico and denim. I told them about the accident and about my mail pouches, which would have to be taken to a railroad station. They assured me that the rural mail carrier would be along shortly with his horse and rig and would willingly help me. The couple were very solicitous. Almost apologetically the wife brought out a big bowl of tiny wild strawberries, a jug of clotted cream, and a loaf of fresh home-baked bread.

Sure enough, the mail carrier came along in due course, with a sturdy mare pulling an old-fashioned hack. The old man and the mail carrier helped me bring the mail sacks down to the road and load them in the hack. Luckily there were only three or four sacks, hardly a hundred pounds. Westbound air mail was expensive that day.

After my thanks and good-bys, we drove about ten miles to Pithole, a little town on the railroad, where the stationmaster accepted the mail shipment. I used my Post Office travel commission to get a train ticket to Cleveland. It was quite a trip, my first flight with the mail. I was beginning to understand why the boys at the Flying Club had given me a farewell party.

FROM

Beyond Horizons

LINCOLN ELLSWORTH

To be the first to reach the North Pole by air was the dream of the veteran Norwegian polar explorer Roald Amundsen and his American partner, Lincoln Ellsworth. At 5:15 p.m. on May 21, 1925, Amundsen and Ellsworth and four crewmen took off from King's Bay, Spitzbergen, and headed north in two Dornier-Wal seaplanes. Eight hours later, 136 miles short of the Pole, they were forced down in the great Arctic ice field. One plane, the disabled N 24, was abandoned. The damaged N 25 was repaired and had fuel for the return to Spitzbergen. But it was trapped. There was never sufficient open water for a take off in the lead between the shifting ice floes; and when the lead froze over, the ice, though smooth, was not thick enough to support the plane. Desperately, the men debated whether to stay with the plane or attempt to reach Greenland by foot and canoe. Here is Ellsworth's account of their narrow escape.

Escape from the Ice

JUNE 6. We had been on the ice fifteen days, and our position was hopeless as ever. No lead had yet exposed water broad enough for a seaplane's run. The ice of the frozen leads would not bear the weight of the ship. The plane could not reach flying speed on the snow.

Nine days to June 15, when we must take the supreme decision. Riiser-Larsen had already announced his intention to start for Greenland on June 15—on foot. If one man went with him, the remaining four might not be able to launch the N 25, if the providential lead appeared. If that man happened to be Dietrichson, there would be no pilot left with the ship. It was becoming evident that we must all set out on that frightful journey. I didn't like to think about June 15.

Wings brought us into the trap; wings must carry us out, if we were ever to see civilization again. That was the only conclusion common sense could draw. We still had left our third alternative, the superhuman one of clearing a runway on the old thick ice of the floes. But in fifteen days of moving around we had not seen a floe big enough to serve as a flying field.

A dense fog shrouded the ice on the morning of June 6. As soon as they had swallowed their breakfast chocolate, Riiser-Larsen and Dietrichson strapped on their skis, growled a word or two of farewell, and disappeared into the smother. They were off on a do-or-die hunt for what might well prove to be the unfindable—an ice cake that could serve our forlorn purpose.

The rest of us stayed with the N 25, which floated in the lead channel we had last broken—the last we were going to break. Now and then one of us pumped out water entering through the leaky joints of the mistreated hull. Amundsen and I wrote in our diaries, took a sounding through the lead, snapped a few pictures when the fog thinned at noon. Feucht brooded within his own spiritual fog. Omdal wiped and greased the engines. With some apprehension we noticed that the lead was slowly closing. Omdal started the Therm-X heaters to warm the engines ready for a quick pull.

Late in the afternoon Riiser-Larsen and Dietrichson returned, and we knew by their faces that they bore good news. Skiing in thick fog, they had had but little luck, but during a short break after noon they saw a big cake shining in the distant sunlight. They made their way to it, explored it, and estimated its north-and-south diameter at three hundred yards. This was none too long for a runway; but, on hard ice and lightened of all excess cargo, the ship might fly in that distance.

The good news was not entirely unmitigated. In the first place, this ice cake was more than half a mile away. Between it and our lead lay two floes separated by wide crevasses. These would have to be bridged. One pressure ridge lay as a barrier wall across the route. In addition, we had to lift the ship out of the lead and upon the first floe. And when we reached the big cake, the problem of a runway had still to be solved.

In other words, we were confronted with a job of Arctic road building. Instead of rock, gravel, and cement, our road metal was ice and snow. For tools we had such things as frail wooden shovels and sheath knives tied to the ends of ski poles. And it was no one-car lane we were called upon to construct, but a way wide enough to accommodate the 60-foot spread of an airplane's wings.

Because of the menacing movement of the ice, the main body of the pack now being only thirty feet away, we decided to move the plane up on top of the first floe that night. It was well we did, for during the night solid ice moved in where the N 25 had been. We started the engines and worked slowly up the lead to the point where we must build our ramp. By midnight we had the plane up safely on Floe Number 1. For our six hours of heavy toil we rewarded ourselves with a mug of hot chocolate apiece. That night we set no outside watch. Every man crawled into his sleeping bag and fell instantly into a veritable coma of exhaustion.

Next morning we were up early and at it again. We tackled first the most stupendous work we had yet undertaken—the cutting of the passage through the pressure ridge. It was a wall of ice fifteen feet thick. It took us an entire day to accomplish this —bitter work, on our knees, chopping with the pocket ax and the ice anchors, our legs wet to the skin from the melting ice, our hands, always soaking in icy brine, red, raw, and swollen from handling the tools. The leveling of sixty feet of this wall accounted for a great percentage of the three hundred tons of ice Amundsen estimated we moved during our stay.

The bridges across the crevasses required less grueling work but offered much more hazard and excitement. These chasms in the ice were really narrow leads, with open or thinly skimmed water at the bottom. It was a question of filling them up with ice until we gained a solid surface level with the floes.

We floated in big blocks as a foundation, hoping they might freeze in position. On top of these we threw down blocks we could drag or carry in our arms. As the upper weight increased, the foundation ice sank, so that we had to heave in a far greater quantity of ice than the mere cubic volume of the crevasse itself. It was also necessary to build the bridges extra wide, since the sides tended to slide off.

When we had a bridge level and bound it with packed snow, though it supported the six of us, there was every reason to believe that it would sag down under the weight of the plane. Therefore, it was necessary to send the ship across with all the speed its engines could muster through the snow. Moreover, it had to stop almost instantly on the other side. There was always danger of the crevasse opening wider and destroying our bridge, so we could spare no time to remove ice blocks and level a coasting runway ahead.

Riiser-Larsen took the N 25 across the bridges alone, the rest of us holding lines attached to the tail, ready to dig in our heels and brake when the ship was over. Thus we negotiated both safely, and before supper time on June 8 our plane stood at last on the lip of the big cake.

I have neglected to mention that this floe was south of the original position of the N 25 in the frozen lead. Therefore, the plane rested at the northern end of our proposed runway. This was favorable for the take-off, since the wind still continued to blow from the south. Riiser-Larsen had never lost belief in the essential ability of the seaplane to rise from snow. The wind blowing rather briskly that afternoon, he wanted to give it the chance then and there. I think none of us had much confidence, but we agreed. God knows, nobody wanted to stay there a moment longer than we had to.

We went over the course with our chopping implements, knocking off the heads of such ice lumps that projected through the snow. Then we went back to the plane and once more took our places. It was no use. The wind had died down, and the engines could hardly drag the hull through the sodden drifts. We merely bumped across the cake to the southern edge, stopping abruptly beside another lead when Riiser-Larsen shut off the power.

We now had to face the task we had been trying to avoid all along—that of shoveling off two and one-half feet of snow, heavy from thawing, and then leveling a runway in the blue ice below. Riiser-Larsen looked the ground over and, instead of taking the north-south diameter of the ice cake, chose a slightly quartering course, which, he estimated, would add a distance of over three hundred feet to our fairway. Speaking in metric-system terms, we would have a runway 400 meters long instead of one of 300 meters. We all knew more or less about flying, and each must have felt in his heart that 400 meters was none too long a run for a take-off.

On the morning of June 9 we began this work. Our chopping tools were of no use to us now. We had only our three wooden shovels. We set out to clear the blue ice along a path 39 feet (12 meters) wide. But this was no job of cutting in with a shovel and tossing the snow to one side. The shoveler had to walk to one edge and then throw the snow far, for it was necessary to leave on each side of the cleared track a 20-foot shelf to accommodate the wing spread.

Three men worked with the shovels while three rested or tossed out big snowballs. The wet summer snow was heavy as lead. So weakened were we by starvation and continued physical strain that after a few shovelfuls a man had to stand and lean on his shovel, panting for breath and gazing drearily out over the labor ahead. At the end of our first day of such effort, we stared disconsolately at only a hundred feet or so of runway cleared. At that rate it would take us from ten days to two weeks to make the runway.

To prevent the ship freezing into the wet snow, in the event of a cold snap, we decided to move it that evening over on the cleared ice. We found it impossible to turn the hull in the snow, ruining another pair of skis in the attempt. Then somebody thought of trampling down and packing the snow next to the hull, and presently we were all beating down with our feet a track to the runway. Over this, we discovered, the hull slid easily.

That gave us the idea that saved us. We decided to pack down the entire runway. Next morning we started it. We adopted a system. We marked out the work in squares, and each man was responsible for stamping down hard every inch of his area. Everyone could keep busy now, and that evening we had the satisfaction of seeing nearly three hundred and fifty feet of runway completed in addition to the stretch cleared the first day. We figured that we would complete the course in five days.

Next morning we had the further satisfaction of observing that the packed snow had frozen to the consistency of brick during the night. It thawed out during the day's rise in temperature but froze again the second night, and this succession kept up regularly. On that first day of trampling we heard a bird's cry overhead and through the mist saw a little auk flying northwest. Next day two wild geese dropped out of the fog and lighted near the plane. Somebody spotted them from afar, and Dietrichson, who was a crack shot, crept back to the ship for the shotgun. The geese seemed tame and stayed close, but this rich prize was too much for the famished hunter's nerves. He fired and missed, and the birds flew off to the northwest. We wondered if there were land in that direction.

At the end of the day, June 14, the last square inch of snow on the runway had been packed down. Five of us wearily plodded back to the N 25 at the southern end; but Riiser-Larsen stepped on ahead of us, carefully pacing the distance. At camp he greeted us with the closest approach to enthusiasm he had shown. He had made an error in his original calculation of the cake's diameter. We had a course not 400 meters long but 500 meters. The rest of us had been too dull-witted, too sunk in fatalistic resignation to events, to notice the discrepancy between his estimate and the amount of work we had done.

Amundsen expressed the feelings of all of us.

"If somebody offered me a million kroner for those extra hundred meters," he said, "I would not accept."

After our evening mugs of chocolate, we took our places in the plane to taxi to the northern end, to be ready to take off into the wind early next morning, when the runway would be frozen. When about to start the engines, Riiser-Larsen suggested that instead of taxiing we try to fly. There was no telling how slippery this surface might prove to be. If we could get off now, why wait until morning? Amundsen and I nodded, and the pilot gave her the gun.

But the runway was soft from the day's thaw, and the strakes bit into it. The plane made no effort to rise. To lift, the wings needed mile-a-minute speed. We did, however, slide at thirty-six miles an hour, which was much faster than any speed we had attained before. When we stopped at the north end, Riiser-Larsen turned around to me and said: "I hope you are not disappointed, Ellsworth. We will do better next time."

I believed him. That night I had the outside watch. With my feet thrust loosely into the ski straps and a rifle slung over my shoulder on the chance that I might get a shot at a seal or wild goose, I shuffled round and round the big ice cake. Our night patrols were doubly anxious now, since the floe was beginning to show signs of the protracted thaw. Crevasses were opening in it here and there. Should a wide crack run across our fairway, it would be the supreme tragedy.

That night I had occasion to observe the solicitude and fidelity of Riiser-Larsen, his conscientious devotion to duty. While the others slept like the dead, several times our pilot drew himself up through the manhole in the plane's deck to observe the wind and feel the temperature. Weary as he must have been, responsibility for the morrow lay so heavily upon him that he could not sleep soundly.

Twice or more I visited the thermometer hanging on the side of the hull. We had our usual night drop in temperature—three Fahrenheit degrees of frost. As the sun moved down into the east, the breeze freshened from the south. Thus dawned, to speak of it that way, June 15, our Day of Decision, the day of our final trial.

Long before it was time for me to waken my comrades, Riiser-Larsen dropped down over the side of the hull. Together we inspected the runway. Yesterday's ruts left by our hull in the soft snow were now petrified grooves. The surface was crisp as a tile pavement. A truck would not have left a track in it.

So impatient was Riiser-Larsen to start that we woke everybody up ahead of time and started the primus stove to boil our chocolate. Riiser-Larsen kept urging us to hurry. The daily thaw was normally still two or three hours distant, but we shared an unreasoning dread that it might start earlier this morning. We gulped down breakfast and prepared for the great test.

The N 25 *had* to get off this time, that we all knew; and yet I think we all confidently expected her to. For now, for the first time, we stripped the ship of everything with which we could possibly dispense. Beside the runway we piled the expensive movie cameras, all the unexposed film, both rifles and one of the shotguns, all the ammunition except one hundred shells, both sledges and one of the folding canoes, half of our provisions, all the remaining skis—leaving only the light snowshoes aboard—even our field glasses. As an afterthought, we threw out our sealskin parkas and our stout ski boots, wearing only moccasins. In the mild weather the hull had long since dripped dry of the sea water taken in through its leaks. We could not have safely got rid of another ounce of weight.

It was not only for the sake of a take-off that we lightened the N 25. Riiser-Larsen was apprehensive about our fuel supply. We had burned plenty of gas during our various movements and take-off runs. It was questionable if we had enough to reach Spitzbergen. We could not afford one excess pound of weight, since it costs fuel to fly a pound six hundred miles.

We turned the ship south into the slightly quartering wind, and the hull slid easily on the packed frozen snow. Then we took our places for a long flight. Dietrichson, who was to do the navigation, got into the observer's place in the bow. So confident was he of success that he unfolded his charts, ready in the cockpit beside him. Amundsen took the co-pilot's seat beside Riiser-Larsen. This time I did not stay with the mechanics in the gondola. Whether I could not bear to see another disappointment or had a superstitious notion that it was bad luck to watch, I crawled back to Riiser-Larsen's sleeping quarters in the tail of the plane, where it was dark and I could see nothing.

The engines leaped into action. The hull moved, scratching and grating at first, then bumping—mighty bumps, spaced farther and farther apart. I did not need Omdal's shout, unintelligible in the tumult, to tell me that we were in the air. The bumping had stopped. Afterwards I found out that we took flight in those final million-kroner 100 meters. But then I did not care much. I experienced no particular elation but only a dull happiness when I felt the plane lift. We were all beyond sharp emotions.

I looked out through the manhole and saw that we were flying through thick fog, dark and clammy. From time to time during the next two hours I looked out again. Always the same fog. Sometimes we flew so low that we skimmed the ice for Dietrichson to make drift observations. It was a great job of blind flying the two airmen did in that fog, since for guidance they had only the magnetic compass, theretofore deemed useless in the Arctic because of its variations.

After a while I saw the manhole opening above me sharply bright. I looked out into clear sunshine. Below us was the fleecy ceiling of the fog bank, with the same double aureole following behind us and the jumping shadow of the plane in their common center. Up forward Amundsen was pointing the periscope toward the sun. I crawled back to my place. After a final day of punishing toil I had been on my feet all night, and I asked only to lie there torpid on the cold aluminum floor, too exhausted for true slumber.

The engines sang their steady song. Hour after hour, how many I neither knew nor cared, I lay there, my hairy, grimed, and salt-caked cheek pillowed on my arm. A confusion of shouting roused me, and I saw Omdal waving me forward. I crawled toward him.

"Land!" he yelled.

It shocked me to my senses.

"Spitzbergen?" I yelled back.

Omdal only shrugged his shoulders. But Feucht, still an image of gloom, yelled as if angry: "No Spitzbergen! No Spitzbergen!"

Again I stuck my head up through the manhole. Fog and ice were gone now, and below us tumbled a gray wind-flecked ocean. Off the nose of the plane, indistinct beneath the southern sun, was a faint shore line.

Something hit my moccasined foot. I drew down in and saw Omdal tossing cakes of chocolate at me. With safety in sight, our ration restrictions were off, and Amundsen broke open a carton of chocolate and distributed the cakes. I ate seven as fast as I could munch them down. As I squatted there, the engines cut off and began choking and backfiring in descent. Omdal gestured to me that we were landing, which meant that I must screw shut the roof deadlight to keep out spray. I treated myself first to a look. We were not at the shore, as I had supposed, but still some miles out, and as we dropped lower I could see that the ocean was rough. A little later I learned the reason for this maneuver. Even as the N 25 had had a forced landing near the Pole, so it was making another on the return. The stabilization rudders had jammed, and Riiser-Larsen preferred to taxi the rest of the distance rather than risk a dive.

I closed the deadlight, and the plane sat down roughly on the racing waves. The engines spoke again, but I was only regretting those seven cakes of chocolate. The light hull pitched like a cork on the combers, and in the airless dark tail I instantly became as seasick as I ever was in my life. For thirty-five minutes I had to endure this final misery, and then the plane taxied into still water.

We reached shore on our final spoonfuls of gas. Then we realized how much we owed to the skill at the plane's controls. Had Riiser-Larsen and Dietrichson not held a true course through those two hours of fog, we should probably have never come back.

FROM

The Spirit of St. Louis

CHARLES A. LINDBERGH

May 20, 1927. At Roosevelt Field, Long Island, a light rain fell through the dawn's haze. Ceiling was low, visibility poor; the ground was soft and muddy. But along the great circle route to Europe the fog was lifting, and the storms that had tossed the North Atlantic for the past week were suddenly stilled. The single-engined, silver monoplane, the Spirit of St. Louis, *squatted heavily on the grassy runway. Would this little plane be the first to fly nonstop from New York to Paris? Charles Lindbergh, a twenty-five-year-old air mail pilot, considered the chances. His plane had been built especially for this flight and it was ready. But he had had only two hours of fitful sleep, and before him lay perhaps forty hours of solitary flying, much of it over the ocean. At best, the weather along his route was uncertain. No one expected him to fly today. Darkness still shrouded the hangars housing the proud multi-engined ships of his rivals, awaiting the completion of meticulous preflight tests, awaiting ideal weather. Let them wait, Lindbergh decided. This was the day!*

Take Off

THIRTY revolutions low! The engine's vibrating roar throbs back through the fuselage and drums heavily on taut fabric skin. I close the throttle and look out at tense faces beside my plane. Life and death lies mirrored in them—rigid, silent, waiting for my word.

Thirty revolutions low—a soft runway, a tail wind, an overload. I glance down at the wheels. They press deeply, tires bulging, into the wet, sandy clay.

The wind changed at daybreak, changed after the *Spirit of St. Louis* was in take-off position on the west side of the field, changed after all those barrels of gasoline were filtered into the tanks, changed from *head* to *tail*—five miles an hour *tail!*

A stronger wind would force me to the other end of the runway. But this is only a breath; barely enough to lift a handkerchief held in the hand. It's blowing no faster than a man can walk. And if we move the plane, it may shift again as quickly as it did before. Taking off from *west* to *east* with a tail wind is dangerous enough—there are only telephone wires and a road at the far end of the field—but to go from *east* to *west* would mean flying right over the hangars and blocks of houses beyond —not a chance to live if anything went wrong. A missing cylinder and—"Hit a house. Crashed. Burned." I can hear the pilots saying it—the end of another transatlantic flight.

And there's no time. There's no time to move the plane—so small, so delicate, so heavy—two and a half tons on those little tires, with all the fuel in. It would have to be towed, and towed slowly, five thousand feet over the muddy runway. We'd have to send for a tractor; I couldn't taxi—the engine's too light—it would overheat—the fuel tanks would need topping off again— hours lost—night would fall on the Irish coast. I'm already late —it's long past dawn—and the weather reports say *clearing*.

My cockpit quivers with the engine's tenseness. Sharp explosions from the exhaust stacks speak with confidence and precision. But the *Spirit of St. Louis* isn't vibrant with power as it's always been before. I'm conscious of the great weight pressing tires into ground, of the fragility of wings, of the fullness of oversize tanks of fuel. There is in my plane this morning, more of earth and less of air than I've ever felt before.

Plane ready; engine ready; earth-inductor compass set on course. The long, narrow runway stretches out ahead. Over the telephone wires at its end lies the Atlantic Ocean; and beyond that, mythical as the rainbow's pot of gold, Europe and Paris. This is the moment I've planned for, day and night, all these months past. The decision is mine. No other man can take that responsibility. The mechanics, the engineers, the blue-uniformed police officers standing there behind the wing, everyone has done his part. Now, it's up to me.

Their eyes are intently on mine. They've seen planes crash before. They know what a wrong decision means. If I shake my head, there'll be no complaint, no criticism; I'll be welcomed back into their midst, back to earth and life; for we are separated by something more than the few yards that lie between us. It seems almost the difference between the future and the past, to be decided by a movement of my head. A shake, and we'll be laughing and joking together, laying new plans, plodding over the wet grass toward hot coffee and a warm breakfast—all men of the earth. A nod, and we'll be separated—perhaps forever.

Thirty revolutions low! "It's the weather," the mechanic said when I climbed into the cockpit. "They never rev up on a day like this." But his encouraging words failed to hide the apprehension in his voice and eyes. Now, the expression on his face, out there behind my silver wing, shows more clearly than any words what is passing through his mind. He's gone over the engine piece by piece, helped tear it down and put it back together. He feels sure that every part is perfect, and firmly in its place. He's squirmed into the tail of the fuselage to inspect structure and controls. He knows that wheel bearings are freshly oiled; that air pressure is up; that tires are rubbed with grease to keep the mud from sticking. He's double-checked the thousand preliminary details to a flight. His work is done, done with faithfulness and skill. Now he stands there helplessly, intent, with tightened jaw, waiting for my signal. He feels responsible for the engine, for the plane, for me, even for the weather that holds the revolutions low.

I lean against the side of the cockpit and look ahead, through the idling blades of the propeller, over the runway's wet and glistening surface. I study the telephone wires at its end, the shallow pools of water through which my wheels must pass, and the top-heavy black column of smoke, rising from some source outside the field, leaning indifferently in the direction of my flight. A curtain of mist shuts off all trace of the horizon.

Wind, weather, power, load—how many times have I balanced these elements in my mind, barnstorming from some farmer's cow pasture in the Middle West! In barnstorming a pilot learns to judge a field so accurately that he can tell from the size of his passenger, and a tuft of grass tossed to the wind, just where his wheels will leave the ground, just how many feet will separate them from the boundary fence and trees beyond. But here, it's different. There are no well-established standards from which to judge. No plane ever took off so heavily loaded; and my propeller is set for cruising, not for take-off. Of course our test flights at San Diego indicate that it *will* take off—theoretically at least. But since we didn't dare try a full load from Camp Kearney's stony ground, the wings now have to lift a thousand pounds more than they ever carried before—five thousand pounds to be lifted by nothing more tangible than air.

Those carefully laid performance curves of ours have no place for mist, or a tail wind, or a soft runway. And what of the thirty revolutions lost, and the effect of moisture on the skin? No, I can turn to no formula, the limits of logic are passed. Now, the intangible elements of flight—experience, instinct, intuition— must make the final judgment, place their weight upon the scales. In the last analysis, when the margin is close, when all the known factors have been considered, after equations have produced their final lifeless numbers, one measures a field with an eye, and checks the answer beyond the conscious mind.

If the *Spirit of St. Louis* gathers speed too slowly; if the wheels hug the ground too tightly; if the controls feel too loose and logy, I can pull back the throttle and stop—that is, I can stop if I don't wait too long. If I wait too long—a few seconds will decide—well, another transatlantic plane crashed and burned at the end of this same runway. Only a few yards away, two of Fonck's crew met their death in flames.

And there's the added difficulty of holding the wheels on the runway while sitting in a cockpit from which I can't see straight ahead. A degree or two change in heading could easily cause a crash. The runway is narrow enough under the best of conditions; now—with the mud—and the tail wind—and the engine not turning up—

I lean back in the wicker seat, running my eyes once more over the instruments. Nothing wrong there. They all tell the proper story. Even the tachometer needle is in place, with the engine idling. Engine revolutions are like sheep. You can't notice that a few are missing until the entire flock is counted. A faint trace of gasoline mixes with the smell of newly dried dope—probably a few drops spilled out when the tanks were filled. I turn again to the problem of take-off. It will be slow at best. Can the engine stand such a long ground run at wide-open throttle, or will it overheat and start to miss?

Suppose I *can* hold the runway, suppose I *do* get off the ground—will fog close in and force me back? Suppose the ceiling drops to zero—I can't fly blind with this overload of fuel; but the wheels have doubtful safety factors for a landing. Shall I cut the switch and wait another day for confirmation of good weather? But if I leave now, I'll have a head start on both the Fokker and the Bellanca. Once in the air, I can nurse my engine all the way to Paris—there'll be no need to push it in a race. And the moon's past full—it will be three weeks to the next one; conditions then may be still worse.

Wind, weather, power, load—gradually these elements stop churning in my mind. It's less a decision of logic than of feeling, the kind of feeling that comes when you gauge the distance to be jumped between two stones across a brook. Something within you disengages itself from your body and travels ahead with your vision to make the test. You can feel it try the jump as you stand looking. Then uncertainty gives way to the conviction that it *can* or can't be done. Sitting in the cockpit, in seconds, minutes long, the conviction surges through me that the wheels *will* leave the ground, that the wings *will* rise above the wires, that it *is* time to start the flight.

I buckle my safety belt, pull goggles down over my eyes, turn to the men at the blocks, and nod. Frozen figures leap to action. A yank on the ropes—the wheels are free. I brace myself against the left side of the cockpit, sight along the edge of the runway, and ease the throttle wide open. Now, in seconds, we'll have the answer. Action brings confidence and relief.

But, except for noise and vibration, what little effect the throttle has! The plane creeps heavily forward. Several men are pushing on wing struts to help it start—pushing so hard I'm afraid the struts will buckle. How can I possibly gain flying speed? Why did I ever think that air could carry such a weight? Why have I placed such reliance on a sheet of paper's curves? What possible connection is there between the intersection of a pencil's lines in San Diego and the ability of *this* airplane, *here, now,* to fly?

The *Spirit of St. Louis* feels more like an overloaded truck than an airplane. The tires rut through mud as though they really were on truck wheels. Even the breath of wind is pressing me down. A take-off seems hopeless; but I may as well go on for another hundred feet before giving up. Now that I've started, it's better to make a real attempt. Besides—it's just possible—

Gradually, the speed increases. Maybe the runway's not too soft. Is it long enough? The engine's snarl sounds inadequate and weak, carrying its own note of mechanical frustration. There's none of the spring forward that always before preceded the take-off into air—no lightness of wing, no excess power. The stick wobbles loosely from side to side, and slipstream puts hardly any pressure against rudder. Nothing about my plane has the magic quality of flight. But men begin stumbling off from the wing struts. We're going faster.

A hundred yards of runway passes. The last man drops off the struts. The stick's wobbling changes to lurching motion as ailerons protest unevenness of surface. How long can the landing gear stand such strain? Five thousand pounds crushing down upon it! I keep my eyes fixed on the runway's edge. I *must* hold the plane straight. One wheel off and the *Spirit of St. Louis* would ground-loop and splinter in the mud. Controls begin to tighten against the pressure of my hand and feet. There's a living quiver in the stick. I have to push hard to hold it forward. Slight movement of the rudder keeps the nose on course. Good signs, but more than a thousand feet have passed. Is there still time, still space?

Pace quickens—turf becomes a blur—the tail skid lifts off ground—I feel the load shifting from wheels to wings. But the runway's slipping by quickly. The halfway mark is just ahead, and I have nothing like flying speed—The engine's turning faster —smoothing out—the propeller's taking better hold—I can tell by the sound. What r.p.m.? But I can't look at instruments— I must hold the runway, not take my eyes from its edge for an instant. An inch off on stick or rudder, and my flight will end.

The halfway mark streaks past—seconds now to decide—close the throttle, or will I get off? The wrong decision means a crash —probably in flames—I pull the stick back firmly, and—*The wheels leave the ground.* Then I'll get off! The wheels touch again. I ease the stick forward—almost flying speed, and nearly 2000 feet of field ahead—A shallow pool on the runway—water spews up from the tires—A wing drops—lifts as I shove aileron against it—the entire plane trembles from the shock—Off again —right wing low—pull it up—Ease back onto the runway—left rudder—hold to center—must keep straight—Another pool— water drumming on the fabric—The next hop's longer—I could probably stay in air; but I let the wheels touch once more— lightly, a last bow to earth, a gesture of humility before it— Best to have plenty of control with such a load, and control requires speed.

The *Spirit of St. Louis* takes herself off the next time—full flying speed—the controls taut, alive, straining—and still a thousand feet to the web of telephone wires. Now, I *have* to make it—there's no alternative. It'll be close, but the margin has shifted to my side. I keep the nose down, climbing slowly, each second gaining speed. If the engine can hold out for one more minute—five feet—twenty—forty—wires flash by underneath— *twenty feet to spare!*

Green grass and bunkers below—a golf links—people looking up. A low, tree-covered hill ahead—I shallow-bank right to avoid it, still grasping the stick tightly as though to steady the plane with my own strength, hardly daring to drop a wing for the turn, hardly daring to push the rudder. The *Spirit of St. Louis* seems balanced on a pin point, as though the slightest movement of controls would cause it to topple over and fall. Five thousand

pounds suspended from those little wings—5000 pounds balanced on a blast of air.

The ground's farther underneath; the plane's climbing faster—I'm above the trees on the hilltop! Plenty of height, plenty of power—a reserve of it! Two hundred feet above the ground. Now, if the motor starts missing, there are places I might land—level fields between the hills and highways. The landing gear would give way, and the fuel tanks would burst; but if I cut the switch, at least there's a chance that the fuselage would skid along and not catch fire.

Now I'm high enough to steal glances at the instrument board. The tachometer needle shows 1825 r.p.m.—no sign of engine overheating. I move the throttle back slowly—a glance at the terrain ahead—a glance at the tachometer in my cockpit—1800—1775 r.p.m. Pull the stabilizer back a notch. The air speed's still over 100 miles an hour—I throttle down to 1750—the tail stays up—the controls are taut! Then the curves are right. If the *Spirit of St. Louis* can cruise at 1750 r.p.m. with this load, I have *more* than enough fuel to reach Paris.

On the instrument board in front of me, the earth-inductor compass needle leans steeply to the right. I bank cautiously northward until it rises to the center line—65 degrees—the compass heading for the first 100-mile segment of my great-circle route to France and Paris. It's 7:54 a.m. Eastern Daylight Time.

FROM
Come North with Me

BERNT BALCHEN

At Spitsbergen, the base for his flight over the North Pole with Floyd Bennett in 1926, Richard Byrd met a young member of the Amundsen-Ellsworth-Nobile expedition, a flight lieutenant in the Norwegian navy named Bernt Balchen. Balchen's advice and help contributed much to the success of Byrd's venture. Impressed by his knowledge of Arctic flying, the American invited Balchen to return with him to the United States. In 1927 Balchen piloted Byrd's trimotored Fokker monoplane America across the Atlantic, taking the place of Floyd Bennett, who had been injured in a plane crash. Bennett died of pneumonia in 1928, and Balchen was again called upon to take his place, this time as chief pilot of Byrd's first Antarctic expedition. Having been the first to fly over the North Pole, Byrd was eager to repeat the feat at the South Pole. In December 1928, Byrd set up his base camp, Little America, on the Bay of Whales. There he and his men holed up during the long Antarctic winter of 1929. Early in November—spring in that hemisphere—the camp began to stir with preparations for the flight to the Pole. Balchen's account of that perilous exploit follows.

To the South Pole

ON August 24 we have a few minutes of daylight, and now spring comes fast to the Antarctic. The northern horizon grows redder, and one day, at high noon, a shaft of sunlight comes streaming across the snow, turning the sastrugi purple-blue and gilding the lower sides of scattered clouds in the cold turquoise sky. At last the time has come to make ready for the grand climax of the expedition.

During the winter I have been working on the performance computations of the Ford for the polar hop. I have rechecked them in detail with the previous performance tests, made up my fuel consumption curves, and determined which revolution and power settings will be needed for the various stages of the flight. The total weight of the plane, counting fuel and crew and all our equipment, should be in the neighborhood of 15,000 pounds —twice the weight for which the commercial model, with its smaller engine, is certified. No less than 1400 pounds of this overload will consist of the essential survival gear and supplies for use in case we run into bad luck and are forced down on the ice. In addition to tents, sleeping bags, and extra clothing, we must load into the plane enough emergency food supplies to last for forty-five days if necessary. This would be far from an excessive amount in the event of a forced landing on the high, glacier-rimmed polar plateau. It represents, however, the maximum weight that four men could expect to haul by their own efforts if they were forced to hike back. As a means of transporting the emergency gear and rations in the event of disaster, the plane will carry a light but rugged hand sled that I have designed especially for a party of men to drag over the ice. It is just about the worst method of traveling there is—man-hauling your own supplies.

Now we start working on the Ford in the snow-hangar. We change the gasoline system to a central collector type, with fuel lines leading to all the tanks—five in the wings and one 126-gallon tank in the fuselage—which can be refilled by hand with 5-gallon cans. With this central system we can pump the fuel into any wing tank we desire by means of wobble-pumps located next to the pilot's seat. A glass-tube gauge measures the exact amount of fuel in each tank at all times. I have completely reworked this system during the winter, considerably simplifying it from the factory design. The outside temperature is still thirty or forty below, and every time we touch the frozen metal it peels the skin from our fingertips. We fire up the big blubber stove until the hangar is reasonably warm, and use blowtorches as close as we dare to the engine, so we can work with our bare hands.

On the fourth of November, Dr. Larry Gould and a six-man party, traveling with a total of forty-two sled dogs, take their final departure from Little America for a 450-mile journey of exploration southward to the Queen Maud Mountains. The main purposes of this overland geological expedition are four: first, Gould and his men will establish a series of depots along a line pointing from Little America toward the Axel Heiberg Glacier, at the foot of the massive Queen Maud Range. Meanwhile, at the foot of the Glacier, supplies and gasoline will be landed by plane from Little America.

In addition, from their position between Little America and the Pole, the geological party can give the plane crew the weather conditions at the mountain range itself, the most critical point of the whole flight.

A third important assignment for the geological party, after they have set up their line of caches, is to stand ready, during the flight to the Pole and back, to act as an emergency rescue team in the event of a forced landing. The abrupt termination of its radio tone will serve as the signal that the plane has landed on the ice. Should this happen on the polar plateau, the geologists will attempt to take dog sledges up the Axel Heiberg Glacier, as Amundsen did on his push to the Pole. Then, pushing on across the plateau, they will leave another emergency food cache for the fliers at the southern end of Mt. Helland Hansen, between the Queen Maud Mountains and the Pole.

The first party to reach either this cache or the one at the foot of the Glacier will leave word there as to its further plans. In this way, there is a remote chance that if the worst happens and the *Floyd Bennett* is forced down on the high polar plateau a rescue can be effected by dog sledge, though it will inevitably be a desperate attempt.

Finally, quite apart from their operations in support of the South Pole flight, Gould and his geologists are responsible for an important and extensive program of exploration and surveying. They will work eastward along the Queen Maud Range and into the virtually unknown Carmen Land area adjoining it. They plan to remain in the field, in all, close to three months.

On the same day that we see the Gould party off from Little America, all hands turn to and begin to dig out the Ford from its winter cocoon of snow, in preparation for the polar flight. The wing sections are still on the sleds, just as they were hauled from the Bay of Whales, but buried now under eight-foot snow-drifts. We shovel them free and lift them onto empty gas drums. With blowtorches, working under a tarpaulin, we melt the snow inside the wingtips. Then we bolt the wings to the fuselage. To get the plane out of its frozen prison, we dig an incline from the snow revetment in which it lies, and I start up the center engine. The power of the big Cyclone pulls it up the ramp without difficulty, and I taxi it to its parking place beside the take-off strip.

Now, from a design I have made during the winter, based on my experience in the Royal Norwegian Air Force, we build a shelter on runners—a framework of two-by-fours covered with tarpaulins, with a workbench and vise in the rear. This shelter we slide on the runners over the nose of the *Floyd Bennett* and cover the engines: it is high enough for us to turn the propellers inside. The door is closed, and the shelter is heated with blow-torches so that we can work on the engines with our bare hands. In the Norwegian Air Force we have always called this type of shelter a "Noah's Ark"; and soon everybody here uses that name.

Working inside the Ark, in a few days I have all the engines tuned smoothly. Now I take the big trimotor up for its first hop, making load and speed and fuel consumption tests, and find that all my earlier computations are correct. The *Floyd Bennett* is ready for a depot-laying flight to help establish the emergency cache of food and gasoline at the foot of the Queen Maud Range.

Byrd has not yet announced who will fly him to the Pole, but it is generally assumed that the honor will go to Dean Smith. The choice of Smith as the pilot on the depot-laying flight is now announced. Harold June will be his copilot and I am to remain in camp.

The *Floyd Bennett* takes off on schedule with Byrd, Smith, June and Captain Ashley McKinley on board. Some hours later they report by radio that they have set up the cache and are returning, and at seven o'clock in the evening, that they are passing a crevassed area about a hundred miles from Little America. When they fail to arrive, I warm up the Fairchild and set out in search, keeping in constant radio contact with Little America in case they get any further news of the long overdue Ford. At the very edge of the crevasses, I sight a black patch on the snow, and land beside them. They are unharmed, but their tanks are bone-dry, and it is good that I have brought an extra hundred gallons of gasoline for just such an emergency. After they have refueled I offer to give them a hand to get their engines started; but they insist that they can take care of this themselves, and so I head back to Little America.

Still the Ford does not show up. We wait all day, puzzled, and at night Carl Petersen and I take off again, carrying more gas and also repair tools in case there has been an accident. They are still in the same place, unable to start the engines and so busy trying to get to the bottom of the trouble, that they barely speak to me when I arrive. We put on the heaters, and in less than an hour all three engines are turning smoothly. Commander Byrd and the others pile into the Ford and take off so fast that Pete, who is working inside the tent, doesn't even hear them leave. We pick up the gear left on the snow, jam everything into our little Fairchild, and rejoin them at Little America long after midnight.

Next morning, with the air of someone who has important business on his mind, Byrd takes me for a walk. He is still concerned about last night, I can see, and he demands to know why their fuel consumption was higher than expected. I reply that I cannot give the answer immediately. Since the flight tests before the depot-laying trip bore out the correctness of my computations, perhaps the trouble was that the mixture was not leaned properly. I am still confident of the accuracy of our test results. However, I promise Byrd that to make doubly certain, we will again go over the *Floyd Bennett's* entire fuel system and recheck the engines completely. Obviously, if there is anything wrong it must be eliminated before undertaking the South Pole flight.

"I am going to assure both you and whomever is piloting that plane," I tell Byrd, "that our figures are right, before the *Floyd Bennett* takes off."

Byrd pauses and then raises another big question that is bothering him. Why, he wants to know, were the pilots not able to get the engines started last night? For that I can offer no explanation except the obvious one that the motors have to be heated properly before being cranked up.

Byrd keeps on walking, his lips firm, his expression thoughtful. Then he turns to me, and some of the strain seems to have left his face.

"All right," he says, "get started right away with those fuel and engine checkups—just to make sure." I sense that the conference is over, and we turn back toward the barracks. "Oh, and by the way," he adds, "I'll want you to pilot the plane. You will fly to the South Pole with me."

"28 November, 1929. Weather okay, preparing polar take-off."

This is Thanksgiving Day, and it is a special Thanksgiving for sure. Last night we received a radio message from Larry Gould, on the dog-trail a hundred miles from the Queen Maud Range, reporting that weather conditions in that general area are ideal. Cyclone Haines weighs Gould's information, watches a couple of weather balloons dwindle to pinpoints in the sky, takes a reading on his barograph, wets his finger in the wind, and gives his official verdict at noon. The weather may be better or it may be worse, but he guesses that right now it is about as good as it probably ever will be. So we will either make it or not.

Now the final arrangements get under way. The mechanics check and recheck every inch of the Ford from nose to tail. An exact setting is made on the plane's chronometer, against a time-tick broadcast from the United States. Everyone in camp wants to be in on the take-off, and a volunteer ground crew forms a bucket line, passing 5-gallon cans of fuel to other volunteers on

the wing who top off the tanks. Another group of eager helpers feeds a steady stream of equipment into the plane, every item carefully counted and weighed. At the last minute Byrd decides to add two 150-pound sacks of food, as a still further precaution, and now we are carrying more weight than planned.

The three engines have been run up, and the rest of the crew boards the *Floyd Bennett*. Harold June sits beside me on the right as copilot and radio man; Captain Ashley McKinley is in his position as photographer; and Byrd will be navigator and flight leader. Shortly after three o'clock he comes out of his headquarters in a big fur cap and parka and polar bear pants, poses a moment beside the plane as the movie cameras grind, and waves to the crowd. The door slams behind him, and I rev up the engines.

The skis jerk loose, and the heavy plane slides forward over the snow. I taxi in a wide circle and up a little incline at the end of the flying strip to get full advantage of the slope. I look back at Byrd. He nods, and I give it the gun.

"28 November. Take-off, 1529, heading due south, wind ESE."

The plane hesitates a moment, pointing eastward into the eighteen-mile wind, and I flip the rudder to break the skis loose. A few seconds later the tail ski is off the snow. I nose up, quickly gaining altitude. The weather is clear and ideal, and after a few minutes we pick up Gould's dog-trail, a tiny scratch in the snow, and follow along its meridian, at that point 143° 45′ W. We pass his 20-mile food depot, then the 44-mile depot. We have climbed steadily to 1500 feet, heading for the South Pole.

Hour after hour the ribbed expanse of the great Ross Shelf rolls under us. Byrd has spread Amundsen's old charts on his navigator's table, and we are looking down on the sledge-route he blazed, doing ninety miles an hour where he made twenty-five miles on his best day. I take my pocket slide rule from its worn leather case, and make a quick check. Our dead reckoning figures correctly. Everything is right on the nose.

Three hours and forty-five minutes out of Little America, we

sight some dark specks on the Shelf ahead. It is Gould's survey and support party, waving to us as we roar overhead. We drop some chocolate and cigarettes, and a few messages which have come into camp since they left twenty-four days ago. We have flown the first transocean mail, I reflect, and now we are pioneering the airmail service in Antarctica.

"*28 November. Sight Queen Maud Range, 2050. Climbing full throttle.*"

Soon the Queen Maud Mountains loom ahead, ranked in stately file against the horizon; here and there the brilliant blue flash of glacial ice lights dark gaps in the range. It is a land of a million years ago, right out of the ice age. June, with his earphones strapped to his helmet by a long cord, moves fast to empty the last of the 5-gallon cans of gas into the fuselage tank, and drop the empty tins through the trapdoor. A pound of weight less could make the difference over the Hump. McKinley adjusts his big mapping camera, ready to aim it to port or starboard.

The engines have been operating at cruising speed, 1580 r.p.m. for the center Cyclone and 1600 for the outboards. I hope the big Cyclone will stand up all right; it is brand-new and I have not had time to break it in fully. So far, it gives no sign of heating. I open up all three engines full throttle, 1750 for the biggest one and 1700 for the two smaller, and we rise steadily toward the only two passes in the Queen Maud Range. We are about fifty miles north, holding course on meridian 163° 45′ W. I watch the altimeter needle climb: 3000, 4000, 5000.

Ahead lies the big decision. One approach to the Pole is over the Axel Heiberg Glacier, the pass which Amundsen chose. He reported this pass to be 10,500 feet at its highest point. It is a long and gradual ascent, flanked by towering peaks far higher than the maximum altitude of the Ford, and its summit is hidden in clouds. The other approach is over the Liv Glacier to its right, named by Amundsen for Dr. Nansen's daughter and completely unsurveyed. We can see it bending in a wide curve to the west of south, mounting to the top of the Hump, and disappearing in a white blur that may be the polar plateau. We estimate its elevation to be about 9500 feet, and the summit is clear. We decide to swing right.

The Liv Glacier is like a great frozen waterfall, halted in the midst of its tumbling cascade and immobilized for all eternity. Sheer cliffs rise above us on either side, and the canyon narrows as we wind our way upward. A cataract of ice looms ahead, and there is no room to turn around now. We are at 8200 feet, just about the Ford's ceiling with its present loading. I wave frantically to catch the attention of June, who is bent over his radio, and signal him to jettison some of our weight. His hand reaches for the gasoline dump-valve, and I shake my head and point to the emergency food. He kicks one of the 150-pound sacks through the trapdoor, and the plane lifts just enough to clear the barrier.

A final icy wall blocks our way, steeper than all the others. A torrent of air is pouring over its top, the plane bucking violently in the downdraft, and our rate of climb is zero. June jettisons the second sack, and the Ford staggers a little higher, but still not enough. There is only one thing left to try. Perhaps at the very edge of the downdraft is a reverse current of air, like a back-eddy along the bank of a rushing river, that will carry us upstream and over. I inch my way to the side of the canyon, our right wing almost scraping the cliff, and all at once we are wrenched upward, shooting out of the maelstrom of winds, and soar over the summit with a couple of hundred feet to spare.

On the other side of the Hump lies the polar plateau. The snow meets the sky in an empty horizon, and somewhere in its center, about four hundred miles away, is the Pole. We set our course along the 171st meridian, leading south like all meridians to the axis of the globe.

"29 November, 0100. Approaching South Pole."

Since midnight the mountains have been fading away behind us, and by one o'clock they are out of sight. During the climb over the Hump we were on maximum power setting for almost ninety minutes. The right outboard engine backfires, and misses a couple of beats, and June reaches for the dump-valve again. At our altitude of 11,000 feet, two engines could never keep the Ford airborne. I figure that I may have leaned the mixture a little too thin, and adjust it just a fraction. The right outboard picks up and runs smoothly once more.

According to my dead reckoning, we should be at the Pole in another fourteen minutes. Our position is Lat. 89° 40′ S., about twenty miles away, so our goal must actually be in sight at this moment. I send a message back to Byrd on the trolley cable that connects the cockpit with the navigator's compartment. Fourteen minutes later, at 1:14 in the morning, Byrd sends a message forward on the trolley for June to broadcast to the base:

"We have reached the South Pole."

We make a circle in the direction which would be westward, except that here everything is north. The trapdoor behind me opens, and Byrd drops an American flag on the spot, weighted with a stone from Floyd Bennett's grave, and we turn north again. I am glad to leave. Somehow our very purpose here seems insignificant, a symbol of man's vanity and intrusion on this eternal white world. The sound of our engines profanes the silence as we head back to Little America.

From Little America, Byrd's message has gone to the outside world. Russ Owen tells us later that the signal from the *Floyd*

Bennett was actually picked up at *The New York Times* station, direct from the South Pole, and transmitted by loud-speaker to the jammed streets in Times Square. All over the world the headlines are carrying the news; and when we arrive back at camp shortly after ten in the morning of the 29th, the members of the expedition are lined along the strip, cheering as we taxi to a halt. The whole flight crew is picked up and carried on swaying shoulders to the mess hall for a celebration.

I have been sitting so long in the pilot's seat that I am cramped and sore, and so I slip out of the mess hall quietly and take my skis. With Sverre Stroem and Chris Braathen I head out for a couple of hours on the white slopes. This I like better than all the celebrating.

FROM

The Sky Beyond

SIR GORDON TAYLOR

As the range and reliability of aircraft increased, fledgling air-lines in the early 1930s eagerly traced intercontinental routes on the world's map. Before regular mail and passenger service could be inaugurated, however, survey flights had to test the various possible routes and demonstrate to the public the feasibility of transocean flying. The Australian pilot Gordon Taylor was one of those who pioneered air routes over the Pacific and Indian oceans in the 1930s. "Jubilee Mail" is his account of one such flight, a harrowing journey over the Tasman Sea in 1935 in the trimotored Fokker monoplane Southern Cross.

Jubilee Mail

VERY soon after I returned to Australia a proposal came up for another trans-Tasman flight, this time with two aircraft carrying a special mail, to commemorate the Jubilee of Their Majesties King George V and Queen Mary, in May 1935. Jack Percival, who had been in the *Southern Cross* on the Gerringong Beach–New Plymouth flight in January 1933 (when I was learning to navigate the airplane) conceived and planned this Jubilee Mail flight, which was designed also to create further public interest in the inauguration of a regular mail and passenger service between Australia and New Zealand.

It was intended to be the last trans-Tasman flight of the gallant but aging *Southern Cross*—and it was.

Kingsford Smith, of course, was taking the *Cross*; and I was invited to go in command of the second aircraft, *Faith in Australia*, Charles Ulm's modified Fokker, in which he also had made a number of pioneer Tasman crossings and other flights. The trustees of his Estate had made the aircraft available for this special commemorative mail.

On the day of departure we flew both aircraft to the Royal Australian Air Force Airdrome at Richmond for night take-offs, estimating daylight landings at New Plymouth.

Soon after our arrival at Richmond it was revealed that Kingsford Smith's navigator was ill and could not go on the flight. A period of high drama, typical of such situations, prevailed for several hours. Eventually it was decided to take only the *Southern Cross*; with Smithy as commander, John Stannage as radio officer, and myself as navigator and relief pilot.

I could hardly have been more apprehensive about this turn of events. While supervising the work on my own aircraft, I could not help noticing that the day before departure one of the engines of the *Southern Cross*, lying dismantled in pieces on the hangar floor, was being assembled by John Stannage, an incredibly good radio operator and technician, and by Jack Percival, a first-class official correspondent on the flight, and the man who had conceived and very efficiently organized the whole project; but neither was an engineer. Kingsford Smith had a way of making such situations work out perfectly well in practice, but from the moment I realized I was not taking Ulm's aircraft and was committed to travel in an airplane one engine of which had been assembled in circumstances which absolutely horrified me, I could see little future in the whole thing.

I unloaded all my gear from the *Faith in Australia*, set myself up in business in the airplane, and was as ready to go as a navigator with any imagination could be in such circumstances. But I had to admit to myself as we prepared for take-off that there was something about this airplane—something good inhabiting it—which made me feel that, for no reason I could put my finger on, the *Southern Cross* would not fail us.

As midnight approached Kingsford Smith started the motors. I took my take-off position in the starboard pilot's seat and listened to the tearing snarl as each engine ran up to full throttle, and their shattering blast came through the open sides of the cockpit. Very heavily overloaded with fuel, and now with all the mail, and some freight, she taxied slowly out for the take-off; and into position for the longest run on the airfield. There she faced the night with a steady, bellowing roar and slowly moved away.

There was the familiar thunderous stress as she fought her way to speed for flight, and near the end of the airfield the change came with relief, from earth to air; from all doubts and confusion, to an aircraft, airborne and passing into the quiet intimacy of the night where the sound of the motors and the air-stream becomes an unnoticed accompaniment to living.

The night was clear and bright as the *Southern Cross* moved across the light-studded land north of Sydney with a steady purpose in her flight. Soon the coast of Australia came in below and we passed out into the Tasman night. I went below to take back bearings for departure on Norah Head and Macquarie Light. Both stayed bright on the horizon till we were far out from the land, but an hour from Richmond the last flicker disappeared with the world we had left.

The *Cross* was alone, a thing apart from land or sea, steady and sure in space, having no connection in my mind with an aircraft one of whose engines had been strewn in pieces on the floor of a hangar only a few hours ago.

A hundred miles out we ran under a layer of scattered cloud which built up as we flew into the east. As this suggested some southerly weather I went below to let go a flare and check the drift.

The first was a dud. No light showed upon the sea. I let go another, and waited for the point of light to show in the darkness down behind the tail. Far back in the night it seemed to leap up out of the sea in flame; then fade to a glowing point of light moving away astern and to the south.

I reckoned eight degrees of port drift, gave John Stannage the course and dead-reckoned position for transmission, and went forward to give Kingsford Smith the new course to steer. The cloud had shut in to scattered showers of rain and Smithy was flying her on instruments, holding three thousand feet of height above the sea. It was too soon yet with the still heavy overload to think of making height for the westerly.

At about five o'clock I took over to give him a spell from the flying and he went below to see about some wireless messages to Sydney. Between the blind regions of the rain showers it was just possible now to see a faint horizon over the nose of the aircraft, and from the pilot's seat I could see the flame-heated exhaust manifold glowing brightly out over the center motor.

Lifting my eyes occasionally from the flight instruments to take in the early morning weather as signs of light came into the east, I saw nothing unusual in the red glow of the exhaust ring. All my senses were in harmony with the sound, the sight, and the touch of the aircraft and the air, and I sat relaxed and happy, flying into the dawn.

But suddenly I was alerted to a change. Just one small spot on top of the exhaust manifold on the starboard side of the center motor was glowing with a lighter, brighter color than all the other visible parts of the exhaust ring. I looked quickly to the manifolds on the outer motors. The glow was steady and clean, with no light spots on the metal. With all the warning signals up, I flew the aircraft instinctively, concentrating on the exhaust of the center engine. The unusual light was there, and could not be denied. But since nothing could be done about it I kept a close watch on it and began to take in the now visible weather effects upon the navigation. I wanted to pick up the wind force and direction from the appearance of the sea, since there would be little, if any, variation at our low altitude, below the cloud base.

As the light increased, the surface of the sea showed a strong breeze from a little west of south, almost dead abeam. I signaled back to Smithy that I needed to go aft for a drift sight. But at the same moment the importance of any normal working of the aircraft was canceled by unmistakable signs on the manifold. The welded edge of the pipe had split, and through it the exhaust was blowing in a flickering slit of light from the trailing edge. Even as I watched, the blow of the flaming exhaust was gradually forcing open the crack and bursting open the whole top of the manifold.

At that moment Kingsford Smith returned to the cockpit and took over so that I could go aft for the drift sight. But when he was settled at the controls I drew his attention to the state of the center manifold. We both sat fascinated but without comment, watching the rapidly disintegrating pipe, till in a few moments the whole top section was blasted out by the flame, flicked away in the airstream and was gone.

Instantly the most terrific vibration shook the aircraft as though some giant, invisible hand had reached out to shake the life out of her. Mentally, my hand flew to the throttles, but Smithy was flying the Cross and his sure hand was there. He drew off the starboard throttle and we both looked out to the motor. It leapt and struggled in its mounting as though it had gone mad and was trying to wrench itself out of the airplane.

Through the fuselage a sickly, pulsating wobble shook the Southern Cross as the slowing propeller lashed the air: and as we finally saw the blades and they came to rest, one stuck out toward us in broken, splintered wood; a jagged stump, like a lightning-struck tree.

Smithy held up the Cross with two engines at full throttle, but she started to sink toward the sea. A few words passed between us and he turned her away and headed her back for Australia. As an approximate course I clapped 285 degrees on the compass to keep the wind no worse than abeam and to give us the best speed toward the nearest land. It seemed quite theoretical, to be heading for land more than five hundred miles away when at full throttle the altimeter needle was steadily sinking down from the level of three thousand feet.

Weight. That was the thing. Somehow we would have to get rid of weight. Smithy was fully occupied holding the Cross up to the best attitude for flight, and was holding every possible inch of the falling height; but we were obviously destined for the sea within less than half an hour. I shouted across to Smithy, "Have to dump some weight. Shall I go ahead?"

His voice came back in the snarling roar of the extended motors, "Anything except the mail."

I slipped below to the cabin, passed the word to Stannage to dump everything except the mail, and then turned on the dump valve of the main cabin fuel tank. How much to dump? That would have to be worked out immediately before too much drained away.

We had been in the air nearly seven hours. Say seven hours at thirty gallons an hour; 210 gallons gone; 390 gallons left.

I went to the chart and estimated our position and distance out; from Australia—590 miles. Nearly half the distance to New Zealand: but best to go for Australia. Weather and head winds the New Zealand end. Say, six hundred miles to the Australian coast. Speed, with the nearly stalling aircraft, about sixty-five. Wing abeam. Make good her airspeed. Reckon it at sixty. Six hundred miles at sixty. Ten hours.

Ten hours on two motors! Best not to think too much about that. I remembered the rate of flow of the dump valve, and turned off the cock till I got it all sorted out. A glance up into the cockpit to the altimeter. About two thousand feet now.

Ten hours at 28 gallons an hour on two engines. She'd use that, taking out all that power: 280 gallons. Say three hundred. We must keep at least three hundred gallons.

It may appear very risky to have left only enough fuel to reach the coast with so narrow a margin, but this was a risk which had to be accepted against the certainty of descent into the sea. I knew the aircraft would sink within a few minutes. We had no dinghy; nor even life jackets, in the *Cross*. So the picture was clear. The mail had to be kept until the very last emergency. So we had to dump the fuel.

I reckoned up the amount in the top tanks, unscrewed the filler cap of the cabin tank and dipped it with the measuring stick. We could let go more fuel. So I turned on the dump valve again and kept a watch on the decreasing level, with the dip stick.

Finally, leaving a little more than the total of three hundred gallons, I turned off the valve and checked the altimeter. She was down to five hundred feet now, but holding the height: so I left it at that. The few extra gallons would not put her in the sea now. Luggage, tools, freight, and all articles not essential to

flight had gone out into the Tasman Sea. Only the mail remained; the bags lashed down in the cabin behind the big tank.

I went up front, to tell Smithy about the fuel, and to let him
know everything had gone overboard.

There, it was as I had expected. He was settled down, but extended; holding the *Cross* in the air; and his aircraft, feeling the
master touch, leaned heavily on the air, staggering; but flying.
He held her with the wheel, feeling just where her strength
lay; using that, and not overburdening her weakness. He felt her
through his hands and feet, and the seat in which he sat, trying
for support from the slowed-up airstream: and he lay her wing
upon it at exactly the right angle, the only angle, at which she
could fly and maintain height.

Down in the cabin again, I went back to John Stannage and
his radio. We exchanged a smile of appreciation. We found some
humor now in the fact that we were not immediately going down
in the sea. This reprieve brought with it a delicious light-
heartedness that was in strong contrast to the threatened disintegration of our world only a short time ago. The airplane now
was not shaking itself to pieces; it was not losing height; and
that was enough. We really felt quite lighthearted, and did not
yet choose to look into the future at all.

Stannage had been in contact with Sydney, reported the
broken propeller and the precarious situation of the aircraft;
and had given our position, course, and speed. Our clear objective now was to reach land: not Sydney airport, but Australia.
The nearest land was at Port Stephens, where the coast bends
out to the northeast at Stephens Point. There was little difference in the distance; but by laying off north of the track to
Sydney we could bring the wind more abeam and make a better
speed. I gave Smithy a compass course for Seal Rocks, 120
miles north of Sydney, and when he straightened the *Cross* up
on this course the wind was slightly better than abeam.

Up there in the cockpit the two throttle levers were still right
forward, taking all the power the two remaining engines could
give. There was a drastic finality about the sight of those throttle
levers, proclaiming the fact that we had no reserve and were just
maintaining height at three hundred feet. But the old motors of

the *Cross* were snarling defiance at the ocean in the harsh, blaring crackle of their exhausts. We were afloat in the air, even though precariously, and flying; and we did not think too much about how long the engines would keep going, dragging a dead motor and propeller on the starboard side, a still heavy load, and a wing obliged to meet the air at an attitude of great resistance to fly at all. But we hoped they would last till the reduction of weight as they burned down the fuel would allow us to ease them down from continuous maximum power.

As we made some distance westward the showers of rain passed, and through the broken cloud shafts of sunlight brought life to the dull gray world of the ocean. The sun was nearly abeam to the north on a bearing suitable for a position line to check the track of the aircraft. There was too much turbulence for accurate results with the bubble sextant; so, to give me the natural sea horizon, Smithy eased the *Cross* down to a few feet above the sea and I was able to get a good set of sights. Worked, and laid down on the chart, the resulting position line showed us to be making good the track for Seal Rocks.

Over the radio from Sydney we learned now of the action being taken for our rescue. The pilot vessel, *Captain Cook*, had left to intercept our track; H.M.S. *Sussex* would be under way in three hours; and *Faith in Australia* would leave as soon as a suitable pilot could be found for her. All this warmed our hearts considerably and was in principle very reassuring, but to stay in the air and reach land was not only the clear objective for survival, but we were now to have ambitions for return to Sydney airport and a normal landing. It was not long before we were back on the single objective of survival, for the aircraft and ourselves.

For some time I had noticed a steady stream of blue smoke in the exhaust of the port engine. There wasn't much; but it was there, coming away in a continuous streak and very visible in the clear air. It was obvious that this engine was burning oil. There were no quantity gauges on the oil tanks, each situated inside the cowling behind its engine, and therefore no way to measure the amount of oil remaining in the tank. It was assessed from the known consumption of the engine, and normally there was a big margin of oil beyond the range of fuel. Each tank held eleven gallons of oil and normal consumption was less than a quart an hour. Now, with the evidence of this ominous blue stream from the port exhaust, my imagination saw right into a tank with not enough oil to reach Australia. Suppose the engine was burning a gallon an hour. An old engine, wide in the clearances, being thrashed to death at maximum power: it could be burning a gallon an hour; and we had been in the air now for nearly eleven hours. Even allowing for more normal consumption over the first seven hours, at high cruising power, the outlook was not good.

I thought around this problem a good deal, and it kept coming back at me. Eventually I tried to accept this blue smoke and hope that I was wrong about the consumption; but the oil pressure gauge of the port engine now had a fatal fascination for me, and my eyes were never long away from it. I said nothing about it to Smithy or John, because talk could not improve the situation, and in the remote event that they had not noticed it there was no point in passing on such depressing possibilities in a situation already loaded with sinister implications. But the confidence and relaxation which I was beginning to experience as the *Cross* continued to stay in the air and put more of the Tasman Sea behind her were completely ruined by this infernal blue stream of oil smoke, since even the most optimistic wishful thinking could not admit the remotest possibility of the aircraft remaining in the air on one engine. The sea was again the final abyss, and the *Cross* our world hanging precariously above it.

Earlier in the situation I had attempted to cut off the ends of the starboard propeller blades with a hacksaw. I thought that if I could trim off the shattered blade, and cut the other to the same length, we could at least let this propeller windmill, and might even get some thrust from it using some throttle with the engine.

One of Smithy's problems in flying the aircraft was to prevent the airstream turning the broken propeller; for, immediately it started to turn, the unbalanced forces of the blades set up the most appalling vibration which soon would have started the disintegration of the aircraft. Any increase in airspeed above the absolute minimum for flight would set this propeller windmilling and Smithy would have to haul the *Cross* up almost to stalling speed to stop it, and then very carefully ease her down again to the very narrow margin between stalling and windmilling the propeller. This was a terrific strain for a pilot and I had tried to eliminate it by trimming the blades to a more balanced condition.

To attempt this operation I had gone partly out into the airstream from the open side of the pilot's cabin; but the blast of air, and the fact that the propeller would turn every time I tried to work on it with the hacksaw, finally convinced me that there was no future in this idea, and I just slumped back into the cabin, exhausted and frustrated.

But now, with the evidence of the blue smoke trail continuously before me, I began again to think of some way to improve our situation. It was quite uncomplicated, really. If the port motor used all its oil the engine would be destroyed. With the center motor alone we would be in the sea within a few minutes. There the aircraft would sink, and if we happened to survive the ditching with a fixed undercarriage aircraft, we would stay afloat just as long as we could go on swimming in a rough sea without life jackets. There was a strong incentive to do something about oil for the port engine.

I began to speculate about the possibility of somehow getting oil from the tank in the cowl behind the useless starboard engine. There should be at least nine gallons of oil there. If some way could be devised to get this oil, and somehow transfer it to the tank of the port engine, we should have enough oil to keep the port motor going to reach the coast.

Every way I looked at it there was obviously no straightforward way to make this oil transfer, since each engine was a complete unit of its own, with no lines or pipes interconnected. The outboard engines were isolated alone, far out in the airstream under the wing.

After developing every line of thought without any tangible result, it wasn't long before I reached the alarming conclusion that the only way to do this oil transfer was to go out and get the oil from the starboard side and go out again to put it into the tank on the port side. With the results of the propeller-trimming episode fresh in my mind this final conclusion was a very unattractive prospect, but rather than live with defeat in my mind, and with what I now believed was the certainty of being forced down in the ocean, I let this idea of going out in the airstream to the engines support my morale, which was in need of some hopeful outlook at this time. As the idea gained some momentum I found myself starting to work out the details of some practical plan. In the beginning it seemed entirely theoretical, like thinking of flying to the moon (not so theoretical now); but as the plan developed in my mind it began to seem less impossible, and as we flew on low over the ocean I began to see it as something which was at least positive thinking, which freed me from a dumb acceptance of ending up in the bleak and threatening Tasman Sea.

The outboard engine nacelle could not be reached directly from the open side of the pilot's cabin; but out from the fuselage below this window a streamlined horizontal steel tube extended to the frame of the engine mounting. It was part of the lateral bracing system for the engine and the undercarriage leg, and was quite strong. I wondered whether I could get out the side window of the pilot's cabin, stand on this strut in the airstream with my shoulders against the leading edge of the wing, and somehow move out sideways and reach the engine. If I could do that, and hold on out there, I could unclip the side cowl, perhaps reach the drain plug of the oil tank, undo it, and drain out some oil in some sort of container. Then, if I could get back along the strut and into the cabin again, it would mean going out the other side, unscrewing the oil tank filler cap, and pouring in the oil I had collected from the starboard tank. Apparent impossibilities came back at me from this plan—the force of the slipstream, the precariousness of trying to stand on the strut, how could I collect the oil while somehow holding on out in the blast of air? How could I get back with the oil? Then there was the other side.

Impossible. The whole thing.

Then the alternative stared me in the face—the sea.

It had to be possible, somehow; if the port engine burned up all its oil. When was the time to attempt this oil transfer? Now: or when we had evidence of the port engine failing?

I looked again at the outboard engines; away out from the fuselage, at the end of the strut: and I weighed up the chances, both ways. The chance of slipping, of being blown off the strut or the engine mounting, seemed infinitely greater than all my theories of running out of oil. After all, the engines were still roaring away at full throttle, and the only evidence of possible failure was the trail of blue smoke in the port exhaust. Perhaps I was putting it off, staying in the relative safety of the cabin: but I decided it wasn't worth it; unless the oil pressure began to fail.

The wind now had come more into the east, so, with some favorable component in its direction, we decided to alter course for Sydney. I gave Smithy the new course to steer and passed to John Stannage the necessary information for transmission.

For five hours Smithy had been flying the *Cross* in her disabled condition, concentrating for every moment of that time on keeping her in the air. He had lived and felt with his aircraft every effort of her struggle for survival. Knowing his feelings about the *Southern Cross* I rather diffidently suggested that I take over to give him a spell, and try to keep her in the air. He hesitated for a moment; then let me take her.

Immediately I laid my feet to the rudder bar and took the wheel in my hands, I realized the narrow margin by which the two remaining engines were holding her in flight. For a few moments I was lost in my endeavor to react to the needs of the aircraft; but gradually I began to pick up the sensitive signals, and finally to anticipate them and so to hold her in level flight a few hundred feet above the sea.

As I became more accustomed to the feel of the aircraft I was able to relax a little, and my eyes set off on the habitual round of the gauges on the instrument panel. The port oil pressure gauge, the danger point in my mind, was holding steady at 63 pounds to the square inch. Pressure on the gauge of the center motor was approximately the same. The needle of the starboard lay flat at zero on the gauge. The motors sounded healthy and I began almost to feel that the most critical situation was passing, as the engines burned down the weight of the fuel. We were able even to ease the throttles very slightly back from maximum power and still maintain height at three hundred feet. But my eyes continued regularly on the round of the gauges, and I still saw in my mind from the starboard seat the blue smoke trail from the exhaust of the port engine. Apart from its numerical reading, I had noticed a small spot on the face of the port oil pressure gauge, exactly where the needle was pointing. Each time I looked I had mentally checked the holding of the pressure by the needle against this mark.

Now, when I looked again, my eyes were rooted to the gauge and my whole body froze into a rigid warning. The needle was flickering, and as it wavered about the mark on the dial it was very gradually falling below that mark. The oil pressure was definitely falling. No need now to be frozen with doubt and anticipation. The port engine was obviously close to the end of its lubricating oil; close to the end of its life as an engine.

Feeling a dull and futile hostility, I attracted Smithy's attention and pointed to the gauge. A hardness came into his expression as he took over his aircraft from me. He throttled back the port motor, gave it several bursts, and then opened to full power again. The pressure was down to slightly below sixty pounds. We looked at each other across the cockpit with an exchange of expression which obviously agreed, "Well, it won't be long now."

I went below to the cabin, let Stannage know the situation; and he immediately transmitted the signals, "Port motor only last quarter of an hour. Please stand by for exact position."

I then worked up and handed him the estimated position, which he transmitted, "Latitude 34°8'S., longitude 154°30'E."

When I went up to the cockpit again the pressure was down to 35 pounds, and Smithy was starting to take off his heavy flying boots.

Suddenly all reasoning, fear, and emotion of any sort left me, and were replaced by a clear feeling of elation; an obsession which listened to the promptings of nothing but itself: "Get the oil from the starboard tank. Go out and get it."

I slipped below to the cabin, took off my shoes, belted up my coat tightly, unlashed some light line from the mailbags, and went back to the cockpit. Smithy was sitting there, flying the *Southern Cross*, preparing himself to put her down in the sea. I shouted across to him, "Going to have a stab at getting some oil."

He shook his head and tried to stop me, but when he saw my determination he accepted it, and while we still had the port engine he tried to gain a little height.

It amuses me now to remember that I lashed the mailbag line round my waist and made fast the other end in the cockpit. It would have snapped with the slightest jerk, but it had a good moral effect, at the time. Then I stood on the starboard pilot's seat and put one leg over the side, feeling for the streamlined tube to the motor. The airstream grabbed my leg and for a moment a wave of futility swept over me. But it passed and again I was driven by the single purpose of oil for the port motor.

I finally got my right foot on the strut, held fast to the edge of the cockpit with both hands, and managed to get my other foot out, and hang on in the airstream. The blast from the center motor screamed round my ears and pushed with a numb, relentless force against my body. A wave of sudden panic surged within me and I felt the utter madness of attempting to move anywhere but back to the cockpit; if I could get back. I stood on the strut, with my shoulders braced against the rounded leading edge of the wing, with a screaming hurricane threatening to blow my eyes out if I looked ahead. Then the panic passed and I felt no sense of height nor any particular fear of the precariousness of my position: only again the obsession to reach the tank behind the motor.

I braced my shoulders against the wing and tried to wrap my toes around the strut; let go my right hand from the fuselage and edged my feet along till at the full extent of my left arm to the cockpit edge I found I could not reach the engine by reaching out with my right. I was horrified to discover that there was a short distance in the middle of the crossing to the engine where I would have no handhold and would have to move on out with only my feet on the strut and the back of my neck against the wing.

Momentarily, again there was a sense of defeat. It seemed

almost certain that I would never make it, but just be blown off the aircraft and fall into the sea. Then I thought, well I'm going in the sea anyhow; so it's better to take a chance on reaching the engine. I braced my neck well against the wing, got a firm footing on the strut, and very carefully let go my handhold on the cockpit. There was an immediate impulse to make a desperate rush and grab at the engine mount; but I resisted that, and thoroughly steadied myself into the position without any handhold. Then I very carefully moved sideways towards the engine. Those few seconds seemed an eternity and the distance infinite, but I reached the engine mount, and clung to it with both hands. Then the worst feeling of panic of the whole operation swept over me—that of being isolated out there clinging to the engine with no way back but another horrifying foot-and-neck crossing of the strut.

But there was no time for panic. Smithy and John were making signs to me that the oil pressure was dangerously low and I knew something had to be done about it immediately. I hung on with one hand, and with the other tried to get the side cowl pin out so I could reach the oil tank. With maddening deliberation the pin resisted my attempts to undo it, but somehow my fingers dislodged it. The other pins came away quite easily and I wrenched out the side cowl and let it go in the airstream. Under the tank I located the brass drain plug.

I made signs to Stannage for a spanner, but he had anticipated this and by colossal luck had found a shifting spanner which we kept for dismantling the hand pump on the cabin fuel tank. I moved back as far as I could along the strut while still holding on with one hand; and with the other reached out to meet Stannage's hand with the spanner. The combined lengths of our arms saved me another passage without handhold. I slid back to the engine, got the spanner adjusted to the drain plug and eased it back till I could undo it with my fingers. Then I needed something for the oil.

Again John Stannage was ready. I saw he had some sort of metal container (which I afterwards found was that of a thermos flask he had for coffee). By the same process as we exchanged the spanner, I got the flask and quickly had it under the drain

plug. To do this I had to hook one arm through the tubular engine mount, hold the flask in that hand and unscrew the drain plug with the other while sitting astride the strut. It was not particularly difficult really, but the airstream blew the oil away as soon as it came out of the plug hole. But I wangled the container up to the drain hole, got it full of oil, and put back the drain plug to a finger tight position. We could not afford to waste oil, with some hours ahead and the hungry port engine.

Now I had to get this container of oil back to Stannage. This we accomplished in the same way as passing the spanner and the container. After collecting and passing back to Stannage several containers of oil I had then to make the full return crossing to the cabin. I was fairly exhausted by that time so I cared less about the risk of the neck-and-foot crossing, and finally reached the cabin just about all in.

Stannage had been pouring the oil into a small leather suitcase which he kept for his radio gadgets and, again luckily, it did not leak. But the oil pressure was down to 15 pounds.

For a few minutes I simply could not move, or do anything but try to regain my breath. But that gauge got me on my feet again, and I climbed round Smithy in the port seat and tried to get my foot over the side for the passage out to the port engine. The howling blast of both slipstreams, center and port engine, hurled me back against the bulkhead and left me gasping and cursing in futile desperation.

Angry and frustrated by this setback, I looked out across the gap to the failing engine, still obsessed with the one idea of getting there. I forced my leg over the side and pushed with every ounce of my strength; yelled and cursed at the roaring flood of air; but was beaten back to the cockpit; stunned and defeated. Then I saw Smithy's hand go forward to the throttles and push them wide open again. He couldn't let her pick up speed to start an attempt to climb because it would have started the broken propeller windmilling. So he immediately hauled her back and willed and lifted her for height. He looked across at me as I still waited, gasping and hostile against the bulkhead; and I understood his intention.

At about seven hundred feet he shut down the port engine,

leaving her flying at full throttle on one, and immediately starting to lose height. But this was my opportunity to reach the port engine, with its propeller now just whistling round without the blast of its powered slipstream. I went over the side and found I could force a passage against the blast from only the center motor, as I had done on the other side. I reached the engine just as Smithy shouted at me to hold on. I draped myself over the cowl against the V-struts and lay as flat as I could with my head behind the exhaust ring. The engine opened up again with a shattering roar, and looking down from my strange situation on the streamlined cowl section behind the engine I saw the gray surface of the Tasman only a few feet below me. The *Southern Cross*, flying only on one engine, had lost almost all the height as I was making the crossing to the engine. I lay on the cowl, not caring about anything but the temporary relief of not struggling against the airstream, and hung on with the breath being sucked out of my body, behind the roaring exhaust. I remember feeling something pressing against my ribs hurting terrifically, but it didn't seem to matter. There was only hanging on, and breathing, to consider.

Having gained a few hundred feet of height Smithy shut down the engine again. I had my back to the cockpit but it was obvious what he was doing to make it possible for me to transfer the oil. Relieved again of the worst airstream, I struggled up and attacked the cowl over the oil tank filler cap. It came away easily and I bent it back and was able to unscrew the cap.

Stannage was ready. He dipped a flask of oil from the case, I moved back along the strut and we both reached out till I took the flask from him and moved back to the engine. We lost a lot of the oil as it was sucked out of the flask by the airstream, but there was still more than half left as I reached the motor again and held the tin against my body. I climbed up into position over the oil tank, cupped my hand round the opening to avoid losing more oil, squeezed in the top of the flask and poured the oil into the tank. I looked back to the cockpit waiting for the reaction, but with just the ghastly thought now that it might not be shortage of oil in the tank, but a failing oil pump or a blockage in the system. But in a few seconds there was a great shouting and waving from the cockpit, and John Stannage held both his hands out with thumbs up.

Pressure! Oil pressure back on the gauge. It worked!

But Smithy signaled again to hold on. We were almost in the sea. I flung myself down on the cowl again and the motor came in with a booming roar. I could see the surface of the ocean skimming by a few feet below: then I buried my head from the torrent of air and waited for more height and a chance to transfer the rest of the oil in the suitcase. As I lay there jammed against the struts I felt a magnificent exhilaration and a reckless enjoyment of our success which made me want to stand up and laugh and shout at the roaring mass of air that tore at everything around me. In my mind I could see the pointer on the gauge rise up and register the pressure in the oil system. Then the pressure of the strut against my ribs began to crush my body so that I began to feel that I could not hold on any longer. The ocean seemed to be moving faster: then faster, and sinking farther away. A strange ease and resignation came over me. Nothing seemed to matter. It was all some fantasy in a strange retreating background from which I was floating away.

Then a sharp stab of fear hit me and I realized I was letting go, and I felt again a choking numbness in my body, but something telling me to hold on. Just to hold on; to fight the unconsciousness into which I was slipping away.

Suddenly the roar of the engine ceased and I realized that Smithy had throttled back and I had to get more oil. It shocked me back to action and I lifted myself from the cowling and turned to move out and reach for the oil.

In a few minutes Stannage and I had transferred all the oil in the case, about a gallon; but some had been sucked away in the airstream. Then Smithy's shout came again and I had to lie over the cowl again and hear the blast of the exhaust a few inches from my ear. But I was past caring now, and there was the exhilaration of knowing we could keep the *Cross* in the air. When he had a few hundred feet of height he shut down the engine again and I safely made the passage on the strut back into the aircraft. My eyes went to the pressure gauge and I saw the needle at 63 pounds. Then I just lay back on the big fuel tank in the cabin, and let go.

Stannage was again in touch by radio and informed Sydney that we were still in the air. That contact with the world by radio seemed at first to give us some physical connection with Australia, and therefore some basis of security: but one quickly realized that the signals coming in through the wireless set were the faint sounds of a world with which we had no connection, and only impressed upon us the vast solitude of our surroundings.

Fascinated by the oil pressure gauge, my eyes kept coming back to it for a reading, and I started to work out how long it would be before the oil transfer would have to be done again, and how many times it would have to be done in the distance we were still out from Sydney. Because I had lost so much oil in the airstream, only a little over half a gallon actually reached the tank. The engine had burned eleven gallons in twelve hours: so about half an hour seemed like the limit of her endurance on the half gallon of oil.

I checked the speed, time, and distance made good, and estimated that the aircraft was still two hundred miles east of Sydney. We went over all the possible alternatives to this method of transferring the oil, and were forced back to the original conclusion that there was no other way to do it. We either kept on getting the oil or we lost the port motor and went in the sea.

In about half an hour I was horrified to see the oil gauge starting to flicker again. Till I actually saw it happening I had stayed in a kind of neutral state of mind, accepting the respite, and not really facing the fact that I would have to do it again. Now it stared me in the face. I made an effort to throw off all thought, and just act.

Again I reached the starboard engine, collected the oil, went out the other side, and finally completed the second transfer without incident. But I found that this time, to keep the aircraft out of the sea, Smithy had to tell John Stannage to dump the mail. It was a bitter experience for him, but it had to be done, to keep the Cross in the air, because now the port engine was occasionally misfiring and showing signs of packing up. Full throttle for more than a very few minutes brought ominous bangs from the exhaust.

And so we flew on, making the oil transfer about each half

hour, throttling back the port engine to cool it off, and losing height: then bringing it up again and trying to gain a few feet on the altimeter.

About 120 miles from Sydney we sighted the smoke of a ship on the horizon, and later flew over her. (We later learned that she was a small New Zealand vessel, *Port Waikato*.) Smithy spoke of putting the *Cross* down in the sea alongside this vessel, to give us a chance of being picked up: but I knew he was thinking this way so that I would not have to risk more oil transfers. Strangely enough, I had gained confidence in being able to go through this act without slipping or being blown off the airplane, and felt quite exhilarated at the possibility of our reaching Sydney and landing on Mascot airport in good shape. It was typical of Kingsford Smith that he was prepared to lose his aircraft rather than let me risk any more oil transfers; but I felt very sure of myself now, and preferred to go on getting the oil than deliberately to land in the sea with a "wheels down" aircraft. Had we ditched the *Southern Cross*, Kingsford Smith's chance of coming out of it from the pilot's seat would have been small. Stannage and I might possibly have made it, but it had no appeal to me and after a short discussion it was decided to proceed for Sydney.

Our real problem now was the port engine. Smithy had to cool it off by reducing power and each time he throttled it back we began to lose height, with the center motor still blasting away at full throttle. There was little point in worrying about the oil left in its tank. There was just no way of reaching it.

About three o'clock in the afternoon, while Smithy and I were

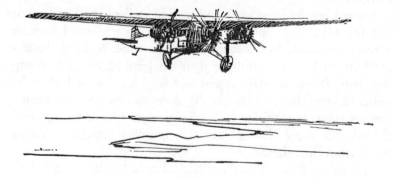

both up in the pilot's cabin, we saw a low purple streak on the western horizon. John Stannage came up, and our eyes never left this vision till we positively identified it as the coast of Australia. The sight of land impressed upon us the truly disabled condition of the *Cross*; but in nearly forty years of life it was one of the best sights I had ever seen. Now that we had actually seen the land it seemed infinitely far away; the aircraft seemed barely to be moving, and unlikely ever to reach it.

The intervals between the choking spasms of the port motor were closing upon us, and Smithy was forced to throttle it back every few minutes to prevent its complete collapse. Then it would cool off and gather strength for another burst, and respond again to the throttle, to keep us out of the sea. But the *Cross* had burned down most of her fuel now and was flying light, and gradually the land grew up out of the sea till we were able to identify the higher land off the port bow as the hills behind Bulli. The desolation of the sea began to be more distant, though it still lay only a few feet below us; and the world we had left in the night only fifteen hours before began to creep back into my mind as a possible reality.

About thirty miles off the coast the engine was calling for oil again and it was obvious that at 60 knots we could not reach the land. Smithy was against my making this last passage for oil and again was prepared to put his aircraft in the sea, since rescue, if we got out of the ditching, was almost certain now. With a wry smile he accepted my suggestion that we do the oil change and go right on in. We were quite close to the land when the pressure gauge settled again on sixty-three pounds. I watched the yellow sands of Cronulla Beach come in and pass under the aircraft as Smithy coaxed its last effort from the banging port engine.

With a perfect approach, he brought her in over the threshold of the airport and feathered her onto the ground. He turned the *Cross* from her last ocean flight, and brought her to rest by the hangar.

The engine which had kept going at full throttle was the one which had been strewn in pieces on the floor of the hangar and assembled mainly by John Stannage and Jack Percival.

FROM

Wind, Sand and Stars

ANTOINE DE SAINT EXUPÉRY

Antoine de Saint Exupéry's books, both fiction and autobiography, have won a permanent place in modern literature for their poetic evocation of the experience of flight—indeed, for their profound commentary on all human experience. Trained in the French air force, Saint Exupéry became a commercial pilot in 1926 and pioneered air mail routes in France, North Africa, and South America. He was lost during World War II on a reconnaisance flight over the Mediterranean. His encounter with a cyclone, related here, occurred in Argentina in 1930.

Cyclone

WHEN Joseph Conrad described a typhoon he said very little about towering waves, or darkness, or the whistling of the wind in the shrouds. He knew better. Instead, he took his reader down into the hold of the vessel packed with emigrant coolies, where the rolling and the pitching of the ship had ripped up and scattered their bags and bundles, burst open their boxes, and flung their humble belongings into a crazy heap. Family treasures painfully collected in a lifetime of poverty, pitiful mementoes so alike that nobody but their owners could have told them apart, had lost their identity and lapsed into chaos, into anonymity, into an amorphous magma. It was this human drama that Conrad described when he painted a typhoon.

Every airline pilot has flown through tornadoes, has returned out of them to the fold—to the little restaurant in Toulouse

where we sat in peace under the watchful eye of the waitress—
and there, recognizing his powerlessness to convey what he has
been through, has given up the idea of describing hell. His de-
scriptions, his gestures, his big words would have made the rest
of us smile as if we were listening to a little boy bragging. And
necessarily so. The cyclone of which I am about to speak was,
physically, much the most brutal and overwhelming experience
I ever underwent; and yet beyond a certain point I do not know
how to convey its violence except by piling one adjective on another, so that in the end I should convey no impression at all—
unless perhaps that of an embarrassing taste for exaggeration.

It took me some time to grasp the fundamental reason for
this powerlessness, which is simply that I should be trying to
describe a catastrophe that never took place. The reason why
writers fail when they attempt to evoke horror is that horror is
something invented after the fact, when one is re-creating the
experience over again in the memory. Horror does not manifest
itself in the world of reality. And so, in beginning my story of
a revolt of the elements which I myself lived through I have
no feeling that I shall write something which you will find dramatic.

I had taken off from the field at Trelew and was flying down
to Comodoro-Rivadavia, in the Patagonian Argentine. Here the
crust of the earth is as dented as an old boiler. The high-pressure
regions over the Pacific send the winds past a gap in the Andes
into a corridor fifty miles wide through which they rush to the
Atlantic in a strangled and accelerated buffeting that scrapes the
surface of everything in their path. The sole vegetation visible in
this barren landscape is a plantation of oil derricks looking like
the after-effects of a forest fire. Towering over the round hills on
which the winds have left a residue of stony gravel, there rises a
chain of prow-shaped, saw-toothed, razor-edged mountains
stripped by the elements down to the bare rock.

For three months of the year the speed of these winds at
ground level is up to a hundred miles an hour. We who flew
the route knew that once we had crossed the marshes of Trelew
and had reached the threshold of the zone they swept, we should

recognize the winds from afar by a gray-blue tint in the atmosphere at the sight of which we would tighten our belts and shoulder-straps in preparation for what was coming. From then on we had an hour of stiff fighting and of stumbling again and again into invisible ditches of air. This was manual labor, and our muscles felt it pretty much as if we had been carrying a longshoreman's load. But it lasted only an hour. Our machines stood up under it. We had no fear of wings suddenly dropping off. Visibility was generally good, and not a problem. This section of the line was a stint, yes; it was certainly not a drama.

But on this particular day I did not like the color of the sky.

The sky was blue. Pure blue. Too pure. A hard blue sky that shone over the scraped and barren world while the fleshless vertebrae of the mountain chain flashed in the sunlight. Not a cloud. The blue sky glittered like a new-honed knife. I felt in advance the vague distaste that accompanies the prospect of physical exertion. The purity of the sky upset me. Give me a good black storm in which the enemy is plainly visible. I can measure its extent and prepare myself for its attack. I can get my hands on my adversary. But when you are flying very high in clear weather the shock of a blue storm is as disturbing as if something collapsed that had been holding up your ship in the air. It is the only time when a pilot feels that there is a gulf beneath his ship.

Another thing bothered me. I could see on a level with the mountain peaks not a haze, not a mist, not a sandy fog, but a sort of ash-colored streamer in the sky. I did not like the look of that scarf of filings scraped off the surface of the earth and borne out to sea by the wind. I tightened my leather harness as far as it would go and I steered the ship with one hand while with the other I hung onto the *longeron* that ran alongside my seat. I was still flying in remarkably calm air.

Very soon came a slight tremor. As every pilot knows, there are secret little quiverings that foretell your real storm. No rolling, no pitching. No swing to speak of. The flight continues horizontal and rectilinear. But you have felt a warning drum on the wings of your plane, little intermittent rappings scarcely audible and infinitely brief little cracklings from time to time as if there were traces of gunpowder in the air.

And then everything around me blew up.

Concerning the next couple of minutes I have nothing to say. All that I can find in my memory is a few rudimentary notions, fragments of thoughts, direct observations. I cannot compose them into a dramatic recital, because there was no drama. The best I can do is to line them up in a kind of chronological order.

In the first place, I was standing still. Having banked right in order to correct a sudden drift, I saw the landscape freeze abruptly where it was and remain jiggling on the same spot. I was making no headway. My wings had ceased to nibble into the outline of the earth. I could see the earth buckle, pivot—but it stayed put. The plane was skidding as if on a toothless cogwheel.

Meanwhile I had the absurd feeling that I had exposed myself completely to the enemy. All those peaks, those crests, those teeth that were cutting into the wind and unleashing its gusts in my direction, seemed to me so many guns pointed straight at my defenseless person. I was slow to think, but the thought did come to me that I ought to give up altitude and make for one of the neighboring valleys where I might take shelter against a mountainside. As a matter of fact, whether I liked it or not I was being helplessly sucked down towards the earth.

Trapped this way in the first breaking waves of a cyclone about which I learned, twenty minutes later, that at sea level it was blowing at the fantastic rate of one hundred and fifty miles an hour, I certainly had no impression of tragedy. Now, as I write, if I shut my eyes, if I forget the plane and the flight and try to express the plain truth about what was happening to me, I find that I felt weighed down, I felt like a porter carrying a slippery load, grabbing one object in a jerky movement that sent another slithering down, so that, overcome by exasperation, the porter is tempted to let the whole load drop. There is a kind of law of the shortest distance to the image, a psychological law by which the event to which one is subjected is visualized in a symbol that represents its swiftest summing up: I was a man who, carrying a pile of plates, had slipped on a waxed floor and let his scaffolding of porcelain crash.

I found myself imprisoned in a valley. My discomfort was not less, it was greater. I grant you that a down current has never killed anybody, that the expression "flattened out by a down current" belongs to journalism and not to the language of flyers. How could air possibly pierce the ground? But here I was in a valley at the wheel of a ship that was three quarters out of my control. Ahead of me a rocky prow swung to left and right, rose suddenly high in the air for a second like a wave over my head, and then plunged down below my horizon.

Horizon? There was no longer a horizon. I was in the wings of a theater cluttered up with bits of scenery. Vertical, oblique, horizontal, all of plane geometry was awhirl. A hundred transversal valleys were muddled in a jumble of perspectives. Whenever I seemed about to take my bearings a new eruption would swing me round in a circle or send me tumbling wing over wing and I would have to try all over again to get clear of all this rubbish. Two ideas came into my mind. One was a discovery: for the first time I understood the cause of certain accidents in the mountains when no fog was present to explain them. For a single second, in a waltzing landscape like this, the flyer had been unable to distinguish between vertical mountainsides and horizontal planes. The other idea was a fixation: The sea is flat: I shall not hook anything out at sea.

I banked—or should I use that word to indicate a vague and stubborn jockeying through the east-west valleys? Still nothing pathetic to report. I was wrestling with chaos, was wearing myself out in a battle with chaos, struggling to keep in the air a gigantic house of cards that kept collapsing despite all I could do. Scarcely the faintest twinge of fear went through me when one of the walls of my prison rose suddenly like a tidal wave over my head. My heart hardly skipped a beat when I was tripped up by one of the whirling eddies of air that the sharp ridge darted into my ship. If I felt anything unmistakably in the haze of confused feelings and notions that came over me each time one of these powder magazines blew up, it was a feeling of respect. I respected that sharp-toothed ridge. I respected that peak. I respected that dome. I respected that transversal valley opening out into my valley and about to toss me God knew how violently as soon as its torrent of wind flowed into the one on which I was being borne along.

What I was struggling against, I discovered, was not the wind but the ridge itself, the crest, the rocky peak. Despite my distance from it, it was the wall of rock I was fighting with. By some trick of invisible prolongation, by the play of a secret set of muscles, this was what was pummeling me. It was against this that I was butting my head. Before me on the right I recognized the peak of Salamanca, a perfect cone which, I knew, dominated the sea. It cheered me to think I was about to escape out to sea. But first I should have to wrestle with the gale off that peak, try to avoid its down-crushing blow. The peak of Salamanca was a giant. I was filled with respect for the peak of Salamanca.

There had been granted me one second of respite. Two seconds. Something was collecting itself into a knot, coiling itself up, growing taut. I sat amazed. I opened astonished eyes. My whole plane seemed to be shivering, spreading outward, swelling up. Horizontal and stationary it was, yet lifted before I knew it fifteen hundred feet straight into the air in a kind of apotheosis. I who for forty minutes had not been able to climb higher than two hundred feet off the ground was suddenly able to look down on the enemy. The plane quivered as if in boiling water. I could see the wide waters of the ocean. The valley opened out into this ocean, this salvation. And at that very moment, without any warning whatever, half a mile from Salamanca, I was suddenly struck straight in the midriff by the gale off that peak and sent hurtling out to sea.

There I was, throttle wide open, facing the coast. At right angles to the coast and facing it. A lot had happened in a single minute. In the first place, I had not flown out to sea. I had been spat out to sea by a monstrous cough, vomited out of my valley as from the mouth of a howitzer. When, what seemed to me instantly, I banked in order to put myself where I wanted to be in respect of the coast line, I saw that the coast line was a mere blur, a characterless strip of blue; and I was five miles out to sea. The mountain range stood up like a crenelated fortress against

the pure sky while the cyclone crushed me down to the surface of the waters. How hard that wind was blowing I found out as soon as I tried to climb, as soon as I became conscious of my disastrous mistake: throttle wide open, engines running at my maximum, which was one hundred and fifty miles an hour, my plane hanging sixty feet over the water, I was unable to budge. When a wind like this one attacks a tropical forest it swirls through the branches like a flame, twists them into corkscrews, and uproots giant trees as if they were radishes. Here, bounding off the mountain range, it was leveling out the sea.

Hanging on with all the power in my engines, face to the coast, face to that wind where each gap in the teeth of the range sent forth a stream of air like a long reptile, I felt as if I were clinging to the tip of a monstrous whip that was cracking over the sea.

In this latitude the South American continent is narrow and the Andes are not far from the Atlantic. I was struggling not merely against the whirling winds that blew off the east-coast range, but more likely also against a whole sky blown down upon me off the peaks of the Andean chain. For the first time in four years of airline flying I began to worry about the strength of my wings. Also, I was fearful of bumping the sea—not because of the down currents which, at sea level, would necessarily provide me with a horizontal air mattress, but because of the helplessly acrobatic positions in which this wind was buffeting me. Each time that I was tossed I became afraid that I might be unable to straighten out. Besides, there was a chance that I should find myself out of fuel and simply drown. I kept expecting the gasoline pumps to stop priming, and indeed the plane was so violently shaken up that in the half-filled tanks as well as in the gas lines the gasoline was sloshing round, not coming through, and the engines, instead of their steady roar, were sputtering in a sort of dot-and-dash series of uncertain growls.

I hung on, meanwhile, to the controls of my heavy transport plane, my attention monopolized by the physical struggle and my mind occupied by the very simplest thoughts. I was feeling practically nothing as I stared down at the imprint made by the wind on the sea. I saw a series of great white puddles, each per-

haps eight hundred yards in extent. They were running toward
me at a speed of one hundred and fifty miles an hour where the
down-surging windspouts broke against the surface of the sea
in a succession of horizontal explosions. The sea was white and
it was green—white with the whiteness of crushed sugar and
green in puddles the color of emeralds. In this tumult one wave
was indistinguishable from another. Torrents of air were pouring down upon the sea. The winds were sweeping past in giant
gusts as when, before the autumn harvests, they blow a great
flowing change of color over a wheatfield. Now and again the
water went incongruously transparent between the white pools,
and I could see a green and black sea bottom. And then the
great glass of the sea would be shattered anew into a thousand
glittering fragments.

It seemed hopeless. In twenty minutes of struggle I had not
moved forward a hundred yards. What was more, with flying as
hard as it was out here five miles from the coast, I wondered
how I could possibly buck the winds along the shore, assuming
I was able to fight my way in. I was a perfect target for the
enemy there on shore. Fear, however, was out of the question.
I was incapable of thinking. I was emptied of everything except
the vision of a very simple act. I must straighten out. Straighten
out. Straighten out.

There were moments of respite, nevertheless. I dare say those
moments themselves were equal to the worst storms I had hith-
erto met, but by comparison with the cyclone they were moments of relaxation. The urgency of fighting off the wind was
not quite so great. And I could tell when these intervals were
coming. It was not I who moved towards those zones of relative calm, those almost green oases clearly painted on the sea,
but they that flowed towards me. I could read clearly in the waters the advertisement of a habitable province. And with each
interval of repose the power to feel and to think was restored to
me. Then, in those moments, I began to feel I was doomed.
Then was the time that little by little I began to tremble for
myself. So much so that each time I saw the unfurling of a new
wave of the white offensive I was seized by a brief spasm of panic

which lasted until the exact instant when, on the edge of that bubbling cauldron, I bumped into the invisible wall of wind. That restored me to numbness again.

Up! I wanted to be higher up. The next time I saw one of those green zones of calm it seemed to me deeper than before and I began to be hopeful of getting out. If I could climb high enough, I thought, I would find other currents in which I could make some headway. I took advantage of the truce to essay a swift climb. It was hard. The enemy had not weakened. Three hundred feet. Six hundred feet. If I could get up to three thousand feet I was safe, I said to myself. But there on the horizon I saw again that white pack unleashed in my direction. I gave it up. I did not want them at my throat again; I did not want to be caught off balance. But it was too late. The first blow sent me rolling over and over and the sky became a slippery dome on which I could not find a footing.

One has a pair of hands and they obey. How are one's orders transmitted to one's hands?

I had made a discovery that horrified me: my hands were numb. My hands were dead. They sent me no message. Probably they had been numb a long time and I had not noticed it. The pity was that I had noticed it, had raised the question. That was serious.

Lashed by the wind, the wings of the plane had been dragging and jerking at the cables by which they were controlled from the wheel, and the wheel in my hands had not ceased jerking a single second. I had been gripping the wheel with all my might for forty minutes, fearful lest the strain snap the cables. So desperate had been my grip that now I could not feel my hands.

What a discovery! My hands were not my own. I looked at them and decided to lift a finger: it obeyed me. I looked away and issued the same order: now I could not feel whether the finger had obeyed or not. No message had reached me. I thought: "Suppose my hands were to open: how would I know it?" I swung my head round and looked again: my hands were still locked round the wheel. Nevertheless, I was afraid. How can a man tell the difference between the sight of a hand opening and the decision to open that hand, when there is no longer an exchange of sensations between the hand and the brain? How can one tell the difference between an image and an act of the will? Better stop thinking of the picture of open hands. Hands live a life of their own. Better not offer them this monstrous temptation. And I began to chant a silly litany which went on uninterruptedly until this flight was over. A single thought. A single image. A single phrase tirelessly chanted over and over again: "I shut my hands. I shut my hands. I shut my hands." All of me was condensed into that phrase and for me the white sea, the whirling eddies, the saw-toothed range ceased to exist. There was only "I shut my hands." There was no danger, no cyclone, no land unattained. Somewhere there was a pair of rubber hands which, once they let go the wheel, could not possibly come alive in time to recover from the tumbling drop into the sea.

I had no thoughts. I had no feelings except the feeling of being emptied out. My strength was draining out of me and so was my impulse to go on fighting. The engines continued their dot-and-dash sputterings, their little crashing noises that were like the intermittent cracklings of a ripping canvas. Whenever they were silent longer than a second I felt as if a heart had stopped beating. There! that's the end. No, they've started up again.

The thermometer on the wing, I happened to see, stood at twenty below zero, but I was bathed in sweat from head to foot. My face was running with perspiration. What a dance! Later I was to discover that my storage batteries had been jerked out of their steel flanges and hurtled up through the roof of the plane. I did not know then, either, that the ribs on my wings had come unglued and that certain of my steel cables had been sawed down to the last thread. And I continued to feel strength and will oozing out of me. Any minute now I should be overcome by the indifference born of utter weariness and by the mortal yearning to take my rest.

What can I say about this? Nothing. My shoulders ached.

Very painfully. As if I had been carrying too many sacks too heavy for me. I leaned forward. Through a green transparency I saw sea bottom so close that I could make out all the details. Then the wind's hand brushed the picture away.

In an hour and twenty minutes I had succeeded in climbing to nine hundred feet. A little to the south—that is, on my left—I could see a long trail on the surface of the sea, a sort of blue stream. I decided to let myself drift as far down as that stream. Here where I was, facing west, I was as good as motionless, unable either to advance or retreat. If I could reach that blue pathway, which must be lying in the shelter of something not the cyclone, I might be able to move in slowly to the coast. So I let myself drift to the left. I had the feeling, meanwhile, that the wind's violence had perhaps slackened.

It took me an hour to cover the five miles to shore. There in the shelter of a long cliff I was able to finish my journey south. Thereafter I succeeded in keeping enough altitude to fly inland to the field that was my destination. I was able to stay up at nine hundred feet. It was very stormy, but nothing like the cyclone I had come out of. That was over.

On the ground I saw a platoon of soldiers. They had been sent down to watch for me. I landed nearby, and we were a whole hour getting the plane into the hangar. I climbed out of the cockpit and walked off. There was nothing to say. I was very sleepy. I kept moving my fingers, but they stayed numb. I could not collect my thoughts enough to decide whether or not I had been afraid. Had I been afraid? I couldn't say. I had witnessed a strange sight. What strange sight? I couldn't say. The sky was blue and the sea was white. I felt I ought to tell someone about it since I was back from so far away! But I had no grip on what I had been through. "Imagine a white sea . . . very white . . . whiter still." You cannot convey things to people by piling up adjectives, by stammering.

You cannot convey anything because there is nothing to convey. My shoulders were aching. My insides felt as if they had been crushed in by a terrible weight. You cannot make drama out of that, or out of the cone-shaped peak of Salamanca. That peak was charged like a powder magazine; but if I said so people would laugh. I would myself. I respected the peak of Salamanca. That is my story. And it is not a story.

There is nothing dramatic in the world, nothing pathetic, except in human relations. The day after I landed I might get emotional, might dress up my adventure by imagining that I who was alive and walking on earth was living through the hell of a cyclone. But that would be cheating, for the man who fought tooth and nail against that cyclone had nothing in common with the fortunate man alive the next day. He was far too busy.

I came away with very little booty indeed, with no more than this meager discovery, this contribution: How can one tell an act of the will from a simple image, when there is no transmission of sensation?

I could perhaps succeed in upsetting you if I told you some story of a child unjustly punished. As it is, I have involved you in a cyclone, probably without upsetting you in the least. This is no novel experience for any of us. Every week men sit comfortably at the cinema and look on at the bombardment of some Shanghai or other, some Guernica, and marvel without a trace of horror at the long fringes of ash and soot that twist their slow way into the sky from those man-made volcanoes. Yet we all know that together with the grain in the granaries, with the heritage of generations of men, with the treasures of families, it is the burning flesh of children and their elders that, dissipated in smoke, is slowly fertilizing those black cumuli.

The physical drama itself cannot touch us until some one points out its spiritual sense.

The Flying Years

LOU REICHERS

It was a period, Lou Reichers wrote of the 1920s and 1930s, when the greatest danger in flying was that the flyer would starve. All sorts of promoters labored to persuade a skeptical public that aviation had a future. Aircraft manufacturers, the armed forces, commercial airlines, newspapers, and wealthy sportsmen were happy to encourage such attention-getting activities as stunt flying, transocean flights, and air races. For a time, endurance flights were popular, with aviators seeking a short-lived notoriety and a little cash by trying to stay aloft longer than anyone had done before. The grueling endurance flight of 1930 that Reichers describes here was organized by a prematurely graying Irishman named MacPail, a veteran of the baling-wire days of aviation, and by Captain John S. Donaldson, a World War I pilot. Two high-winged monoplanes driven by Lycoming 200-horsepower engines were to be involved. Philip Watson, an ex-army pilot was to fly the mother plane and the Lycoming Engine Company had sent one of their field representatives, Captain Kane, to help out where necessary. Reichers and fellow pilot Bob Black were to attempt to stay aloft for a full month, for which they were to receive $3.00 each per hour—$72.00 a day—and a share of the profits from endorsements offered by companies providing them with oil and gas, a two-way radio, a storage battery and spark plugs. Here Reichers recalls the record-setting flight in which he and Black flew an estimated 31,350 miles nonstop, spending 313 hours and 35 minutes—thirteen days and thirteen nights—in the air.

Two Weeks in the Air

For six days we worked like Trojans, making minor changes and perfecting our method of contact. At eighty miles per hour, the fifty-foot length of hose assumed a trailing angle of about forty-five degrees. We would fly about thirty feet below and to one side of the mother plane, and gradually skid under her, allowing the hose to drag along the trailing edge of the left wing until the nozzle struck the fuselage. When the pilot felt the nozzle strike, he would hold his position and fly formation on the mother plane. The one in back would reach for the hose and put the nozzle into the filler neck. While gas was flowing into the tank, the mother plane would lower a canvas bag, guided to the hose by a large ring. In this bag was our food and drinks. Donaldson had arranged with a doctor to prescribe a diet—something special for folks who can't exercise.

The advance publicity had created considerable interest, and crowds were driving to the field every evening, hoping to see us take off. We were ready on the twenty-first of July.

Our wheels left the ground at 7:00 P.M. Donaldson had prevailed upon us to take off light and make an immediate refueling contact over the field for the benefit of the sight-seers and the morning newspaper reporters. We transferred seventy gallons of gas, took on board sandwiches and coffee, and settled down for our first night. Since we had to check over the field every hour, we soon worked out a series of sight-seeing trips to relieve the monotony of aimless circling. We flew over nearby communities, spotting homes of our friends, buzzing them, and checking the time they turned their lights out.

The first night was a hot one. New York was in the throes of a heat wave. We tried various altitudes and found that 5000 feet was the most comfortable. When dawn was breaking, we radioed for a six o'clock contact at 2000 feet over the field, ordered breakfast, and the morning newspapers. Due to the heat and excitement, neither of us had slept much, and our attempt to make contact with the mother plane was very ragged. Watson flew his plane too slowly; I was having difficulty maintaining our relative position. Donaldson, whose job it was to pay out the hose from the mother plane, was sitting in the open doorway, and I motioned with my hand for more speed. He relayed the information to Watson and Phil opened the throttle too fast, jerking the hose out of Bob's grasp. In a split second, the hose tangled with our propeller. Before Donaldson could shut off his emergency valve, my windshield and the top of our plane were liberally doused with raw gasoline. All that I could think of was— fire! I yanked the throttle back and cut the switch. The hot engine kept turning over and jumping around in its mount— the propeller blades had been damaged. It was a miracle that we hadn't caught fire and fortunate that we were within gliding distance of the field. I made a dead-stick landing, ending our first attempt to establish a new record.

Mac and Kane "pulled" the propeller. Both blades had been badly nicked and bent. The prop had to be replaced. While Kane was checking the motor to make sure the propeller shaft hadn't sprung, Bob and I went over the contact speed and signals once again with Donaldson and Watson. The bad news spread fast, and our well-wishers of the day before became our critics today. We could overhear snatches of conversation: "There go the damn fools." "What are they trying to prove?" "Who cares about refueling in the air?" "They'll bust their butts before the week's out."

I took Bob by the arm. "Come on, Phil has a couple of cots in the rear of his office. Let's get away from these bums for a while and rest. They'll be wishing us in our graves, next."

"Yeh," answered Bob. "Particularly those reporters. They actually looked disappointed that we hadn't caught fire."

The plane was ready to go again by noontime, but Donaldson asked us to delay until evening. "People will have read about your close one in the early editions. They'll be out here in force right from work to watch your take-off and first contact." He patted us on the back. "Make it a good one, right over the field."

We took off again at 6:30 P.M. and made our first refueling

contact over the field two hours later. If anything, it was hotter than the night before, and we were soon stripped down to our shorts. Coney Island and Jones Beach were crowded with families seeking to escape the heat of the city, and by daylight we could still see thousands of them sleeping on the sand. The early morning contact was made without a hitch. We took turns flying, eating our breakfast, and reading the morning papers.

Donaldson had been right about creating public interest, only most of it was unfavorable. Newspaper editorials were tearing us apart. Residents adjacent to the field complained about the motor noise and asked that we be adjudged a public nuisance. The Nassau County authorities threatened to prevent the refueling plane from taking to the air, thereby forcing us to land. Donaldson called us on the radio, happy as a lark. "Keep it up, fellows, you're doing great. We've got a real rhubarb going and the press is playing it up to the hilt. Just be sure you don't break any of the Department of Commerce regulations."

"But John," I replied over the radio. "Suppose they ground Watson. What then?"

"Don't give them any reasons to and they won't dare. We'll sue if they do! And listen," he continued excitedly. "This report just came in—they've gone overboard! This is what the county district attorney said: 'Effective immediately, civilian flights after 11:00 P.M. banned by airports on residents' complaints, and after September first, at 10:00 P.M.,' and here's the soft soap he's added, 'It must be kept in mind that private fields are undoubtedly here to stay and that we, the public, must put up with some degree of annoyance from them.' So you see, Lou, he knows he can't make that ban stick. Now don't bust any of the regulations!"

"O.K., John." I cut off the radio. It was time to crawl out and service the engine.

"Bob," I said, "head for the mud flats while I switch tanks and dump this old oil. Then stay away from these towns while I give the 'mixmaster' out front a few shots in the arm. And tonight, I think we'd better forget about checking the time our friends go to bed and stay over the open countryside. I wouldn't put it past Donaldson to have started all this. Bet he's made over half those complaining phone calls to the district attorney himself. I can almost see him now, sitting down and writing phoney letters of complaint to the editor. Anything for a story —that's Donaldson."

After refilling the oil tank and tossing out the empty cans, I crawled out on the catwalk to service the motor. Squirting the penetrating oil on the valve stems wasn't such a tough job, for I could hold the can and operate the plunger with one hand, leaving the other free to hang on. The only trouble was, the slip stream blew half the thin oil back in my face and smeared my goggles. The next time I carried a rag to wipe them clear.

But greasing the rocker arms required both hands. I soon worked out a satisfactory scheme of straddling the cowling in back of the engine, riding it like a horse, and leaning over almost on my face, I could grease all the rocker arms except those on the bottom cylinders. To reach the lower ones on the right-hand side, I had to lie face down on the catwalk, wrap my legs around the tubing to hang on, and feel with my hands for the grease fittings. Through this whole operation I remained uncomfortably conscious of the spinning prop less than six inches from my head. After burning my arms a few times on the hot exhaust stack, I managed to fit the flexible tube to the cap and force the grease through. To reach the lower cylinder on the left side, I pulled myself over the cowl and lay down on the catwalk on that side. It was a lot tougher doing it in the air than on the ground.

After greasing the magneto cam shaft, I crawled back through the window. "Bob," I said, "I dread the thought of changing those spark plugs. That fan out front gives me the willies. I just don't like it!"

"I don't like any part of that business out front," he replied. "How about you doing all the servicing? You make it look so simple."

"Nuts! This is a fifty-fifty job. It's your turn next. I'm going to check the battery and then sleep. Wake me up in four hours. Sooner if you get tired."

Bob let me sleep the full four hours, then woke me. "Time for our noon contact. How did you sleep?"

"Pretty good. Did you radio the field?"

"Yes." As we changed places, he added, "I can see Phil warming up. Wonder what they'll lower us to eat?"

We transferred fifty gallons of gas, and Donaldson lowered to us creamed chicken, rolls, cake, milk, a gallon of drinking water, and water to wash with. After lunch Bob took a nap. I soon tired of sitting in one position and radioed the field to talk to Donaldson again. "I'm built too close to the bones and my rear end is getting sore. Buy me one of those round rubber air cushions they use in hospitals."

"O.K., Lou," he laughed. "I'll lower one on your next contact. Need anything else?"

"Yes, more distilled water for the battery. It's evaporating fast in this heat."

"Right. And how are your cigarettes holding out?"

"We've quit smoking for the duration, but you could send down some mints. And double up on the water this evening. We're drinking more than we planned. What does the weather bureau say—any chance of a break in this heat? What's the official temperature?"

"Hottest July 23 on record. Official temperature is ninety-nine degrees. Why don't you fly higher and cool off? I'll see that you get the extra water and mints."

"Thanks, John. And you might tell those radio people that their set is working fine, only the next one should be designed with a broadcasting channel. Then we could help pass the time away by listening in on the local broadcasting stations."

"Yeh, too bad," was his sarcastic reply.

The air cushion added measurably to our sitting comfort. After the dusk contact I lay down for my four hours' sleep. Suddenly Bob remarked, "You know, Lou, I think I'm pregnant."

"What?"

"Yup, I think I'm pregnant. I keep wanting the damnedest things, now that I can't have them. Like now—I'd give an arm and a leg for a strawberry soda. Just a while ago I was wishing for a corned-beef sandwich on rye with a big juicy kosher pickle."

"Chew some mints, you bum, and let me sleep. Don't call me until 1:00 A.M."

And it was precisely 1:00 A.M. when Bob awakened me. I hung my head out of the window for a few minutes to blow the sleep out of my eyes. After checking the gas gauges and engine instruments, I flew while Bob pumped gas from the fuselage tank into the wing tanks. Then he went to sleep.

We had settled down to a prescribed routine. One of us flew for eight straight hours, while the other performed all the necessary chores—handling the hose, the food, changing oil, and servicing the motor. This left him about four hours of uninterrupted sleep. It was a tough grind, and the results began to show up on the third day. It was becoming increasingly harder to awaken the sleeping one, and it was with difficulty that I aroused Bob before daybreak on the fourth morning.

"Bob, gas!" I yelled, and grabbed a handful of hair and shook his head violently. "Gas! Wake up! Bob! The wing-tank floats are almost to the bottom. Look!" I turned my flashlight on the outside wing-tank float gauges.

He jumped up and grabbed the fuselage-tank hand pump and went to work. I flashed my light on the gauge again on my side, and noticed a thin spray coming from the underside of the wing near the float. I was able to lean far enough out of my open window to reach it with my hand. Then I put my hand to my nose. It was gas!

"Bob!" I cried. "This tank has sprung a leak! How much gas do we have in the fuselage tank?"

"Nearly empty!"

"Pump the rest into the right wing tank while I radio the field. Be sure you get every drop."

I called the field and stood by while they awoke Mac. "We are in trouble, Mac. The left wing tank has sprung a leak during the night and we're running out of gas. Get Watson up here, pronto!"

"But it's dark!" replied Mac. "You can't see to make a contact. You'll never find the hose!"

"We've got to—or land! I don't think we have more than a half-hour of gas left. Do this! Tie some flashlights to the hose, about ten feet apart, and I think we can do it. In fact we have to, so don't waste any more time arguing. We need gas! I'll wait over the field at 3000 feet. Hurry!"

Bob was worried. "Do you think we can do it in the dark?"

"Sure! We've done lots of night formation flying and those flashlights will stick out like sore thumbs. Are you wide awake now?"

"Yes, I'm plenty awake."

"Good. Now this is how we'll do it. We're going down to 3000 feet and meeting them over the field. Without jockeying for position, I'll slide under him. Don't lose any time grabbing for the hose. When you want me to break contact—bang on the side of the fuselage. Then quick like a mouse, pump some into the right wing tank. If necessary, we'll contact again. From the looks of that gauge, this is going to be touch and go. I wish they'd hurry!"

Watson actually lost no time in getting off the ground, and we met over the field. The night was as black as the ace of spades, but the string of flashlights was easy to find. I slid under his plane, keeping one eye on his exhaust flame, and Bob grabbed the hose before the nozzle struck the side of the fuselage. I heard his, "I've got it!" over the noise of the exhaust. Not more than five gallons could have been transferred when the engine started cutting out—starving for gas! Bob banged on the fuselage and then frantically transferred the small amount to the wing tank.

In the meantime, I had closed the throttle and started gliding toward the field. I was lining up for a landing when Bob yelled, "O.K., Lou! Try her now!" I hit the throttle. The motor took hold once again. I chased after Watson and slid into position once again. This time we completed the transfer. I waved my flashlight to Donaldson and broke contact.

When Bob came forward I said, "You fly. I'm shaking all over, can't keep my legs still."

He wasn't in much better shape, but took over and I flopped on the floor alongside. When Phil landed, I watched his navigation lights until he taxied over to his hangar and then waited for Mac to call me on the radio.

"We transferred fifty gallons of gas, and Donaldson lowered to us creamed chicken, rolls, cake, milk, a gallon of drinking water, and water to wash with." —*Two Weeks in the Air*

"That was a close one, Lou," said Mac when he called. "How does it look? Will you have enough until daylight?"

"I think so. The right tank looks O.K. I'll call you at the crack of dawn when I can see better. Now listen carefully. Tell everyone who knows anything about this to keep his mouth shut! The Department of Commerce will take a very dim view of what we have just done, if they hear about it. And be sure you put a muzzle on Donaldson."

"O.K., Lou, we'll contact you again at the regular time. Meanwhile, we'll stand by with loaded tanks in case you need us again. That was nice flying, you guys."

"Thanks, but remember: mum's the word! This district attorney would jump on us with both feet if he ever found out about this."

We surveyed the situation in the daylight. Our left tank was useless. It had cracked near the gauge. This was going to work an additional hardship, for it meant that we would have to pump gas from the fuselage tank every two hours. Gone were those four hours of uninterrupted sleep, and I radioed Mac the bad news.

"Do you birds think you can stick it out?" he asked.

"I don't know," I replied. "I've talked it over with Bob, and we feel we'd like to try it for a few days. Maybe we can stand it. We'd hate to throw the last four days and nights overboard and start from scratch again."

"O.K., I'll talk it over with Donaldson. I know he'll want you to keep going if at all possible. Now that you've passed the hundred-hour mark, we're beginning to get inquiries from other possible sponsors. I'm sending each of you birds a wrist watch —they're shockproof and waterproof. The manufacturer wants to advertise that due to the close timing with his watches we were always able to make contact. You know, the usual baloney. Anyway, the watches are yours, and furthermore, your food isn't costing anything now. The restaurant is giving us the food now for allowing them to put up a sign saying that they are feeding you two, and we're talking to the people who sell the coffee you're drinking. So stay up there, Lou, and you'll be rolling in dough."

"Speaking about money, Mac, reminds me. Our three bucks an hour. Where is it?"

"Don't worry about your money, it'll be here when you come down. Besides, you can't spend it where you are now."

"That may be true, but Donaldson owes us over three hundred dollars apiece, and we think he should deposit the money in a bank to our accounts."

"I'll tell him when he shows up. In the meantime, keep flying."

Donaldson radioed shortly before our noon contact and talked about contracts with sponsors and then went into a pep talk. "Stay up there at least a month, but don't take any chances. This endurance craze has hit everyone. Some kids have started a tree-sitting contest in Nassau County, and in New Brunswick, New Jersey, they've started a bicycle-riding contest. At Rock-away Beach pool there's a water-endurance contest, and in Bloomfield, New Jersey, the kids have come up with a baseball-pitching deal. Parents are complaining, but the publicity is piling up. One boy fell out of a tree and broke his arm, and another is charging reporters twenty-five cents an interview. You're doing great. Two-hour naps will get you by, and you've plenty of time for those." He cut the switch before I could ask him about our pay.

Afternoon thunderheads were piling up in the west, and before going to sleep, I remarked to Bob, "If that storm starts coming our way—wake me."

It seemed as though I hadn't had any sleep at all when Bob woke me. He had a handful of my hair and was banging my head against the side of his seat. "Damn it, Lou, but you're hard to wake up! That storm is almost on top of us and you have to pump some gas. Besides, it's your turn to fly." And he banged my head some more.

Half-awake, I pumped while Bob watched the wing-tank gauge. When the tank was full, he said, "O.K., we'd better change places before this hits. It's going to be a lulu. Look at that lightning!"

I was wide awake now and just had time enough to fasten my safety belt when the deluge struck. Rain? It was a cloud-burst! And rough? We bounced around like a cork on the ocean.

We were now at 500 feet and occasionally losing visual contact with the ground. The lightning was playing all around, and I headed for the high-tension wires that bordered the field: at least the towers were well grounded and would keep the surrounding atmosphere free of static, lessening the chance of our being struck. At 100 feet we were barely able to see the ground. Turning parallel to the wires I picked out two towers and started flying figure eights, using the towers as pylons. It took a half-hour for the center of the storm to pass over the field and then I was able to climb back to 500 feet. In another half hour I was back to the safer altitude of 1000 feet. The rain was now letting up and the air wasn't so rough. We began to relax and breathe more freely. "After going through that one," Bob remarked, "we can fly through anything."

I nodded in agreement, but I was glad it hadn't hailed. In storms like that one, you sometimes hit hailstones as big as golf balls, and with those linen wings . . .

We flew directly over the field. It looked like a lake. All airplanes had been hangared and the doors closed. We circled aimlessly, waiting for the rain to stop and the static to clear up, for our radio was useless until it did. I was worried. What if the mother plane was unable to take off in time for our next refueling contact? In spite of the static, I managed to make a radio contact. "Mac," I asked, "how does it look down there? In about one hour we're going to need gas!"

"We'll make it," he replied. "It's draining off fast. Stick close to the field; we may have to take off with a light load and contact you twice. That one was a pip. How did you like it up there?"

"Like it? We didn't!"

From the spray the mother plane threw up on take-off, she looked like an amphibian, but somehow Phil managed to stagger into the air. He transferred twenty gallons, enough to last us another two hours. By then, the field had drained sufficiently for Phil to take off with a full load and we filled our fuselage tank for the night.

We read the next morning's papers with interest. The headlines said, "Violent Electric Storms, High Winds Hit City," and

"Freak Storms Flood Subways." Then there was one about us. "Endurance Flyers Ride Out Season's Worst Electrical Storm. Now in Their Sixth Day." It was Sunday morning, and the papers were nice and fat. Lots of comics and the rotogravure sheets were loaded with pictures. The sports news wasn't all bad; even though Cleveland did take a double-header from the Yanks— Babe Ruth had smacked out his thirty-sixth home run. Another piece interested me. "Bob," and I nudged him, "did you read this article about the possibility of night baseball?"

"Nope, I'm more interested in these new cars. Look at this one! Isn't it a dandy? A Marmon straight eight for only $950. That's what I'm going to buy. How about you, Lou, what are you going to do with all your money?"

"I want a new car too, but I'm going to look them all over first. Now that we're up here and can't spend any money, everyone has a sale on. Look! Davega has a matched set of MacDonald irons for only $9.94, and Wallach Bros. have a sale of Hart Schaffner & Marx suits, with plus fours, for only $24.50. And here's Douglas Aircraft stock on the Curb—the asking price is twenty-one and the bid is nineteen. I'm going to buy some of that. Half of the money I make on this flight, I'm going to save. The other half, I'm going to blow in.

"And that reminds me, those bums down there haven't said a word about depositing our pay in the bank. Hand me the mike, Bob. I'm going to call Mac."

When Mac answered, I asked, "Did you say anything to Donaldson about our money?"

"Yes I did, and John said you'd have to sign personally to open an account. What are you worrying about? Donaldson will take care of your pay."

"We'd still like to know that it's in the bank. Now listen. Sometime tonight, at 1:10 A.M. to be exact, we will pass the endurance record set by Major Carl Spaatz and Captain Ira Eaker in that Army Fokker at Los Angeles last year. They stayed up for 150 hours and 40 minutes, with the help of the U. S. Air Service. At 6:30 A.M. tomorrow, we will have been in the air for 156 hours and we'll feel better with a bank account. Tomorrow have someone pick up two savings-account applications at the

County National Bank. Send the blanks down to us during our noon contact. We'll sign and return them with the dirty dishes. Multiply 156 hours by three dollars and you'll see that Donaldson owes us $468 each.

"When we make our evening contact, have Donaldson lower us the two bankbooks showing that amount deposited to our accounts. Be sure that you impress Donaldson that if those books do not come down with our supper—we pull the cork and land. Bob and I are not fooling. No bankbooks and the flight is over!"

"O.K., Lou, I'll tell him." I imagined him shaking his head and saying to himself, "Banking by air——"

"And one thing more, Mac, before you sign off. From then on, we want slips lowered every evening showing that the seventy-two dollars we earned the day before has been deposited to our accounts."

With the start of the second week, the business of going no-place and having all day and all night to do it in became more and more monotonous. But the monotony did not last long. Bob was out on the catwalk the morning of the eighth day, servicing the engine. It had been purring along like a kitten when suddenly I began to detect a little unevenness. I lined up the rocker arms of number one cylinder on a distant water tower, sighting them like a gun, and watched. Yes, the engine was jumping a little in the mount. Reaching over, I rested my fingertips lightly on the instrument panel. Feeling a little roughness there, I rocked the plane to attract Bob's attention.

When he poked his head into the cabin, I asked, "What happened out there? The motor has just started running a little rough!"

"I think I put too much grease on the magneto cam shaft," he replied with a worried frown. "Looks like the shaft threw some on the points."

"Very much? Is it going to give us trouble?"

"I don't know, maybe you'd better come out and look."

Bob crawled back into the ship. We changed places and I climbed out. After removing the magneto cover and carefully examining the points, I had Bob switch off the front plugs and then the rear ones—while I tried each time to clean the excess grease from between the points with a strip of cardpaper. But the damage had already been done, the points had started to pit. This looked like the start of the finish, and when I climbed back inside, Bob asked, "What do you think? Will it smooth out again?"

"Nope. Not a chance! In three or four hours that motor will be ready to jump out of the mount. She'll keep running rougher and rougher. We'll have to land soon, before we shake apart."

We were a sad-looking pair. Except for the split wing tank, everything had been going along swell. We were even believing that the month was a cinch. Now this, just a little too much grease, and the flight was over. Eight wasted days! Bob finally broke the silence. "Lou, isn't there something that we can do? There must be something. We can't come in and land. Not for something like that!"

"I don't know, Bob." I felt down in the dumps. "Stick close to the field, and I'll go out for another look."

I went out and studied the magneto for some time and then crawled back. "Bob, I think there's a chance—a slim one! I think we can change the whole damn assembly. I'm going to radio the field and talk to Kane."

When Kane answered, I said, "We're in trouble! We put a little too much grease on the mag cam shaft this morning and the points are beginning to pit."

"Has the engine started to run rough?"

"Yes. Not bad, but I can feel it through my fingertips on the instrument panel—a bad sign."

His silence made me ask. "Did you hear me? Are you still there?"

"Yes, I heard you. What do you want me to do! Come up and hold your hand? You were cautioned about that, you know."

"I know, but the damage has been done. Have you any suggestions?"

"Don't let her get too rough before you decide to land," was his caustic retort. "You might break a gas line or crack the other tank."

"Listen, your sarcasm isn't any help, but I think I've an idea. We'll change the entire breaker assembly! There's only a couple of screws holding it down. I'll remove those, pull out the old assembly, and drop in a new one."

"But, Lou, you can't adjust the points in flight! You know that no two magneto assemblies are exactly alike. Both sets of points have to be adjusted to the thousandth part of an inch. How are you going to get around that?"

"We can't, but here's what we can do! Use the mother plane as a gauge, and have someone check you. Write down every movement you make; list them by the numbers, and time each one with a stop watch. Try to simulate flight conditions—working with one hand and stuff like that. Remove the old breaker assembly and fasten in a new one. Do this a half-dozen times and give me your average time. We'll have to take a chance that the gap set for the mother plane will be accurate enough for us. Also, be sure you send along with the new assembly a well-magnetized screw driver, one strong enough to hold the fastening screws, because there isn't room enough for fingers. Don't waste any more time telling me I'm nuts! I'll stand by on the radio for your answer."

After we had been circling for about a half-hour, Kane radioed. "Here's the dope. It can be done—*if* you can stop the propeller from turning!"

I didn't think that would be a problem, and I let him continue without interruption.

"Taking it very slowly, my average for six tries was three minutes. So if you go up to 10,000 feet, cut your engine, pull her up into a stall and stop the prop, then let the nose drop and hold a minimum glide, you should have plenty of time to make the change and crawl inside before you have to dive to start the motor again.

"We're going to take off in a few minutes and lower the assembly with complete step-by-step instructions and sketches. Study them carefully before trying. And, Lou—good luck!"

The motor was now roughening noticeably. We lost no time in making our contact and effecting the transfer. I studied the instructions, and they looked simple enough. Bob studied them and said, "Looks like there is nothing to it, just as long as I don't drop one of those damn screws."

"You mean—you want to go out there and make the change?"

"Of course! I'm the guy that loused it up!"

We changed places again, and I put her into a climb. At 10,-000 feet, Bob crawled out, fastened his belt to the guardrail, and I handed him the new assembly and the magnetic screw driver. He signaled when he was braced and ready. I pulled the throttle back and cut the switch, then eased back on the control wheel to stall the ship in an attempt to stop the propeller from turning. At the stall, the plane shuddered violently and fell off on a wing. I dove her to regain control, started the engine again and climbed back to 10,000 feet to try again. In the third attempt, the plane fell into a tight spin, glueing Bob against the side of the cowl. I lost two thousand feet in the recovery.

Bob crawled back in, shaking like a leaf. "Bob," I said, "I can't stop that damn prop from turning, the motor is too well worn-in. What do you think your chances are with the motor turning over? You know how tight that assembly fits over the cam shaft. If you get it the least bit cocked, the whole assembly will start spinning—twist right out of your hand. Might tear your fingers off!"

"I think I can do it. Besides, we haven't any other choice!"

Bob pumped more gas into the wing tank and then climbed out again. I cut the switch and held the plane in the flattest glide possible. With the power off, and the drag of the free-wheeling propeller, plus the drag of Bob's body, our rate of descent was a little over 1200 feet per minute. That meant he had to make the change in not much over twice the length of time that Kane took to do it on the ground.

Two minutes went by and the altimeter needle pointed to 7500 feet, but Bob was still hunched over the cowl. He seemed to be having difficulty and was now straddling it. Three minutes. Four minutes, and we were now at 5000 feet and still going down—fast!

Suddenly Bob threw his leg back and slid down to the cat-walk; his movements were hurried and a foot slipped. I thought he was gone, but his safety belt saved him. It wasn't fear that I saw in his face, it was cold fury. He reached a hand through the open window and yelled, "The hammer! Quick! I'll fix the G—" The rest was unintelligible.

I gave him the hammer, handle end first, and shrugged. I had expected too much. Bob must have cocked the assembly and was so damn mad that he was going to beat the hell out of the magneto with the hammer.

I looked over the side to check the wind-sock and then glided for a position to make a dead-stick landing. I leaned my head out the window and shouted, "Come back in here! I can't land with you out there, too nose-heavy! We'll go over on our back!"

He acted as if he didn't hear me, and, holding the hammer by its head, using the handle like a ramrod, he jammed it down— hard! I was resigned now. This was the end of the flight, and I was glad that we were now lined up with the field, and into the wind. At 500 feet, with the edge of the field dead ahead, Bob turned his head and yelled, "O.K., Lou! Switch on!"

I had committed myself to a landing and was hoping that I'd get away with it without hurting Bob, but there was something about the expression on his face that gave me new hope. I reached over and turned the switch on. The motor caught! I hit the throttle and she wound up as if nothing had ever been wrong. After clearing the hangars at the end of the field, I put her into a climb. Bob was still on the catwalk leaning over the cowling and patting it affectionately. I rocked the wings and when he looked back, I motioned and yelled, "Come in here, before I spin you in!" He grinned in reply and waved his hand nonchalantly as if to say, "Nothing to it," and took his own sweet time climbing back through the window.

As soon as my nerves quieted a little, I called the field and talked to Kane. "She's running like a clock again, but we had a tough time. Couldn't stop the prop, and the assembly caught on the cam shaft, but Bob knocked it loose with the hammer handle."

"When we saw you go into that spin we knew you were in trouble, knew you couldn't stop the prop. I still don't see how, under the circumstances, you birds ever made the switch. Send the old one up on your next contact. Everything else O.K.?"

"Yup, but tell Mac we need gas. We used plenty for all that climbing. I'll wait for Watson over the field."

With that crazy stunt behind, we knew that nothing could stop us now. The month was in the bag. We had money in the bank, and were adding to it at the rate of seventy-two dollars a day. While we were discussing our good fortune, Bob asked, "No fooling, Lou, what are you going to do with all your money?"

"I'm going to build a speakeasy, with a peek-a-boo door and everything. When people ring the bell, I'm going to peek at them through my little door and shake my head—no! I won't let anyone in. That's my ambition. To own a speakeasy, and be able to afford not to do any business."

"You've been up here too long, Lou. Are you sure you're feeling all right?"

I grinned—I was too happy to make sense. "What are you going to do with your share?"

"I'm still going to buy a new car. Did you noticed the ad for the new Ford in this morning's paper? It's a brand new model— a de luxe Phaeton with wire wheels. The windshield folds forward. The little beauty sells for only $625. Studebaker is bringing out a new job, too. This one has free wheeling and they say it saves twelve per cent on gas and twenty per cent on oil."

"I thought you were going to buy that new Marmon."

"I changed my mind. I think I'll buy a smaller car."

It was fun squandering our money this way, and it didn't cost anything. But we had to return to realities, to dodging thunderstorms, servicing the "mixmaster," pumping gas, and trying to get enough sleep.

A few nights later, to relieve the boredom of aimless circling, I flew over Brooklyn to Governors Island and then up the Hudson River to about Fifty-ninth Street. I marveled over the advancement of aviation in the short span of twenty years: since that Sunday in 1910, when I stood on a Battery Park bench and watched Glenn Curtiss complete his historic flight from Albany to New York to win the $10,000 prize offer by *The World* for the first person to fly from Albany to New York, or New York to Albany, in a mechanically propelled airship, either lighter or heavier than air.

People were saying that Curtiss was "batty," had a "screw loose," and that if "God intended that we should fly, we'd have been born with wings." But when his flying machine flew past the Battery, not over fifty feet high, and circled the Statue of Liberty before landing on Governors Island, I had made up my mind to become, as they called it in those days, an aeronaut.

The memory of that day had been engraved on my mind. I could still see the black biplane with Curtiss sitting out in front on the leading edge of the lower wing. The motor was mounted directly in back of his neck, and between the bicycle wheels that were his undercarriage he had fastened a canoe in the event of an emergency landing in the Hudson River. Yes, compared with the modern planes, Curtiss' was sure a funny-looking job.

I was glad when day broke and Bob took over. Before dropping off to sleep, I told him, "The motor seems to be running a little rough. And our fuel consumption—I think it's increasing. You check and we'll compare notes when I wake up."

When I awakened, we discussed the engine and Bob confirmed my fears. I radioed the field and discussed the symptoms with Kane. He took all the joy out of my life: "Spark plugs. They're fouling! You passed the 276-hour mark at 7:30 this morning. That's more than we expected out of those plugs, and I advise changing them immediately. We'll lower you a new set at noon-time, and let me caution you once again. Watch out for that propeller while changing those front plugs! Particularly those two lower cylinders!"

I could tell by the set look on Bob's face that he'd call the flight off before he'd crawl out and change the plugs, so I asked him if he could stand a longer trick at the controls while I changed the plugs. He agreed. We decided to make the change at 5000 feet over the ocean off Jones Beach, in case I dropped any of the plugs or the tools.

I crawled out. Changing the rear plugs was a cinch, and when Bob switched the mag to run on the new plugs the motor picked up twenty-five r.p.m.s—a good sign.

"Now," I thought. "Those damn front ones!" But my parachute was in the way. It hampered my freedom of movement, so I climbed back into the cabin and took it off.

"You going out there without your chute?" queried Bob. "Have you gone nuts?"

"Have to! The harness keeps interfering with my arms. If I get clipped by the prop, what in hell good will the chute be?"

"O.K. Want to go any higher? Maybe we can find an altitude where the air is smoother."

At 8000 feet the air was better, and I radioed the field. "We're going to change the front plugs over the water from Jones Beach to Coney Island—back and forth. This is going to be a ticklish job and can't be hurried. Tell the official observer that he can easily see us from the field and that we must have the smoother air over the water. Ask him if he'll waive that one-hour requirement of checking over the field."

Mac inquired and reported, "He said O.K. And, Lou, take it easy."

I crawled out on the catwalk, but felt so insecure without my parachute that I tumbled back in again. "What happened?" Bob asked.

"I felt naked out there, without my chute. I don't like it! I'm going to make myself a couple of safety belts out of this clothes-line I asked for the other day. I had something like this in mind."

I cut two convenient lengths of rope. One I knotted around my waist, leaving the other end free to fasten to the guardrail. The other length I fastened to an ankle and tied the free end to Bob's seat. "This way, Bob, you can feed me slack as I need it, and if the worst comes to the worst—you might be able to pull me back!"

Bob looked at the rope arrangement and shook his head. "Look, Lou, we've busted the Army's record. Let's call it enough and land——"

I gave him a friendly poke and crawled out again. This time I felt more secure, but soon found out that I was short one hand. Since I needed both hands to make the change—one to hold the exhaust valve down, and the other to unscrew the plug—I had no way to hold the new plug. I solved this problem, for the moment, by sticking the plug in my mouth. I started with number one cylinder, the top one, and worked my way down the right side; then crawled over the cowling and worked my way down the left side. I learned a lesson changing the first plug. I removed the hot plug with my gloved hand and, forgetting all about the heat, I put it in my mouth in exchange for the new one. After that, as I removed the plugs, I let them drop over the side to the water below.

It was tedious work. I was always conscious of the three inches of clearance between my knuckles and the turning propeller. It took me almost two hours to change the nine plugs, and I returned to the cabin just in time to pump gas up to the wing tank.

Bob flew over the field and I reported the change completed. Mac answered. "The spark-plug representative is sore because you lost all the front plugs. He wanted them for laboratory tests."

"Tell him that I'm sorry, please, but if he can figure a way to send me another hand, I'll save the plugs for him the next time we have to make a change. How does this change effect our $10,000 contract?"

"Donaldson is going to meet with them tomorrow. You just stay up there and keep grinding away. How's she running since the change?"

"Smoother, but somehow I have the feeling that we're still burning too much gas. Maybe the new plugs will change that. Talk it over with Kane. I think the rings are wearing a little. You know we're pushing the 300-hour mark, and if we're using too much gas, that's a sign of lost compression—worn rings. Or else the carburetor jets are wearing and the mixture is now too rich. You might ask Kane about that, too. Maybe we should lean out our mixture a little—ask him!"

That night I had a long talk with Kane and he sounded concerned. "How is your oil temperature?" he asked.

"Running about five degrees above normal. Has been for the past ten hours or so."

"Then don't monkey with the mixture control. Keep her running full rich. How are you at full throttle? How many r.p.m.s can you get wide open in level flight?"

"I'll try now and let you know. Stand by."

I opened her up wide and waited until she steadied down and then called back. "We're running about seventy-five r.p.m.s short. What does that tell you?"

"Piston rings. Could be the rings, or maybe valves. You're beginning to lose some compression. There's nothing that you can do, except possibly change your oil more often. Might keep your temperature down that way, change it twice a day, instead of only once. I'll check with the factory tonight and let you know tomorrow. They might advise using heavier oil. Stand by for my call around ten in the morning. I should hear by then."

Kane was prompt the next morning. "The factory said your condition was a normal one. You've passed your three-hundred-hour mark and they expect some piston-ring wear, but the chances are it's your valves. They need adjusting. Their only recommendation is to do what I suggested yesterday. Change oil more frequently. How are you running now?"

"The same—a little hot. Do you think we're heading for any trouble?"

"Offhand, no! You'll be starting on your third week tomorrow, and should be good for at least one more—that'll be your month. We'll send you oil twice a day now. Here's Donaldson. He wants to talk to you."

"Hi, Lou. I want to check over some statistics for a special news release. You've more than doubled the Army endurance record, and the newspapers want some comparisons. How do these figures check? Your total number of contacts to date—58. Total number of full meals served—39. Gallons of coffee—26. Gallons of drinking and washing water—312. And boy, have you fellows got mail. We have over 500 pounds of it sitting on the floor. What are you going to do with all the phone numbers? Some of them are real cute, they've enclosed pictures."

"Stick to the statistics, John. Our records show that we've taken on 3100 gallons of gas, but I can't help you on the oil, we've lost track the last few days. Don't mention anything about changing the mag points, that was our fault. You can do as you wish about the spark-plug change. And if you're interested in our general health, we feel fine, except that we're always tired. In fact, we're putting on weight. Not enough exercise. Anything else?"

"That's all for now, and incidentally, we expect a big crowd of sight-seers today. Stick around close to the field."

Late in the afternoon Bob awakened me and pointed to the oil temperature gauge. "Engine is running hotter. What do you think?"

I didn't like it. I turned on the transmitter and called Kane. "The oil temperature has gone up another five degrees. How does that sound to you?"

"Not so good," he replied. "How is your oil pressure? Is that going down?"

"No, it's steady. And maybe I'm imagining things, but I think the motor is beginning to run rough again. Kane, I don't like it!"

"I don't either, Lou. When was the last time you changed the oil?"

"Directly after lunch."

"I'll send Watson up with some more. Change it again and call me back."

While Donaldson lowered the oil, we took on additional gas and then Bob headed for the mud flats. Before changing the oil, I went out on the catwalk and examined the engine carefully. I squirted penetrating oil on the valve stems, greased the rocker arms, and oiled the generator. The inside of the engine compartment seemed hot, and the engine a little rough, everything else was O.K. But I was frowning when I climbed back into the cabin.

Bob looked at me intently. "You're worried, Lou. Anything wrong out there?"

"Nothing that I can put a finger on. Just a premonition. Maybe this oil change——"

I never had time to finish the sentence. The motor skipped a few times, then started backfiring. The engine revolutions dropped in half and we thought the motor would jump out of the mount. Bob cut the switch and the propeller ground to a stop. There was nothing but swamps under us, and it was questionable whether Bob could make the field.

When it became apparent that he couldn't stretch his glide

to Roosevelt Field, Bob shouted, "Salisbury Country Club, dead ahead. I'm going to sit her down on that long fairway. I hope those players clear out of our way!"

"She's your baby, Bob. I'm going to throw all this loose junk out, lighten our load. They'll see it falling and know we're in trouble."

I started throwing oil cans, water bottles, tools, and finally I pitched out the parachutes. Occasionally I'd glance over the side to see how Bob was doing, and I just had time enough to brace myself before we hit. Bob had realized at the last second that he could not clear a high bunker, straight ahead.

"Hang on!" he yelled. As the wheels hit the ground, he pulled back on the controls and bounced right over the bunker. We seemed to hang in the air for an instant, and then we dropped like a ton of bricks, rolled a short way, and stopped. Right side up! The last lucid picture I had of the Sunday golfers was just before we hit the ground. They were throwing their clubs away and running like hell.

Except for a sprung undercarriage and a bent axle, there was no damage to the plane. We were looking the motor over when one of the golfers ran up, all out of breath, and asked, "Your motor quit?"

"No!" I replied in disgust. "We landed to find out what your score was."

Other golfers surrounded us. Out of curiosity I asked one, "What fairway is this?"

When he replied, "The thirteenth," Bob and I just exchanged glances.

FROM

Pilot

TONY LEVIER

Tony LeVier earned his pilot's license in 1930, just as the Great Depression was settling over the country. In the lean years that followed he struggled to support himself by barnstorming, stunt flying, and teaching for as little as seventy-five cents for a five-minute lesson. Though his clothes were threadbare, he considered himself lucky to be flying at all when other pilots were driving trucks. Flying began to pay for LeVier in 1935, when he turned to professional racing. His first big success came in 1938. In that year he won the Pacific International Air Races at Oakland, California, and the Greve Trophy at the National Air Races in Cleveland with a little racer called The Firecracker.

Racer

THE plane was a Keith Rider racer named *The Firecracker*. C. H. "Gus" Gotch, a West Coast pilot, flew it at Cleveland in 1937, winning third in the Greve Trophy Race at an average speed of 231 miles an hour. The owner was Bill Schoenfeldt, a Los Angeles aviation enthusiast, whom I knew through Vernon Dorrell. Bill offered me the chance to fly his plane in 1938, with the understanding that I would take it over and put it in shape and he would back me in the Pacific International Air Races.

This was an act from heaven, a thing I had been dreaming of for years. Now I was going to get my chance in a real racer, a plane capable of more than 330 miles an hour, which at that time was a fantastic speed. After visiting Bill's shop on Western Avenue and getting acquainted with the airplane, I set up a schedule to do the job, as I was the only person who would work on it. Bill bought all the parts and supplies needed for overhaul and I paid for my own labor.

The Firecracker looked like its namesake, with a long, barrel-shaped fuselage, a small, low wing and a couple of small fins for a tail. But it was powered by a Menasco Super-Buccaneer inverted six-cylinder engine developing 550 horsepower, and it was the fastest plane in the world for its size and engine displacement. I completely reconditioned this airplane and overhauled the engine, and made my first test flight early in May at Long Beach municipal airport.

Up to this time I had not flown a really fast airplane. Sitting in the tiny little cockpit, I started the engine and listened to it roar. I am a fairly large man, and as there was not room for both me and my parachute in the cockpit, I had removed the cockpit canopy for the first flight. I was squeezed in so tightly that Don Reece and Roger Don Rae had to buckle me in my seat.

Roger had flown The Firecracker before, and he was at the field this morning to tell me what to do. He had not yet given me a word of instruction, and finally I turned to him and said, "Roger, I'm ready to go and you haven't told me a single thing."

He bent down so I could hear him over the roar of the engine. "Look," he said. "As you apply power to the engine the nose will want to go down. Hold the nose up by pulling the stick back. The plane will swing to the left. Move the rudder and make the necessary adjustment to keep it straight and hang on to your hat. That is all I know."

That is all he said. I pushed the throttle forward and the plane leaped ahead. It was like being tied to a rocket. This made the Pobjoy feel like a tired old horse. In four or five seconds I had left the ground and was streaking upward. The next time I looked at the airspeed indicator I was going over two hundred miles an hour. After half an hour of tests I landed, thrilled by the performance of this airplane and confident we had a winner. At once I telephoned Bill to tell him how well it flew, and he was so excited that words failed him.

We took the airplane to Oakland on May 24, where we assembled it and prepared to qualify. This was a big day in my life. I had never even qualified, much less flown in a big race before, and had never competed against famous pilots like Roscoe Turner and Earl Ortman, who were among the professional flyers participating in the Pacific International Air Races that year. Some of them knew me but had yet to see me perform, and I have no doubt there was considerable speculation as to what kind of bird was this Tony LeVier.

We were able to do a favor for Roscoe which paid off later for us at Cleveland. When he reached Oakland he found a bad gasoline leak in his plane and half the fuel was in the bottom of the fuselage. We happened to have a supply of the special rubber hose he needed to fix the leak, which we gave him, and through no fault of his own he missed winning the main event by a narrow margin.

There were three main races over a period of three days—the first two for planes in the 550-cubic-inch class and under, which were open to planes like mine, and the final event which was unlimited. I qualified on my first attempt and Roscoe qualified in his Turner-Laird Special. Art Chester was flying the *Jeep*, a midwing monoplane with external bracing, and Steve Wittman was on hand with two planes, the D-12-powered *Bonzo* and the veteran *Chief Oshkosh* with a new Menasco engine. Gus Gotch was entered flying a new midwing monoplane with a good racing record, the *Folkerts Special*.

I knew from previous flights in *The Firecracker* that in order to get the landing gear up after take-off I had to climb out very steeply at a high angle and slow the plane up by pulling the power back. As my first race got under way I performed this maneuver, which slowed me up and permitted the entire field to get in front of me. But once my gear was up I immediately took off and began catching the pack.

I passed Steve Wittman, who was leading, but he put on a little more power and passed me. Then I put on a little more and passed him again. Finally I ran him out of power. He had no more to call on and I was out in front going away when his engine blew up. He was out over the water, but Steve was a good flyer and he got back to shore, where he landed in a potato field. His plane was a wreck but he escaped serious injury, and he raced again in *Bonzo* on the final day.

The second race was very much the same except for Steve. It was here that Gus Gotch ran into trouble out over No. 2 pylon in San Francisco Bay and actually went out of control and spun in. I also won this race easily, as the competition wasn't up to the speed potential of my airplane. *The Firecracker* was certainly living up to its name. With two victories under my belt, all my friends were pulling for me to win the main event and make it a clean sweep. I got one telegram reading, "Congratulations make it three straight we are all for you," and signed, "Boys Los Angeles Eastside Airport." Another said, "Dearest Tony love and best wishes for your success God bless you," and was signed "Mama."

Now, however, I was up against the big boys, such as Roscoe Turner, three-time winner of the Thompson Trophy Race, and Earl Ortman in a Keith Rider Special built for the London-Melbourne international air races. But the thing that bothered me most was the fact that I could not wear a parachute in the cramped cockpit of my airplane and still close the canopy over my head. When I sat on the 'chute there just wasn't room for both of us. Another problem was a gasoline leak behind the engine firewall that developed at the last moment. There was no time to fix it before the race, so I stuffed rags around it to soak up the leaking gasoline and said another prayer.

Bill and I had planned that I would hold a certain speed and allow Turner and Ortman to lead if they chose, up to the fifth lap of the eight-lap race, when I would make my spurt and catch them. Turner, Ortman and I all left the ground at the same time. I had to slow up to retract my gear as usual, and the whole field got ahead of me. Then I took out after them and quickly passed everyone but Earl Ortman. I was holding my own against him when Turner went by me, and we continued in this order through the fifth lap.

As I entered the sixth lap I opened up my engine for the first time and began gaining on the leaders so rapidly I knew that in another lap I would catch them. At that moment my oil pressure suddenly dropped to nearly zero. Faced with a quick decision to reduce power or go ahead and possibly damage the engine, I decided to take no chances and throttled back to my earlier power rating. I finished the race that way, winning third place.

After the total points were counted I had the highest score for the three-day meet and was awarded the trophy for champion pilot. This so encouraged Schoenfeldt to shoot higher that he immediately entered *The Firecracker* in the national air races.

They were held at Cleveland again in 1938, and interest as usual centered about the Thompson, Greve and Bendix trophy races, the first two of which we planned to enter. Bernarr MacFadden was entered in the Bendix that year but cracked up before the race shooting landings, and Jacqueline Cochran won it in her Seversky low-wing monoplane, the only woman in the field of ten who started. Total prize money at Cleveland increased from $82,000 to over $102,000, and Schoenfeldt had visions of making a real killing. *The Firecracker* carried extra fuel for the Thompson race, which was longer than any we had flown previously, and our plane was nothing but a flying gas tank when we left for Cleveland.

We had also increased the engine power, and it blew sky-high on my first qualifying flight; only luck saved me from a bad accident. Inspection revealed that the No. 2 piston had a hole the size of a silver dollar blown through the head. The No. 2 cylinder was badly scored and required honing before it would be fit for use. There seemed no possibility of repairing it that afternoon, and the deadline to qualify was the next morning.

It was only a few minutes before Roscoe Turner heard of our predicament. In return for our assistance at Oakland he offered the services of his entire crew to help fix our plane. While we dismantled the engine he took Bill and the cylinder in his Packard and drove madly across Cleveland to find a machine shop before closing time. After working all night on the engine it was ready the next morning, and I flew and qualified for the Greve trophy race a few minutes before the deadline.

As race time drew near on Sunday I became excited and very tense. An air race with a racehorse start is considered one of the

great spectacles of competitive sport. Unlike other forms of racing that take place on the ground, air racing is in the third dimen-
sion and requires great alertness on the part of the pilots to avoid
flying into one another.

We were lined up at the starting line—Art Chester in his new
racer, the *Goon*, powered by the Menasco C6S Super-Buccaneer
engine, the same one I was using; Joe Jacobson in Keith Rider's
new creation, a sleek all-plywood Menasco racer called the *Eight
Ball*; Earl Ortman in a Marcoux-Bromberg, the *Jackrabbit*;

George Dory, a newcomer, in the Bushey-McGrew Special, another Keith Rider racer called the *Bumblebee*; and Harry Crosby
in a brand-new all-metal plane of his own design. Harry had
crashed in a similar plane in the 1936 races and had been laid
up for two years with a broken back. He designed this new plane
while in a plaster cast in the hospital.

I was strapped in my seat with the engine running when the
one-minute flag went up. Bill Schoenfeldt was on the field helping the crew hold the plane down. He tried to hide his excitement to ease my own tension, but it wasn't hard to see he was

jumpy too. He shook my hand and called good luck over the roar of the Menasco.

As the seconds ticked away I had my eyes on the official starter with both flags high in the air. My heart was beating so hard I could feel it pounding above the vibration of my powerful engine. Then the flags came down, and my throttle was already forward before they touched the ground.

We took off north toward Lake Erie and the first scatter pylon about one mile away. As *The Firecracker* leaped ahead, I caught

a glimpse of Art Chester's cream-colored *Goon* to my left and slightly behind me. At the take-off halfway point I was still in front of him and gaining. The runway was smoother than I had expected, and I bounced only a couple of times before leaving the ground.

Now I pulled up sharply in the familiar maneuver to get my landing gear retracted; if my speed was over two hundred miles an hour the wheels would fail to close into their wells against the tremendous pressure of the air. I had to crank them up by hand in that airplane, and as I slowed up the other planes flashed past me, with Chester leading. I was momentarily dejected, but then I reminded myself that *The Firecracker* had enough speed to catch all of them if my engine would keep going.

The crank handle turned hard and stopped. With my gear finally up, I banked sharply to the left around the scatter pylon, a striped tower sticking one hundred feet into the air. Leveling out from my first turn I moved the throttle forward again and pointed the nose of my plane down the No. 1 straightaway.

The five other planes were bunched together about half a mile ahead, with Chester still in the lead. My Menasco engine was almost wide open and I caught and passed George Dory and Harry Crosby on the back stretch. Earl Ortman and Joe Jacobson were just beyond them.

I pulled up slightly at the No. 3 pylon and passed Ortman as I rolled into my turn in a near-vertical bank, swinging in with my eye on the pylon to cut it as closely as possible. My plane was still gathering speed as I passed Jacobson on the far side of the turn.

Only Chester was in front of me now, his engine spewing black smoke, and I knew he was "coaling" it, but I had the speed to catch him. No. 4 pylon was still half a mile ahead when I passed him going into my next turn. As I crossed the white starting line I took the No. 1 adhesive tape tab from my instrument panel and stuck it on my metal seat. One lap completed, 10 miles flown—19 laps and 190 miles still to go. This was my first long race—twice as long as Oakland. Could I stand the strain? Even Oakland was an effort in this airplane. It was not designed around a frame as big as mine, and I sat hunched over in the cockpit even without a parachute.

I went by Chester so fast I saw no need to burn up the engine unnecessarily and I throttled back from 3350 to 3000 rpm's. I was in the back stretch on the second lap when he passed me. Easing the throttle forward to 3100 rpm's again, I gained just enough speed to stay with him; if I flew closer to the pylons on my turns I would be able to conserve the engine still more.

I turned inside of him at the next pylon, using elevators and ailerons, and passed Chester again. The laps flew by. At the ninth lap we had both lapped the field. As I entered my eleventh lap he passed me for the umpteenth time, when suddenly without warning my engine misfired.

I snapped to attention and scanned my instruments for signs of trouble—3200 rpm's, oil pressure 45, oil temperature 205 degrees, fuel pressure 12 pounds. I wobbled my auxiliary fuel pump and the pressure surged to 14 pounds, but the engine was still rough and continued misfiring. I checked the cylinder head and base temperatures for each cylinder. The heads were cool at 495 degrees, the bases running much too hot at 230 to 250 degrees. But what could I do about it—no Bill to consult with up here. Just me and *The Firecracker*.

I looked at the stubby little wings as they quivered and shook from the rough air and engine vibration. There was no other choice—I had to reduce power and try to stay in the race by flying a tighter course. There was an oil scum forming on my windshield from the engine, making forward visibility poor, and it was going to be touchy business trying to tighten my turns around the pylons.

As I throttled back I held my own in the turns, but I lost a little on each straightaway. At the end of the fourteenth lap Chester had a substantial lead. My engine was getting rougher every minute, and looking forward over the long nose of the engine cowl I could see the entire assembly twist and shake from the violent power interruption. Would the engine mount stand up under this beating? It was well designed, but the side bracing was light. Grimly I kept on flying.

Chester was more than a mile in front of me, going into his turn around the No. 2 pylon, when I saw him suddenly pull up and veer sharply to the left inside the race course, then pass me going in the opposite direction about three-quarters of a mile away. Was he pulling out of the race? As I followed him into the turn I looked back and saw him get back on course. He must have cut a pylon and had to go back and try it again.

With this lucky break I now enjoyed a comfortable lead, and I eased the throttle back still more to reduce power and save my engine. It was still rough but it didn't have to work quite so hard. Now I devoted all my attention to my course from one pylon to the next—flying each straightaway just right, turning smoothly into the pylon and then tightening my turn, and after passing the pylon picking up the next landmark as I eased out of the turn. There was a turn every thirty seconds at the speed I was flying, and each one had a slightly different problem because of a changing wind blowing across the race course.

After each turn I looked left to check Chester's position. He closed the gap steadily until at last I could not see him and I knew he must be very near. I eased the throttle forward again to 3200 rpm's and the engine roughened noticeably. I was in the nineteenth lap, coming up on the No. 4 straightaway, when I sensed Art's nearness, and as I banked into the home pylon I saw him flash past me.

One lap to go—two minutes to fly—less than ten miles and it would all be over. A sudden urge to win came over me, and I shoved the throttle forward with such force that the engine choked and stuttered for a moment. Then it let out a roar never before equaled. I felt a tremendous surge forward and I knew it was now or never.

My windshield was so smeared with oil I was unable to see through it. I was peeking through a small hole on the left side of the canopy, not daring to start my turns until the pylons came in view. Chester was nowhere to be seen as I rounded the No. 2 pylon. Then I eased into the No. 3 marker and caught a fleeting glimpse of his plane as I crossed his path and turned inside of him. He went wide around the turn and I knew I would win if my engine would stay in the airplane.

Now I was around the last pylon and on the home straightaway. As I roared over the finish line I saw the checkered flag waving for me. I had a wonderful feeling of elation and relief, glad to be the winner, but at the same time happy the race was over. I pulled up into a victory zoom in front of the grandstand, then retarded the throttle and eased the power off my engine.

Circling around the field several minutes to slow up and cool off, the engine got smoother, and I lowered my landing gear and wing flaps to enter the landing pattern and come in. I was ready to come down. My back felt like a pretzel, and I was exhausted by the events of the last half hour. I came over the fence a little too fast, going about 110 miles an hour, and slipped off a little speed but not enough.

The Firecracker settled to the ground in a nice three-point landing, but as it began to roll it hit rough ground. It lurched and pitched completely out of control, first right and then left, and I heard the sound of metal ripping and tearing and wood splintering as the wings broke open. In front of the grandstand the landing gear collapsed and the overwrought little plane crashed into the ground and came to a grinding halt.

Bill rushed up to help me out of the cockpit—I have never seen a happier guy in my life. He told me I beat Chester by four seconds in the most thrilling race ever staged at Cleveland. Roscoe Turner couldn't have been more pleased if he had owned the airplane. *The Firecracker* was in bad shape—much too bad to fly the next day in the Thompson Trophy Race, but no one seemed to mind.

I had set a new record of 250 miles an hour and won $12,000, of which I got 30 per cent. Schoenfeldt was delighted with our victory and quite satisfied to rest on his laurels. It was disappointing to miss the Thompson race, but he said we would come back the next year, which we did. But that is another story.

FROM

Boring a Hole in the Sky

ROBERT LEE SCOTT, JR.

In 1941, Colonel Robert L. Scott's great ambition was to be a fighter pilot with the American Volunteer Group in China, the famed Flying Tigers. Instead, he was assigned to the new Assam-Burma-China Ferrying Command, with headquarters in Dinjan, India; his job was to pilot heavily loaded C-47 transports "over the hump" to China. This, at least, brought him close to his goal. In China he met the almost legendary founder and commander of the Flying Tigers, Claire Chennault.

Flying Tiger

CHENNAULT was the epitome of nonconformists, a man who'd long been accepted as the father of modern fighter tactics.

In 1937 when Chennault was a captain in the Army Air Corps, he was considered the spokesman for pursuit aviation as an instructor in the Tactical School at Maxwell Field, Alabama. Then in the middle of his life's work he had been retired with the flimsy excuse that he was hard of hearing. The real reason was that he was such a nonconformist; he was a staunch proponent of the policies of Billy Mitchell and was dedicated to air power—with emphasis on fighter planes.

At the time of his retirement he was one of the greatest acrobatic pilots in the service. He flew a P-12, leading two others tied to his wings with ropes, through precision maneuvers. As a team they were known as Three Men on a Flying Trapeze.

He left the United States for China at midnight the day he was retired. His mission—to organize a new and modern Chinese Air Force. But he did more than that. He led it too.

After four years of hard work, he was able to prove his theories about fighter planes in aerial combat. In addition, he was instrumental in the construction of airdromes over a great part of China, for which his own country would have urgent use when war came. Most important of all, he succeeded ultimately in organizing the American Volunteer Group.

In July 1941 Chennault flew to Rangoon to prepare for the arrival of his long anticipated First American Volunteer Group —the AVG. There he ran into problems, as usual; the priceless P-40's were still exactly where they'd been unloaded on the docks a whole month before. So he had to set up an assembly line, which was to have been ready, with maintenance facilities. Then he turned to the more difficult task of finding a field in Burma the British would allow him to use. Finally they leased him the abandoned RAF fighter strip at Kyedaw, near Toungoo, seventy miles north of Rangoon, lying in the middle of a pestilential jungle. By late August, when his collection of pilots and mechanics arrived, there was at least a place for them to be trained—as rotten and as dilapidated as it was.

Most of those rambunctious pilots were in for the surprise of their lives. They didn't just walk down the gangplank, climb aboard a P-40 and begin to shoot down Jap planes with a bounty of five hundred dollars each from the Chinese government. Instead, they were herded aboard a Burmese train and taken off to the field at Kyedaw. Then they went back to flying school in an improvised classroom, listening to a "beat-up old Army captain" telling them to forget all they'd learned about combat flying in the services. That is, if they wanted to stay alive.

The genius of the man got through to some even though he never let them know he'd ever met a Japanese pilot in combat. He was able to convert Army bomber pilots, Navy PBY flyers and even Marine Corps transport men into fighter pilots. Many couldn't stand the pace and resigned after a few weeks to go back home; but a few listened to the seventy-two lectures this leather-faced, iron-jawed ex-captain threw at them. Only then did he let them fly the P-40's. Most important of all, he imparted to them the lessons of his experiences during the previous four years, when as a discard of his own country's air arm he had flown aerial combat as a fifty-year-old "has-been" and personally destroyed a great many Japanese planes.*

He insisted that the AVG use the strong points of their own equipment against the weaknesses of the enemy's. He harped on gunnery and formation flying, and he maintained nobody in their business ever had enough of either.

They would be outnumbered, he told them, and would be flying a heavy and cumbersome airplane, compared to the light maneuverable Zero. But they could come out on top if they used their P-40's the right way.

At last, as a sort of exam for his course, he sent his pilots aloft to do mock combat with one another while he studied their techniques from take-off to landing, monitoring them from a rickety bamboo control tower—a pair of field glasses in one hand and a radio microphone in the other.

When they did enter combat with the second-rate planes the British had refused, those who had listened to him were successful. A few who didn't listen and held to old habits were shot down. He came to be almost a god to the best of the group and they went on to become the famous Flying Tigers.

Haynes initiated me next morning exactly as I'd hoped he would. In conventional times and places my indoctrination in a strange ship would have more than likely been a flight around the field. That way I could have flown light and free of cargo, felt out the controls, made a few touch-and-go landings. But out there on the edge of combat, and almost the end of the supply line, gasoline was too important for such a luxury. Any practicing would have to be done with an airplane loaded with freight and en route to where the supplies were needed. C.V. took me to the mud-and-wattle *basha* that was our office, where a crude sign that hung above the door read: "Headquarters, Assam-Burma-China Ferrying Command." We remained only

---

* Chennault's combat record had to be kept confidential. He was a civilian as well as an American citizen; it could never be officially admitted.

long enough for him to check radiograms from New Delhi and then took off for China.

It was one of those flights where you went quickly from one world into another. On a course of a hundred and nineteen degrees we'd hit Kunming after five hundred miles. We climbed out of the valley of the Brahmaputra and crossed five other great rivers all of which were to stamp their names indelibly on my memory; Chindwin, Irrawaddy, Salween, Mekong, and Yangtze. But great as those streams were they didn't impress me as much as the mountains around me. The very foothills which hemmed us in from the outside world were thousands of feet higher than the most lofty peak in the United States. We had to climb to 19,000 feet that morning just to begin our cruise toward China. Ahead and to the left flank, some two hundred miles away, I could see the Kunluns, where Minya Konka, the highest in China, touched twenty-five thousand feet. At least that was what my map indicated. But when we flew close to another one dead on course, I lost faith in the map. For this peak of Talifu was supposed to be 15,100 feet, yet we were flying at better than 16,000 and the snow-covered pinnacle poked up over a thousand feet higher. I skirted Talifu and corrected my map.

Kunming field was a kind of cobblestone runway dug out of the raw red earth of China's Yunnan Province. Before Chennault had come, it had been nothing but acres of rice paddies. Then human hands had scooped out a trench six thousand feet long, a hundred feet wide and deep as a tall man. Then the same hands had filled the ditch with large rocks and the spaces between with smaller ones; next came pebbles and gravel. Finally red mud was poured in to seal all of this. When dry it formed a hard cobblestone surface, and your plane just bounced and rattled as though you had a couple of square wheels. But wet, those rocks loosened and the field became a sort of ballasted quagmire through which your groaning undercarriage slithered.

Never will I forget those Chinese runways, nor the strange superstitions of the people who built them and lived beside them. Sometimes, as I came in to land, I'd see a Chinese coolie waiting beside the paved strip, his load of vegetables or bun-

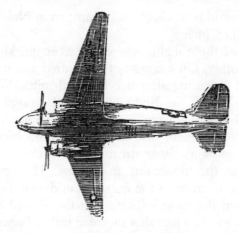

dles of faggots on the two gin-poles across his shoulders. Then, just as the plane was touching down, he'd step out and try to cross to the other side. Most of the time he made it, was fast enough, or we dodged him with wild maneuvers. But we couldn't miss them all; then it was terrible, just as though the coolie had committed suicide. That wasn't the explanation. There was a devil following all those coolies, and if they could just make the crossing in front of all those whirling propellers, wings, and wheels, and cut it close enough, perhaps their personal devil wouldn't be so swift and fortunate.

On that first ferry flight I made to Kunming I was unsuccessful in my personal mission; Chennault wasn't there as Haynes had expected him to be. He was still down at one of the fighter fields in Burma. My meeting with him would have to wait.

The next day seven transports arrived at Dinjan for the new Ferrying Command; six of them were C-47's with full crews that Haynes had with him originally in Aquila. What was more, my old crew chief, Sergeant Aaltonen, was on one of them. Seeing Al was almost as good as getting my B-17 back. Haynes acted like a new man. He hadn't been the same since the new high command in Delhi had taken away all his carefully selected personnel. On the following day he had to stay behind to make the new assignments and brief his recovered men on their future operations, but I took Sergeant Aaltonen and flew back to Kunming, hoping again to encounter Chennault. Again he wasn't there. And for a whole week I made daily ferry flights to Kunming, Lashio or Loiwing. Every time I landed in Burma, Chennault was in Kunming or Chungking. All I accomplished was to become fairly proficient with the Goony bird, and each time I returned to Dinjan the field was looking more like a real airdrome. We had nine transports by that time, and Haynes had been promised the full thirteen of his initial quota would be there before another ten days.

Somehow I'd been lucky and managed to miss interception by enemy fighters. But a good many times I'd felt awfully naked out there alone over Burma, which the Japs had almost completely invaded. Perhaps what saved me was the constant radio alert I maintained on the frequencies used by the Japs and the Flying Tigers. By listening to both of them I could sometimes tell where the fighter contacts were taking place. I had also gotten acquainted with the AVG radio operators, especially Ralph Sasser at Loiwing. I had never met him but just by talking together daily we had devised a code of slang and colloquialisms by which he could tell me areas to be avoided.

My luck didn't run out until the very next time Haynes and I flew together again. We were less than a hundred miles from Loiwing when suddenly I heard one of those little pieces of innocent-sounding news which made me stop appreciating how beautiful the day was. Sasser came on the air and said, "Tally-ho all Florida visitors, especially kissing cousin visitors. Seems like everybody and his brother's coming today. Brother rat should be here in five minutes, heading towards Georgia."

From that I knew Jap fighters were approaching Loiwing from the south while we headed for the same place from the north. Haynes was already craning his neck to search the forward quadrants and I had called Aaltonen and told him to be sure the hand guns were ready; the rubber plugs were pulled from the porthole windows so we could stick the muzzles out to fire. After that I told "Cousin" Sasser we were doing a maneuver known as getting the hell out of there and could be found in Birmingham, which signified Paoshan—just as Florida meant Loiwing. The only trouble was another formation of Japanese was fairly close to the "Georgia" line, but Sasser didn't know it, and neither did we until almost too late.

We set course for Paoshan, which was the first field open to us in China, and I was searching hopefully for clouds, even a wisp of one. Haynes had already seen some enemy fighters and had left me alone in the cockpit to join Aaltonen and our radio operator to protect us with the highly inadequate weapons. I never did see the enemy planes. I could hear the firing, but was too deep down inside the steep Salween Gorge to see anything but the canyon walls, which seemed altogether too close. What ended up worrying me the most, however, wasn't Japanese fighters, so much as the wild firing from our own Tommy guns, pistols and rifles. It suddenly came to me that if one of our own bullets, much less a burst, hit our fuel tanks or the control surfaces we would go down most ignominiously.

Just after landing safely at Paoshan, I looked up to see four shark-nosed P-40's dive the length of the runway. Perhaps they saw us parked on the field and decided to give us a show. In any case, no sooner had they taxied in than I went from ship to ship introducing myself to each pilot and asking where Chennault was. I couldn't help feeling close to every one as well as to the organization they represented, but it never once crossed my mind that they might feel differently about me.

They climbed arrogantly from the saddles of their fighters and swaggered in their western costumes, faded Levis, Texas boots, gaudy shirts and belted six guns. All four had beards.

The boldest one started out with almost friendly kidding about us being VIP's and asked, "What the hell are you doing this far from Delhi, anyway?" I thought it was some joke they had among themselves. I even joined in the laugh. I began passing out cigarettes which were scarce enough out there to make a friend out of a real enemy, and Sergeant Aaltonen had opened our last can of pineapple from the emergency rations on the B-17. Then the jibes grew more pointed until all of us in the Army Air Corps were being insulted.

I finally had all I could stand. I told them that I wasn't any headquarters man from Delhi or anywhere else. What was more I was a fighter pilot and would swap seats with any one of them. "Flying an armed fighter would be a snap compared to wrestling this overloaded Goony bird—and overloaded with stuff for you too. How in hell," I went on, "you think your ammunition, fuel, food or anything else gets this far? You think it comes by itself?"

At that the tall one came over close to me and began waving an empty pineapple can at me. I thought he wanted to fight.

"Colonel, we're happy you're over here. We've waited long enough for any regulars from the Air Corps. But just one mighty moment. Let's take up the subject of this vital cargo you're risking your neck to bring us."

He brushed past me, tossed the can under the transport, and then commenced tearing at one of the bales of cargo which filled the plane. He must have known exactly how to open those metal-banded Lend-Lease supplies, for before I could stop him he'd pulled out a handful of the contents and shoved it in my face. By the time I'd examined what it was, he had two other bales open and the aisle of the cargo space was filled with bundles of gray and purple paper all printed with the picture of Dr. Sun Yat-sen, the father of the Chinese Republic—paper money. The rest of our cargo turned out to be letter-sized stationery, envelopes, filing cabinets of heavy metal and two office safes. Haynes was as surprised as I. At least the earlier cargoes he had flown in had been fuel and machine-gun ammunition; but that had been a week before, prior to the arrival of General Joseph Stilwell's supply people from AMMISCA, the American Military Mission to China for all the Lend-Lease.

For once I was glad I didn't find Chennault. All the way back to Dinjan I talked the situation over with Haynes and we agreed that next day I'd come back and bring the Old Man what he needed and wanted, regardless of blindly established priorities. Only then would I feel free to ask him what I wanted to.

But that wasn't the way it worked out. Haynes received an urgent message during the night which changed all our plans. He was ordered to send an airplane into the middle of Burma and fly out some U.S. personnel threatened with encirclement and capture at Shwebo. General Stilwell and his foot soldiers had waited too long to withdraw. Of course, with orders such as those, C.V. went himself and took me along to help him.

The rescue flight wasn't too difficult even though we had to penetrate further into enemy controlled skies than we had before. Luckily for us the Burmese had already started in with their scorched earth policy. Villages and rice fields were burning and there was plenty of smoke to hide us after we left the comfort of the monsoon clouds. The most difficult part of the rescue came after we found Stilwell. Vinegar Joe didn't want to fly out with the Air Corps.

"It didn't bring me here," he shouted at Haynes and me, "and I don't need any blankety-blank aeroplane to take me out. Dammit, I'll walk!"

For a few minutes we actually considered taking the emaciated Infantryman bodily aboard the transport, but in the end we reneged. We loaded thirty staff officers, who weren't reluctant to ride in an Air Corps ship at all. Then we took aboard their filing cabinets filled with military records, and evacuated them out of Burma and across the many mouths of the Ganges to Calcutta.

That night we flew back to Shwebo again to try to rescue the most important person General Arnold had sent us for. We weren't successful. The bungalow had been burned, the Japanese were almost there, and Vinegar Joe really had set out through the jungles with his men. We did bring out a load of wounded soldiers, however—British, Burmese and Chinese—and land them at Dinjan. But for almost three weeks the whole world wasn't to know whether Stilwell was alive or dead.

That cargo of office supplies and Chinese paper money was still weighing heavy on my conscience. The morning after I came home from Shwebo I again set out to change the military priorities of Stilwell's AMMISCA by insisting to the supply major at the Dinjan godowns (warehouse) that the Ferrying Command be permitted to fly Chennault what he wanted. But I was wasting my nonconformist breath. He stubbornly showed me Lend-Lease instructions and then hid behind army regulations. No matter what a commander needed in the field, he was going to sit right there on top of his mound of freight and see that we fly-boys delivered each item in sequence as it came up on his sacred priority list. I finally realized it was impossible to make him see the light, agreed that orders were orders, and watched him pompously supervising the loading of my ship with more stationery and enough mops, brooms and GI trash baskets to clean up all of Burma.

All I could do was sign the manifest, taxi away from the major, and take off. But I didn't fly toward Chennault. As soon as I was over the Brahmaputra and just out of sight of Dinjan, I signaled to Aaltonen and a couple of helpers he'd brought along to remove the cargo door. After all was ready, I put the Goony bird in a steep bank, doorside toward the earth, and dropped all that useless tonnage into the rice paddies beside the little village of Sadiya. When we were empty I turned back for Dinjan and put the rest of our plan in operation.

Most of the night before Sergeant Bonner had been working with Aaltonen and some of the others from the Ferrying Command to assemble the tonnage that was to be our real cargo that day. Hidden in the tea bushes, close beside the hardstand where we always parked my C-47, were scores of the rusty steel drums of aviation gasoline I remembered from the barge I'd ridden into Dibrugarh. These were soon being rolled up the loading ramp and stood on end along the cargo space of the ship. Sixteen of them filled it. On top of the drums we packed wooden cases of fifty-caliber machine-gun ammunition until we were a good ton overloaded. That time I was confident Chennault was at Loiwing. There had already been a radio message from Sasser in our colloquial code which established exactly the farm the Old Man was plowing that morning. This would be no hit-and-miss delivery today.

The first village I identified in Burma after I'd left the Naga Hills and had set a straight course for Loiwing seemed like a good omen. I read Tagaplung Ga off my map. It couldn't have much to do with the Georgia that I knew, but it made the whole day feel friendly. In twenty minutes more we were over Bhámo on the Irrawaddy; from there the country had towns instead of tribal villages, and there were glittering pagodas. Perhaps a hundred miles away, across the ruby mines of Mogok, was Mandalay. Just north of there I could see a patch of smoke about where we'd been the day before, reminding me that Shwebo must still be burning.

In another twenty minutes I saw the hairpin switchbacks of the Burma Road twisting agonizingly along the mountain ridges to the south and east. That was the most important check point of my dead-reckoning course to Loiwing. All I had to do was line up three of those horseshoe loops in the serpentine with a small river named Nam-Tu and it was time to punch the button and let Sasser know I was almost in. I called the control tower and passed on the code word. A few minutes later I dragged the heavy transport straight into the jungle strip with a power-on approach. That was the best way to hit the edge of the field—not wasting anything. The wheels had barely touched and commenced slinging globs of mud against the bottom of the wings when I saw a vehicle fairly burst from the trees bordering the rain-soaked runway.

My radio receiver came to life simultaneously, but on the ground what Sasser said was garbled; besides I was busy slowing my ship in the heavy going and keeping a wary eye on the "follow-me" jeep. But there was something about the frantic motions the driver was making with one arm that coincided with the tenor of that last radio call. Something must be wrong. And it was. It was no follow-me vehicle, and the driver was Chennault. At last I was about to meet him, but he was waving excitedly that I take off again. He was shouting something too, at the top of his voice. I could barely hear him over the idling engines, the whistle of the props and those mud-slinging wheels.

"Jin-bao! Air raid!"

My head was already sticking out the cockpit window with a hand cupped behind an ear. Then I made all the signs I knew that meant "no," pointed at the cargo behind me and yelled through the spinning prop, "I'm overloaded—two thousand pounds. Have to wait till we're unloaded."

He finally pointed rather disgustedly to a cleared place among the trees, motioning that I pull over there.

I taxied in, swung the tail around, and cut the switches. I

ran the length of the cargo space across the tops of the gasoline drums, going over ammunition boxes like they were low hurdles. When I reached the fuselage door, I told Sergeant Aaltonen to keep it open so Chennault would have no trouble seeing what we'd brought him. Then I jumped out.

Claire Lee Chennault was even more impressive face to face than he'd ever been pictured. His face was sun-cured mahogany, skin as wrinkled as the bark of an oak tree, but what impressed me most was the depth of his dark eyes. I remember thinking, mad as he is at me now, there's a twinkle still there.

"Air raid, I said, goddammit! Jap'll be here any minute. Didn't Sasser warn you on the radio?"

"Didn't hear him, sir. I was already down when he came on the air." I was pointing all the time to Aaltonen in the open door, who was in turn pointing to the markings on the rusty fifty-five-gallon drums.

While the impossibility of a take-off, as well as the nature of our cargo registered, I thought it was time to tell him about me.

"Sir," I said, sticking out my hand, "I'm the fighter pilot who wrote you those letters, tried to join the AVG. I think Colonel Haynes told you about me too . . ."

But my startling announcement made no noticeable impression. He was looking at the sky apprehensively, then saying, as though he wished I hadn't come to bother him, "Suppose you'll have to stay—if you can't get off. But cut some bamboo cover." A truckload of men drove up; he stopped talking to me and shouted at them. "Cover the wings. Take special care of the props and windshield—can't have anything shining down here. And hurry! They're close!" He glanced again at the heavens and buzzed off in the little car, leaving me.

When I found him once more he was in a hole in the ground. It was really a reinforced slit trench, rigged like an underground operations office, where he could maintain contact with his pilots. He stood there just as I'd heard he did during air raids, field glasses in one hand and a portable radio mike in the other.

As I climbed down into the trench I was looking up into the sky, trying to see for myself the enemy planes—or the friendly ones I knew he was directing. That was when I saw the lone

P-40. Its gaudy shark mouth was sticking out from under a tree. That ship had to be waiting for me as though a part of some divine schedule. My feet kept on moving me toward Chennault and I dared grasp his elbow.

"That P-40! Can I take it off the field? It's sure to be strafed if it stays there!"

He didn't answer me but spoke in a low voice to the mike, "Tex, I can hear their engines, southwest."

While I waited for him to answer, I thought I heard them too, a weird sound, more like a high-pitched whistle than the familiar roar of an American Allison. I didn't know then, but that was the distinctive note of the long three-bladed propeller on the Zero. I leaned close to his ear and asked again, pointing at the extra fighter, "I'm current, sir!"

His face hardened as he took the microphone from his mouth and looked me over from feet to the eagles sewn to the shoulders of my flying suit. Then he said, not too unkindly, "I heard you the first time. I'm afraid you're in the wrong uniform, *Colonel.*" Did I only imagine he stressed that last word? "You apparently haven't noticed the markings on that plane."

I looked again and saw what he meant: the insigne of the Chinese Air Force, twelve-pointed blue and white sunburst. But such a minor technicality couldn't matter to him; it was that word "colonel" he'd placed the accent upon. So he was not only down on all regulars but also didn't like so-called kid colonels either. He'd never been higher than a captain when he was retired at the age of forty-seven, and here I was reminding him of it. But not very much—he was ignoring me again.

"Maintain your altitude, Tiger leader, but keep contact with them."

"But I'm a pursuit pilot, sir. Like you. I didn't think it would matter what uniform I wore or what rank so long as I wanted to fight!"

He just stared past me, his expression unconcerned. I thought he was going back to his remote-control operations. Then he seemed to suddenly relent.

"All right, if you're going to keep insisting, go start it if you

can—and get it out of here. If you can't, don't just sit out there when you see them coming, or they'll get you and the ship."

I hardly heard the last admonition. I was already running.

In those old Tomahawks a man needed four hands. First your right toe had to be pressing the inertia starter pedal while your hands were fumbling with switches and working a wobble pump. There was a primer to shoot seven or eight shots into about three cylinders, and you could always feel the cold of the evaporating gasoline, leaking from the plunger onto your fingers and smelling up the cockpit. After the whine of the inertia flywheel reached the right pitch you shifted pressure from toe to heel to engage the clutch and the prop made its first slow, laborious turns. The left hand was busy adjusting the critical throttle, and then poised to shove the red knob of the mixture control at precisely the right instant. Simultaneously the right one had moved to twist the crank of the booster magneto. If all that footwork and hand-changing had been correctly co-ordinated, the prop forgot its sluggish reluctance, caught with almost mechanical laughter and a breath of blue smoke, then smoothed to a roar of steady power. All sixteen short exhaust stacks said the engine was ready to go.

I hit the right combination and the P-40 caught with its wonderful throaty cry. I didn't even remember to look into the sky from where danger might be coming, but kicked off the brakes, and moved away from the trees. With a burst of throttle I blasted across the hardstand and we lunged down the runway. Only after I was making two hundred and forty miles an hour, and still low down against the top of the trees, did I pull up above the familiar switchbacks of the Burma Road and begin my chase. Then it was time to become the hunter. I'd find the Flying Tigers and join up, or failing that, I'd find the Japanese all by myself.

Intent on my search I kept going over my switches and fuel-tank selectors, practicing so I could reach them with my hands without even looking. I turned on the gun toggles, pulled the charging handles back and tried a short burst. I wasn't any novice there. We kept climbing with near full throttle and mixture rich, trying to swap as much of the belly-tank fuel for precious altitude as possible. Once contact with the enemy was established I'd pull the T handle and drop that external tank.

The P-40 passed through ten thousand feet. Carefully I covered the two quadrants of the sky that lay ahead of me and the more dangerous ones behind. I kept working with the radio but there was only static. We climbed through twenty thousand and I could still distinguish Loiwing far below. I failed to see any evidences of the anticipated attack. I didn't see the Flying Tigers either. My head was aching and I thought of my forgotten oxygen mask. At twenty-four thousand—still nothing else in the sky—the headache was worse. It was a battle just to gulp enough of the thin air to live. Only the sputtering of my engine saved me. It frightened me so much that nature gave another shot of adrenalin. But it was only my belly tank running out. I shifted to the internal tanks realizing I'd been out an hour. Still no Tigers; no Japs either. But I had the radio working and I heard voices. They sounded so close I almost broke radio silence and called. Slowly it registered that the high falsetto voices were those of the Japanese. I squinted out into infinity until my eyes burned; I shifted from wing tank to wing tank. When I began to use the fuselage tank, the last, I'd been looking two hours and still there was nothing. I tuned another frequency on the radio.

When Sasser's voice broke through he was calling my name. That was the first I knew of the silent period having ended. The first thing he said when I acknowledged, was, where the hell had I been? "I called you every three minutes for half an hour. Rats intercepted twenty miles south of Lashio but failed to reach here. Better come have lunch with us."

As I took the P-40 down to five thousand feet, it came to me again how good air with oxygen in it tasted. By that time I recognized the roof of Central-Aircraft Manufacturing Company's (CAMCO) Factory Number Ten and could see the hardstand where my Goony bird was being unloaded. There were twelve P-40's lined up—six on each side of the runway, as though waiting for me. I circled, breathing deeper than I'd ever breathed before, let down my wheels and noted I'd been flying two hours and a half. Then I landed in between the two lanes of painted grinning white teeth and laughing red tongues of my welcoming committee.

I'd no more than parked under the same tree when I saw Chennault coming with a couple of Flying Tigers.

All during the introductions I couldn't help wondering why he seemed to be in better humor than when I'd left. After all, his men had only claimed three Japs, much below par for them. Most certainly it was evident I hadn't caught a friend or a foe in the hundred and fifty minutes I'd been trying. What caused the good humor was no secret as soon as he made his next announcement.

"I've been worrying about you, Colonel. After you got our hangar queen* started, I thought maybe it quit on you or that you had gotten lost!"

One of the Flying Tigers, Johnny Petach, added, "Just a half-hour before you arrived in the transport, I tried all the combinations—after the mechanic had given up. It refused to catch. That ship's just a born lemon. Even if I had gotten it cranked up I was going straight to Paoshan and sit out the fight."

I understood now.

Chennault said, "I was doing my best to get out of the trench when you took off, intended stopping you. Why, Scott, I've been sitting here for two hours worrying about having to radio General Arnold tonight that the first regular Air Corps pursuit colonel I ever saw out here was missing over Burma in a Chinese airplane. But come along, we've saved you some lunch."

* A hangar queen is an aircraft with so many mechanical troubles it acquires a reputation of spending most of its time under repair in the hangar.

FROM

Fate Is the Hunter

ERNEST K. GANN

"Am on a lake about five miles long approximately four hundred miles north St. Lawrence on a course of three hundred thirty degrees. All well. No injuries. Urgently require food and supplies."

O'Connor was alive. Somewhere in the uncharted Canadian north, his C-87 transport, with seventeen sick and wounded soldiers returning from the war zone and a crew of five, lay in the snow in subzero temperatures. It was February 1943. From Presque Isle, Goose Bay, and other bases along the North Atlantic route, planes of the Air Transport Command spread out in search. One was commanded by Ernest Gann, like O'Connor a civilian commercial pilot now flying for the ATC. Gann's initial optimism vanished after the first day's search. Empty maps, wandering compasses, the immensity and sameness of the wilderness, the absence of any radio signals from O'Connor persuaded him that the search would be long and difficult.

The Search

WE were aloft early on the following morning, renewed in energy, and with some confidence restored. We were also convinced that O'Connor's course must have been as uncertain as our own. He should have been able roughly to judge his distance flown, but he was possibly somewhere to the east or west of his intended course. We would look for him first in the region around Lac Mistassini, one of the few actually indicated on the chart, and then work eastward.

Presque Isle radio had been in successful communication with O'Connor during the night. They had urged him to send bearings at regular intervals, but he had replied that his batteries were capable of only one more transmission. This was most disheartening, although the fact that he was still able to think shrewdly when his brain should have been frozen cheered us. He said he would crank the Gibson Girl frequently.

A Hudson Bay trading post far to the south of where O'Connor believed his position to be reported a night surface temperature of seventy below zero. Yet the cold brought and maintained one great blessing. The visibility was again excellent.

We knew that several more planes were now in the air although they were unseen. Because we were all on a common frequency, we could hear them chattering as they left Presque Isle and Goose Bay. I recognized the voices of McGuire and Watkins and remembered that Watkins was flying as O'Connor's co-pilot during the same period I had flown with Ross. The numbers, I thought, were becoming curiously jumbled.

Shortly after noon, as the planes approached the most promising area, the radios became silent. Everyone was listening for O'Connor.

Then a lame duck quacked, bursting rudely upon the stillness. It was the intrepid lieutenant complaining of his compass. The disgust of many shook his earphones as he was unanimously rebuked for airing his troubles. We needed silence, absolute silence, lest we miss the faintest signal from O'Connor.

In the cockpit we rarely spoke.

Returning to the same general area should have been an easy business and we did manage at last, thanks to our crudely drawn representation of the more prominent rivers and lakes. Without this aid our visual impression might have tricked us, for every feature of the land seemed to change in conformation and size from hour to hour. In the morning the same lake did not appear at all the same as it had in the afternoon. And every lake seemed to qualify as being "about five miles long."

We had flown as far north as Egg Lake and then turned about to the southeast, our eyes inspecting each feature of the terrain as faithfully as we could chain our flagging interests. Hour

after hour of lakes, each one so similar to its neighbors, passed
beneath us. The total effect was stunning and after a few hours
became so soporific that Johnson had a terrible struggle with
himself. Only the thought of O'Connor's now truly desperate
situation kept him awake.

We began to pass through occasional veils of snow which
trailed downward from the cloudless sky. These crystals glistening in the sun were not really snow but minute particles of ice
formed in the super-cooled air. We had a long and perplexing
session with our right engine, which took on such a spasm of
coughing and backfiring that we despaired of ever taking full
power from it again. The trouble seemed to be created by a
lack of sufficient carburetor heat in the right engine, which in
turn normally supplied heat for the plane's interior. Now if we
turned the heater off, the engine ran fairly well. So we alternately froze and then sweated with nervous concern, and
wished O'Connor would choose less alien places to land his
airplane.

"Hear anything?"

"Negative. . . negative. . . negative. . ."

"HOLD IT!"

We had about thirty minutes of gas remaining for the search,
and the sun was again very low when a faint peeping sound en-
livened our earphones. It endured for no more than twenty
seconds, but it was there—unmistakably O'Connor. We took
a bearing on the signal. It subsided before we could achieve
any degree of accuracy, yet the general direction was straight
ahead. So we flew on, waiting for a repetition, holding our
breath, scratching at the thin coating of frost on our windows
for a better view of the earth. We waited ten minutes; then
the signal came again. It was louder, so we must be flying in
the right direction, but again so short our bearing was only
approximate.

The right engine began another ruckus and threatened to
quit entirely. We disregarded it, so intense was our desire for a
further signal. We were afraid to call the other planes lest our
transmission drown O'Connor's relatively feeble hand set. We
waited ten minutes more, and then another ten. No signal. We

circled once, then flew back over our course in the hope O'Connor would hear our engines and start cranking again. Our eyes searched every lake. Nothing. We rechecked our fuel supply, telling ourselves there were always a few more gallons than shown on the gauges. If we could be positive of our position and assume the winds would hold light, the flying time to Presque Isle would be approximately six hours. It seemed we had exactly six hours' fuel remaining. O'Connor! Damnit, man! Crank!

So easy to demand from our perch of relative comfort. We could not understand why O'Connor would select these last precious minutes to abandon his efforts. But no sound came, and we turned south once more. With numbed fingers we sketched in the general shapes of the larger lakes and marked a low range of barren hills which were the only distinguishing feature of this area. We must locate this same lonely expanse on the morrow. For O'Connor was no longer lost. We knew he was down there, somewhere in that wilderness . . . waiting. And if our hands were numb, his must be ever so much colder.

In spite of his tremendous vitality, O'Connor was far from a youngster. He could, if he had chosen, have remained flying comfortably between New York and Boston. And he could thereby have slept in a bed at night instead of a wilderness. The irony of his position matched that of his radio operator, a man who had left the Merchant Marine because he had been twice torpedoed and considered he had asked enough of fortune. Such men were worth saving, for there were never enough in the world.

Long after nightfall we landed at Presque Isle with some twenty minutes of fuel remaining. Ten of those minutes we would gladly have exchanged for even a glimpse of a plane on a lake. The mechanics worked all night trying to make our right engine behave itself.

So ended the second day of the search. We told Boyd of the signals but confessed we had not known our true position during the whole of the afternoon. The signals could have come from directly below our plane or a hundred miles away. There was no way to prove anything.

We were all agreed that O'Connor's most likely position occupied the center of a unique triangle which would place him almost equidistant from Montreal, Goose Bay, and Presque Isle. Therefore he was so close to the maximum round-trip range of any C-47 we could not devote enough search time on arrival. Boyd eliminated this handicap by commandeering two C-87's in which we could search much longer. McGuire would fly one of these planes, and the other would be mine.

Presque Isle was now swarming with pilots, air crewmen, and various experts on almost everything. There was endless theorizing by these aerial detectives, spiced as frequently as he could find an audience with the latest adventures of our stalwart army captain. We who had tried searching true desolation soon wearied of the elaborate errands of mercy proposed by those who had once spent a summer fishing in Canada, or knew how to drive a team of sledge dogs. No dogs could remove O'Connor from his captivity. Nothing could, except a continuous run of luck and that must begin very soon.

Just before we slept a message came through that O'Connor had been found. Watkins, flying westward out of Goose Bay, had literally stumbled upon him, and dropped food and blankets. Like ourselves, however, he was flying on the last of his fuel and was obliged to leave immediately. This was indeed the greatest of accomplishments, and we had a great deal to say about the luck of the Irish.

There was now only one grievous hitch. After crisscrossing a thousand miles of sky, Watkins did not know his own true position when he saw the stranded airplane. Nor did he pretend that he could ever find the place again.

Binkowski was our flight engineer in the C-87, for which I was most grateful. If Binkowski said the airplane was in good health, then it was nearly a guarantee the C-87 would snort and bellow on schedule and we would not abort this important day of search because of some mechanical outrage. Binkowski was a fair-skinned, blond young man, of deep religious convictions. Behind his little jump seat at the rear of the C-87's flight deck, he had placed a small brass-framed triptych. An unusually bland Madonna panel occupied the center, and I envied Binkowski for the peace she seemed to bring him. I could not decide whether he bore his treasure with him in mistrust of all C-87's or hoped, in the doing, to remind us of our sins. In either case he would have sufficient reason, for most of us were at best irresolute polytheists.

On this morning Wynn had replaced Catchings in our airplane, and Beattie had taken over for Johnson. Wynn was new to the north country and to C-87's, which was the only reason I continued to hold down the left-hand seat. He was much senior to me, yet because of his unique tolerance no protocol hindered our relationship. He was a dynamic and mischievous spirit, so quick of movement and bubbling with the most rapid conversation that he seemed constantly on the brink of physical disintegration—which was a deception, for Wynn was nervous only in his moments of relaxation. On demand he could settle his lean face into the firmest lines of concentration, his eyes would cease their darting, and he would become, in a trice, the coolest of pilots. But he was also an instinctive actor and delighted in holding his listeners spellbound while he passed quickly from the absurd to bleak tragedy.

"A C-87 does not really fly," he explained to the bewildered Binkowski, who had not broken his contemplation of the Virgin since we had reached cruising altitude. "No, indeed, it does *not* fly. It is merely a crude form of levitation."

He favored Binkowski with his most sardonic and evil wink and left him to think his way through such nonsense.

With our extra speed we could reach the search area in about four hours and remain in the vicinity long enough to find O'Connor. Wynn's effervescence was contagious and with a four-engined airplane which thus far behaved perfectly, we proceeded northward in full confidence. We located Boyd Falls and Mount Catchings and the Johnson River, and were much pleased at their familiarity. As our compass began its unpredictable swinging we reached the Wynn Mountains, which their namesake surveyed as if they were truly his own. Then we were again in the wilderness of the lakes and even Wynn fell silent. We were fixed to the windows, staring at the frozen earth, and waiting for the slightest sound in our earphones.

This day the February sky had lost nearly all its former cold blue and was instead a pale and jaundiced white. It was as monotonous as the snows except for a festooning of mare's-tails. Too often they foretold high winds and bad weather. In this region the result could easily be a long series of blizzards which O'Connor was ill-prepared to withstand, and which would certainly halt any attempts at rescue.

Rescue remained a matter for the future. We had still to rediscover O'Connor. The lakes were now beneath, the same lakes in the same area we had been over the day before, but there was no sound in our earphones. Again each one of us knew the certainty of spying an airplane on a lake, only to discover after more careful examination that whatever object we concentrated upon was only an illusion. The process was intermittent but self-creating, causing us to rise suddenly in our seats, gasp, twist our heads this way and that like puppets, and finally subside in embarrassment at our repeated gullibility.

In the middle of the afternoon we picked up a signal which offered more than just a bearing. It said, "Return same place" over and over again. Where was the same place? We believed we were already over the same place. If the message was for Watkins he was far over the horizon also looking for that same place.

Before the signaling ceased we managed a valuable bearing. We called to O'Connor's radio operator begging him to keep up a continuous series of long dashes. We were fishing in the depths, but this was more than a nibble. If they would send long enough for our automatic direction finder to swing, it would all be over.

"He's on again! We've got him!"

Wynn was in a frenzy of excitement, and even Beattie was bereft of dignity when the direction finder swung sharply around and pointed to our right. I banked immediately and put the ship on the exact course indicated by the needle. The signals became much louder. He should be dead ahead. But if he was, we could not see him. The great hoglike snout of the C-87 blocked off our forward visibility. I jinked the ship a few degrees left and waited. A fine sharp signal came once more. We had him now. It was a certainty. I rose slightly in my seat, trying to see past the others who were pressed to the flight deck windows. But none of us could discover an airplane on any of the lakes below.

The signal came again, so loud we were obliged to move our earphones. The needle began a rapid swing until it pointed nearly vertically to our course. Still no one could recognize an airplane.

Binkowski had left his Madonna some time previously and had been observing the earth from the cabin. Now he rushed forward, calling to me and pointing.

"There he is! Right by the shore!"

I pushed the C-87's nose down so we could all see. And still there was nothing to enliven the empty lakes below. I doubted Binkowski, a reaction I should never have believed possible. Yet he was insistent. He kept pointing and we all tried to follow the inclining line of his arm.

Then very suddenly I felt more insignificant than I ever had before. We were all, for one humiliating moment, squashed into our miserable little bone and flesh units and the multitudinous cells of us became one cell, thereby establishing a proper microscopic relationship to all things of creation. We were men

like O'Connor, and as men here in such environment, we were
physically insects of the lowest order. Find O'Connor? Without the radio to guide us and Binkowski's keen and worshipful
eyes, we could have passed over him fifty times in vain. O'Connor, how did you become so small, so Lilliputian in dimensions
that you rudely shock all of our senses? In fact, you are now
shown as a traitor to the vanity of man, for we cannot see you
at all, nor any of your species. Our eyes are only drawn to your
airplane, which is over a hundred feet in breadth and length.
And yet it too is so terribly small. Compare yourself to it, as
you have caused us to do, and weep for your nothingness. Remember you are as we are, which is such a mortifying station
the mind must accept it altogether or reject it altogether. The
hesitant middling ground is strewn with the wreckage of men's
sanity.

I began a large circle over what we at once christened Lac
O'Connor. We radioed every plane in the sky so they could
take bearings on us. Montreal also took a series of long-range
bearings and Sydney in Nova Scotia did the same. All of this
took some time, which we knew to be a strain on O'Connor's
patience, but it was very necessary if he was at last to be exactly
located.

Circling, I had leisure to appreciate O'Connor's almost incredible situation. The lake was as he had described it. His airplane appeared to have stopped just to the south of the shore.
To land a C-87 safely on that lake in the middle of freezing arctic
night was certainly magnificent airmanship. All of the skill of
O'Connor's long career must have been bunched into those
vital last seconds and now he could justly claim a victory.

While we continued to circle I scribbled a note which left
me in considerably better spirits than had a previous communication to the same man. Influenced by Binkowski and his mel-
lowing triptych, I wrote:

> THANK GOD WE FOUND YOU
> MORE PLANES COMING AND
> WE'LL HAVE YOU ALL OUT
> IN A FEW DAYS.

I inserted this note in a box of chocolate bars and asked Wynn, who would supervise unloading our supplies, to drop it first.

When every interested plane and station was satisfied, we had a rare moment of triumphant joy with a C-87. I peeled off fighter-pilot fashion and dived for a low pass at Lac O'Connor. The maneuvering was intended as a salute to every man on the lake. They returned it with much arm-waving. We swept over their heads too fast and hence could recognize no one, but our chandelle when we reached the end of the lake was designed to gratify their excitement. Exhibitionism, I hoped, was here forgivable.

When the show was completed, we slowed and prepared for the serious business of dropping supplies so they would land in convenient places. One thing puzzled me while I waited for word from the cabin that Wynn was ready. I had noticed a long arrow made of what appeared to be pine boughs laid out in the snow. If it had been a cross, then I would have known O'Connor realized how difficult his special lake was to separate from any other. But an arrow?

I banked for the first dumping pass and slowed to a near stall. Beattie frequently called off our flight speed so I could concentrate on a flight path straight for the waiting men. We came in very low and on this descent I could easily recognize O'Connor's face. He was standing beside the arrow pointing to it and alternately waving his arms. I assumed his excitement was overwhelming and thought I understood his gestures as a simple demonstration of joy. Near him stood another man who genuflected like a pilgrim before Mecca and afforded us great merriment. Spirits must have remained very high in that stranded party if they could keep their sense of humor. More credit, we thought, to the indomitable O'Connor.

We made three additional passes over the field before all our supplies had been dropped. Each time O'Connor pointed to the arrow and made gestures which I could only believe were an invitation to land. With Wynn and Beattie I discussed the possibilities. We quickly agreed that a landing could accomplish nothing and might very well end in disaster. O'Connor must

know this. Apparently it had snowed heavily since his arrival,
for there were no visible tracks to mark his landing. He was
standing thigh deep in snow when he made the signals.

While we sought an answer, the first supporting plane arrived. It was Captain Lord of Northeast Airlines flying a C-47.
We welcomed him on the radio.

Lord made his passes over the lake, and we saw O'Connor
signal in the same fashion. Finally Lord called us on the radio
and asked us to stand by. He believed that with his much lighter
and slower plane he could make a successful landing. We
wished him luck and watched apprehensively as he began a slow
descent. If he could land, there would presumably be enough
men on the lake to shovel a short runway. Then he could begin
taking people out a few at a time.

The wheels of Lord's C-47 brushed two light marks near the
end of the arrow. The ship settled ever so gently and then suddenly vanished in an explosion of snow. When it had settled
we saw the airplane buried to its wings and our meek decision
was confirmed by a discouraged voice on the radio.

"Oomph! I'm stuck!"

We now had more mouths to feed. On the long way back to
Presque Isle we watched the torn clouds very high aloft and
found no peace in them.

Factual events rarely arrange themselves in convenient or
dramatic sequence. Yet here the revelation of more important
matters would be justly suspect if the true line of events were
even once adjusted. The various real dangers, displays of courage
and cowardice, plus certain inevitable sacrifices, all occurred *after* O'Connor was located and so composed a sort of grand
anticlimax.

Soon after Lord had joined O'Connor other planes arrived
over the lake, and the pilots felt no temptation to try further
landings. They dropped their supplies and left. All of this
amounted to a fair collection of food, stoves, blankets, and cigarettes. There were also magazines and playing cards to help
pass the time until some scheme could be devised for the actual
removal of the men. The food supplies would be sufficient to

last for a few days, but we would have to return with more at frequent intervals. My own message to O'Connor promising their release within a few days was exceedingly premature. I had written it in a moment of great exhilaration and had failed to analyze the true dilemma.

The little community now existed on a flat cake of ice a very long way from any assistance. Presumably they could continue in good health for so long as they were careful and we were faithful with supplies. If we failed they must resort again to such occasional nourishment as owl soup (which they had tried and found very unappetizing), or if they were lucky they might

shoot a ptarmigan. They could not long survive on such a diet of semi-starvation for their greatest and most frightening enemy—clutching, soundless, and absolutely unforgiving—was the extreme cold. It was with them like a poisonous shroud every moment of the day and night. The haggard O'Connor's battle had just begun.

We set off for the lake on the following day loaded with tents, shovels, axes, and all manner of additional gear to provide shelter. It seemed very possible that the party might be spending a long time on Lac O'Connor, if indeed they could escape before the coming of summer. Against this dismal possibility, arrangements were under way for bush pilots in small ski planes to establish refueling stations on the lakes between Montreal and Lac O'Connor. Hopping froglike from lake to lake, they could eventually fly the entire distance. It was to be a long and laborious operation. Meanwhile our sole business was the continuance of food and shelter.

Our fourth day was an abysmal failure for everyone save the meteorologists, who would have wished otherwise. In spite of the meager reports they received from the general area they had discovered a warm front which they claimed would bring winds of such velocity we could never make our goal and have fuel enough to return. Consequently the two-engined airplanes were grounded, but we believed a C-87 should have ample reserve.

We were wrong. Our heavy, lumbering C-87 became a helpless butterfly. It danced in the air, trembled and bounced and writhed in such a continuous paroxysm of violent fits that there were times when we could not read the instruments. The wings flapped as if they were responsible for our elevation, the great double tail twisted alarmingly, and we were constantly jammed down hard in our seats or thrown against our belts. All four engines nodded angrily on their mounts and the entire assembly of parts seemed determined to separate. Neither Wynn, nor Beattie, nor myself had ever seen anything like such turbulence except in the maw of a thunderstorm, and our half-jokes about the inherent strength of a C-87 became ever more feeble.

At last we surrendered, but not because of the turbulence alone. We estimated the wind to be at sixty miles an hour and directly on our nose. The visibility ahead was fair enough, but the ground was completely obscured in blowing snow. Even if we were lucky enough to find Lac O'Connor under such conditions we could not possibly execute a useful drop. So, with our tails between our legs, we turned back to Presque Isle.

During the night the wind diminished, and it began to snow heavily.

Far to the north of the Saguenay, beyond even O'Connor's special wilderness, a blizzard was conceived because a heavy mass of air met, took, and raped a lighter, more delicate mass of air. It howled down from Hudson Bay and from the Belcher Islands. It swallowed Cape Sandy and obliterated the Great Whale River. It screeched toward O'Connor's refuge, where he waited in ignorance of its being. Its stealth in approach, strewing Christmas card snowflakes before it so prettily, gave no hint of its inner fury. Only science could reveal its spiteful character, and for once we trusted the meteorologists. They said the blizzard had not yet reached Lac O'Connor. Nor would it, they believed, for some twenty-four hours. After this preparatory stage we should accept the fact that O'Connor could not be reached for some time.

Because of the nature of the weather on this fifth day we rejected the unhandy C-87 and returned to our faithful two-engined airplanes. We knew the route now and believed we could follow it well enough if we could keep visual contact with the earth. Hedgehopping, we thought to locate ourselves by the prominences we had named and so be less at the mercy of our untrustworthy compasses. The cloud ceiling at Presque Isle was very low, but we intended to slink along beneath it. The snowfall was spasmodic, becoming quite heavy at times and then subsiding to sprays of little body. It was much warmer than it had been for weeks, yet the dull gray sky and the foreign appearance of our home airport in its new formations of snow depressed us.

We set off with five airplanes, one of which was flown by our bombastic lieutenant. He had been stomping around in the snow long before our actual departure and the clouds of vapor from his anxious breathing served as a fitting background to his words of fire.

If we were to give full credence to his behavior this man was fearless, although he had not as yet once reached even the general vicinity of Lac O'Connor. Something always developed within his airplane—a rough engine or a faulty radio or frozen propeller controls—which forced his return to base. Here too the poor bull of a man must have been at constant odds with the fortitude which obsessed him and the true timidity which ruled him. For we saw him frequently terrified of badge authority, cringing in the presence of Boyd, who was half his size, and ever obsequious to anyone of higher rank. We concluded sadly that he was a worshiper of power and, in his greed for even a sip of the brew, had performed his own emasculation.

None of us cared very much for the first hour of flying. The terrain between Presque Isle and the St. Lawrence was easy and rolling, but the top of the mildest hill can become the rending summit of a mountain when it is hidden in cloud. We were frequently obliged to slip between the hills, taking such advantage of the shallow valleys as we could. The visibility deteriorated to less than a mile as we proceeded, and in the snow squalls became somewhat less. It was not safe flying. All of us knew this and accepted the fact with such wry remarks as came to our minds. Catchings' southern drawl came over the radio.

"There's a very limited future in this."

Someone else: "I forgot my snowshoes."

Another: "On Donner . . . on Blitzen."

We reeled in our trailing antennas for fear of losing them and hugged the contours of the earth. All manner of objects, both human and natural, loomed suddenly out of the white mists ahead. It was as impossible as it would have been unwise to fly in close formation. Each pilot drew away from his nearest companion and sought his separate way between squalls and terrain.

It was no surprise to any of us when the lieutenant's voice rattled in our earphones. And it was full of such honest misery we could only pity him.

This time he made no claim of mechanical difficulties. He

simply stated that we were all crazy. We had no business flying in such conditions and he was getting out. He would climb through the overcast to a sensible altitude and return to Presque Isle.

We urged him to hold a little longer. We told him the weather was bound to improve although we knew as well as he did that any such prediction was based upon pure wishing. We must remain low regardless, believing it impossible to climb to a higher and safer altitude, fly for five hours on instruments, and then descend with any hope of recognizing our location. The course to Lac O'Connor was inflexible. If we lost it visually for any appreciable length of time, our compasses invariably led us astray. And O'Connor desperately needed what our airplanes contained.

The lieutenant said he was sorry. And that was the last we heard of him. I began to doubt my opinion of the lieutenant, for a man could not be altogether lacking in courage who would so publicly display his funk. He knew he could not be forgiven and he must have known his censure would be unspoken, which is the most severe punishment of all. No one would ever ask him why he turned back, or suggest that it would have been more admirable if he had persevered. The guise of politeness, even a touch of jollity, would be his slap in the face and it would sting for as long as he had any contact with those who had been witness to his desertion. He had chosen loneliness and there was nothing we could ever do to regain him. The rest of us continued in hypocrisy, frequently afraid yet compelled onward by our even greater fear of each other.

My own resolution often reached the vanishing point. Beyond the St. Lawrence the squalls thickened, whirled around each other in ghostly dances, and finally united in those meager tunnels through which we managed to squirm our way. We would only occasionally catch sight of each other and more frequently lost the course entirely. It seemed hopeless and even more foolhardy if we dared to approach the Wynn Mountains, but there was suddenly a large break revealing their lower foundations, so that we were momentarily encouraged. But the barren outcroppings of granite, the minor indentations, sheer cliffs, and dark crevasses we had known were smoothed over with snow. Now the range presented only a series of domed teats, joining upon each other until the highest were lost in the overcast. At length we found a promising valley columned with snow showers. We slipped through it to immediate disappointment.

Nothing in the land beyond was recognizable. All of our carefully plotted landmarks had magically disappeared or had been so changed in contour and character by the heavy fall of snow that we failed to identify any of them. Our compasses, bewitched as ever, required us to fly due west or east for a full five minutes before they would settle enough to set our gyros. Then we could carry on north again. The process, in such visibility, caused us to wander back and forth across a course we now could only assume to be correct, and consequently we wasted precious time.

Here in the wastelands of lakes, the visibility finally increased to a mile or so, but the cloud ceiling prevented us from climbing above a thousand feet. Thus we must come upon Lac O'Connor exactly, neither too far to the east nor to the west. An error of two miles would carry us past it, unseen and unseeing. The chances of stumbling upon O'Connor as Watkins had done were about equal to the multitude of lakes against one. We called repeatedly for radio guidance to the lake, but no sound came. It was understandable that we might not be expected guests in such weather, but the rationalizing did little for our spirits. We had found O'Connor only to lose him again.

We milled all about to the limit of our fuel and then turned away in dejection. Actually we were never sure, nor could we ever be, that our searching on this day occurred anywhere near the right area.

Unknown to us, McGuire was searching the same skies in a C-87. He had thought to locate O'Connor by radio alone and was obliged to remain much higher, within the overcast. When no signals came he was also compelled to turn toward Presque Isle and, in the doing, found a measurement of his fortune.

The fuel tanks of a C-87 were constructed of a self-sealing rubberish material, as were those of its bomber counterpart.

Because of the extreme cold on these operations it was customary to seal off the air venting pipes to these tanks with masking tape. Thus, when the airplane was on the ground, moisture condensation could not collect just inside the pipes, freeze, and thereby choke the breathing of the fuel system. When the airplane was prepared for flight, the masking tape was removed.

Just before night fell McGuire's engineer discovered this vital chore had not been performed on two of the tanks. From the astrodome he could see the vents only a few yards away, yet he was helpless to reach them. Horrified, he informed McGuire, who did some rapid thinking and yearned for the simplicity of his Carolina mule. The engines had continued to function only because the rubber tanks were slowly collapsing. How much longer could they squeeze out the needed fuel? McGuire found out soon enough. One engine backfired and quit without further apology. Shortly afterward, the second engine also ceased to function.

McGuire was flying a C-87 on instruments, at night, over unknown terrain, with two engines out on the same side. This was something less than a pleasure, but not his major concern. All of the remaining fuel on the crippled side of his airplane was unavailable to him. As a result he simply could not reach Presque Isle or any other recognized airport. It seemed as if he might be the unwilling imitator of O'Connor.

He radioed his impossible predicament and learned that there was a new field still under construction on the north shore of the St. Lawrence. It was much too small for a C-87, but it did have a radio range. McGuire calculated he could just make it if nothing else happened. This was good, but now there came an additional evil.

When he arrived over the airport he was told the only lights outlining the short and snow-swept runway were a few kerosene flares. And the weather could not have been less hospitable. The ceiling was far below limits—its actual height, unknown. The visibility was half a mile—less, in the periods of heavy blowing snow. The wind was strong across the runway.

Every trick and device McGuire had ever learned since he first clutched the controls of an airplane, all of the knowledge ac-

quired in Lester's school, and his subsequent thousands of
hours' experience as co-pilot and captain now asked for a reckoning. And to this he must add more than a soupçon of luck, plus
a heavy seasoning of pure nerve.

The final ingredient was courage, which McGuire summoned
through his fears when he cut back the two throttles and sank
into a white void.

True to his profession, McGuire said later it was a rotten instrument approach. He was referring to his minor technical mis-
demeanors, as if they were important at the time. His critique
deliberately skipped the fact that the airplane was flying askew,
everything below was foreign to him including the nature of the
terrain, and they had to lengthen the runway before the C-87
could be flown away again. Nor would he mention how he swept
down through the squalls, caught a mere glimpse of the runway,
then somehow squeezed the ship into its limitations, and
landed without scratching the staggering beast of an airplane.
All of these things he passed off as inconvenient tribulations
which it would be in poor taste to discuss. He acknowledged a
surging in his bowels when they passed downward through two
hundred feet and there was still nothing to be seen; but the
thing anyone was asked to understand was his technical clumsi-
ness in wavering from the beam an occasional degree or two, or,
preoccupied with his troubles, momentarily allowing his air
speed to exceed or fall below those exact amounts prescribed
for flying in perfect conditions. It was he who was fraudulent,
anyone must understand, and the ultimate success was achieved
in spite of his efforts rather than because of them. Over-
modesty can easily be the reverse side of pride and hence in-
tolerably false; but if it is contagious and constant to the bearer,
and if he assumes it with wink and humor to conceal honestly
the details of personal exploit, then it may be admirable and
also delightful. It was a code to which nearly all of us were
happily bound.

Two days passed while the snows loaded the earth. We
waited in warm impatience while the mechanics fretted over
our planes. From the overheated operations office with its banging radiators, we could watch the mechanics trudging out to

the line of half-buried airplanes and then jogging stiffly back when they could no longer stand the cold. And they were very cold, for wind had come along with the snow and penetrated every protection. Most of the mechanics were muffled to their bleary eyes and had deliberately rubbed grease on their faces against frostbite. But they suffered it anyway and would tenderly minister to each other when the telltale white areas appeared.

We stood about, smoking and cursing the weather, and kicking at the radiators with our soft flying boots, and saw in the raw-meat faces of the mechanics only a reflection of our uselessness.

We went again and again to the weather room, interfering with and annoying the meteorologists with our questions, prognostications, arguments, and unhappy derision. We stood before the teletype machines, defying them to repeat their dismal utterances of continued bad weather from every station, and the machines, as if in stuttering revolt against such persuasive attempts by human beings, always stood their ground. There were, of course, no reports available from the search area itself, but reports from Montreal and the few Hudson Bay outposts to the west were sufficient to draw a general picture and would normally show the earliest improvement.

I had brooded upon our failure to find Lac O'Connor by hedgehopping. The present storm must alter the appearance of the terrain even more radically and it seemed we might once again be defeated because we could not recognize our way. The capricious behavior of our compasses at a vital point along our route was still mysterious, but it was proven well enough and some means must be found to circumvent it.

We now knew the approximate latitude and longitude of Lac O'Connor. But this was an arbitrary as well as invisible point in space and the problem remained to bring ourselves upon it. Our barnstorming tactics had succeeded and would again eventually, yet the process was dangerous in bad weather and ripe with frustrations when the weather was good.

So we went to Boyd with a plan and found him, as always, receptive. We proposed leaving Presque Isle at night and at an hour which would permit us to arrive over Lac O'Connor, or at least in its vicinity, just after dawn. We would employ celestial navigation to keep our course, using the stars in lieu of our eyes. We would take fixes as frequently as possible, every half hour or so, and thus have an almost continuous warning of any deviations from course. The very last fixes would be taken just before the stars faded, and the concluding distance to Lac O'Connor should then be so short we could hardly miss it. In addition, a message would be sent to O'Connor and Lord describing our intentions and stating our approximate time of arrival. If they would then set up a fuss of radio bearings, an oil fire with as much smoke as they could manage, plus flares when they heard our engines, they would have visitors. Most of us were now convinced O'Connor had no idea how difficult he was to see even when we were on top of him.

To all of this Boyd agreed, and improved in detail. Among other things he suggested better navigators than our already rusty selves. These men would keep us toeing the line.

We took off the following night, climbed above the still-lingering overcast, and placed our trust in the stars. Our compasses could be as clever as they pleased, for now their dishonesties were rediscovered so frequently they could not long deceive us.

For this first attempt, which was admittedly experimental, we used only three airplanes and flew in loose formation. It was a beautifully smooth flight, free of incident for a change, and we were as jovial as we could be about the cold. Ordinarily we would have amused ourselves with complaints of such minor discomforts—the itching misery of our oxygen masks, which were designed only to fit the face of a baboon, the theft of our sleep, the cold coffee, brittle sandwiches, and the slow all-pervading fatigue for which our heavy flying suits were partly responsible. But there was none of this. We were all too conscious of the men on the lake hidden in nowhere, and of their true ordeal.

The last fixes, obtained just before the stars disappeared, placed us some fifty miles south of the area. We started a slow descent toward the broken overcast as the light increased and called to the lake for radio bearings. But the silence in our ear-phones remained undisturbed.

We were in cloud only a few minutes and then slipped out beneath. I began to doubt the wisdom of the plan, for nothing I could see in the half-light was recognizable. The snows had obviously been very heavy and the rippling mass of lakes and low hills might have been anywhere. I wondered if our original estimate of O'Connor's latitude and longitude had been in seri-ous error, or would we in these last few minutes pass right on by because we were again at a low altitude? Already the question of fuel had entered our thinking and each minute of silence subtracted from our ability to remain in the vicinity.

Suddenly the silence was broken and our direction-finder needles swung with wonderful precision. O'Connor was not straight ahead, a situation which could only have been miracu-lous, but he was a mere ten degrees to the left of our course. Moreover, we thought him to be near, since the signals were of strength. We banked at once and followed the quivering needles.

He was farther away than we could have believed, and our impatience stretched the distance. Dawn was well established when we saw a series of red and green flare balls explode and glisten against the white horizon. We could not yet observe their origin, but they were still in descent when we passed over a ridge of intervening hills and at last swooped down upon our quarry.

Two days later I made a final flight to Lac O'Connor and was then assigned elsewhere. O'Connor, Lord, and their companions, were as well found and fed as could be wished under the circum-stances, and a considerable assembly of men and machines was now combining to effect their actual liberation. O'Connor was among the last to be taken from his frozen home, a retreat made in justifiable pride, for all of his charges, even those who were sick and injured before they ever left Thule, emerged in good spirits and health. Their most grievous wounds were a few mild cases of frostbite. They were on the lake, in all, nearly three weeks.

O'Connor rested briefly and then, indefatigable as ever, went out to Assam, where he became chief pilot of an even more difficult and sensitive operation—flying the Hump into China. I did not see him again for a year, and then under quite different conditions.

The doings at Lac O'Connor did not terminate with the departure of its discoverer. Wynn remained in Presque Isle to conclude the adventure in a remarkable and appropriately determined fashion. Everyone was distressed at the idea of an undamaged airplane finally sinking into the lake when the ice melted. So a snowplow was flown to the lake in pieces, reassembled by a crew who made their own acquaintance with pure cold, and a short runway was cut across the lake. The C-87 was filled with a minimum of fuel, the engines revitalized with special heaters, and when all was ready, Wynn took a deep breath in an instinctive attempt to increase its lift and flew the thing out.

The same airplane was eventually sent to the Hump as if in dogged pursuit of its former master.

FROM

Thunderbolt!

ROBERT S. JOHNSON WITH MARTIN CAIDIN

The Republic P-47 Thunderbolt was a big, rugged plane. Behind its four-bladed propeller the massive cowling shielded a Pratt & Whitney engine capable of 2000 horsepower. Each wing carried four .50-caliber machine guns. This was the plane in which Robert S. Johnson shot down twenty-eight German fighters during World War II. And this was the almost indestructible plane that brought him home out of a losing, one-sided fight one terrifying day in June 1943.

Fighter Pilot

Thunderbolts moving out from the perimeter, propellers drenched in sun, grass flattened by airblast. Pilots leaning out of cockpits to see beyond those giant engines weaving their way along, moving into position for takeoff. Orders from the tower, brakes released, throttle forward, go! Hard on the rudder to counteract torque, the needle climbs around, back pressure on the stick. Grass and trees fall away magically beneath my wheels, I work the controls, hydraulics surge in tubes, the gear folds up and inward and tucks away into the Thunderbolt's broad wings.

Left turn, stick and rudder working smoothly, tilting the earth sharply, back on the stick, climb out, and meet in the air. Forty-eight Thunderbolts in formation, sliding and wheeling into neat and precise patterns. No one aborts, no engine fails, the pilot of the forty-ninth Thunderbolt, our standby, mutters unhappily and peels off to return to Horsham St. Faith. We lead today;

the 61st Fighter Squadron holds the low and leading position for this mission. I swivel my head. High to my left, bunched together, the sixteen fighters of the 63rd labor for altitude. To my right, slightly higher than my own formation, wings the 62nd. I am Blue 4 in Blue Flight, stuck on the end slot. My element leader is to my left; sliding smoothly through the air to his left ride our flight leader and his wingman.

It is a tight, well-drilled team. Each flight of four Thunderbolts holds tight formation, four finger tips greasing through the air. Manston falls far behind as the forty-eight fighters drone southward, all climbing at an indicated 170 miles per hour. Our throttles are held back, allowing the Thunderbolts to ascend in a shallow, fuel-saving climb.

Dover below, the cliffs melting into the Channel waters. A day of crystal clarity, scattered clouds far below us, miles between the puffy white. There is absolutely no limit to visibility; the earth stretches away forever and forever. A strange world—made for solitary flight, and yet made also, it seems, of three-dimensional movement, the gliding through space of forty-eight fighters, each alone, each linked also by the unseen thread of metallic, radio voices.

Over the Channel, only a mile or so off the French coast. Still climbing, the altimeter winding around slowly, clocking off the hundreds, the thousands, past ten thousand, reaching for twenty. The coastline drifts by, quiet and almost sleepy in the rich sun, unrevealing of gun batteries and listening posts and radar scanners already reporting of our position, number, height and course, data flashed back to German antiaircraft batteries, to fighter fields, to command posts. From this altitude, France slumbers, beautiful and green.

Le Tréport beneath our left wings, the mouth of the Seine River clear and sharp. "Blue Flight, stay sharp. Nine zero degrees. Let's go." Blue Flight wheels, banks and turns in unison with its squadron, the 61st matching flawlessly the wheeling of its two sister squadrons. Below the formation, the Seine River, occupied territory.

"Open up, Blue Flight." Our radio call, orders to the other flights. Move out, separate into combat formation. Pilots work stick and rudder; the Thunderbolts ease away from one another. Now Blue Flight is in its combat position, each Thunderbolt 200 yards apart. Between each flight of four fighters stretches a space of 500 yards and, even further out, holding a distance of 1500 yards, ride the squadrons. Almost constantly I turn and look, turn and look, watching the position of my own planes, seeking out strange black specks in the sky, alert for the plunging Focke-Wulfs or Messerschmitts.

Marching in precision, the 63rd Squadron flies to the north, very high, in down-sun position. I turn my head, and see the 62nd Squadron, to our south, and slightly above our own altitude. Other things to check as I divert my attention to the cockpit. Gun switch "On." Gunsight "On." Check the chute harness. Shoulder and leg straps tight, catches secure, the harness fastened. Don't make it easy for the Jerries—check the "elephant trunk." I inspect the oxygen tube, start to count: "3-6-9-12-15-18-21-24-27-30." Oxygen okay; the count by threes to thirty clear and sharp, no faltering. Escape kit secured. If—that big "if"—I go down, I want to be sure of my equipment, my procedures, my position. It's a long walk through France and Spain, *if* luck holds.

The Thunderbolts move into the skies of Europe. A moment to myself. Alone, yet not alone, I pray. If He allows, a moment of thanks on the way home. There won't be time to pray once the black-crossed fighters rush in.

Keep looking, keep looking! It's that moment of carelessness, the second of not paying attention, when the fighters pounce. Occasionally I glance ahead, but I am in the end slot, exposed in the Blue 4 position. At all times my head swivels, my eyes scanning every inch of the sky from my right wingtip, rearward, and above, over my canopy, and down. The silk scarf around my neck isn't a hotrock decoration; without the silk to protect my skin, my neck by now would be raw and bleeding from rubbing against the wool collar of my shirt.

Out of the corner of my eye—a speck. There, far to the right! I catch my heart with my teeth, swallow, snap my head to the right. I squint, study the sky. A speck of oil on the windshield, not a fighter. Gratefully, my heart drops back where it belongs.

Fifteen miles inland, the Thunderbolt phalanx due north of Rouen, still over the sparkling Seine. My head continues to swivel, my roving gaze stops short as I notice a formation of sixteen fighters, directly behind and slightly above us. They're coming in fast, flying a duplicate of our own formation. Thunderbolts? I look to the left; the sixteen fighters of the 62nd Squadron are rock steady. To the right; there, the sixteen fighters of the 63rd Squadron. Who the hell are these other people? For several seconds I stare at their silhouettes—they're Focke-Wulfs!

Slow, Johnson, take it slow, and be clear. I press the radio mike button on the throttle, and make an effort to speak slowly and distinctly. "Sixteen bandits, six o'clock, coming in fast, this is Keyworth Blue 4, Over." No one replies, no one makes a move. The Thunderbolts drone on, utterly oblivious of the sixteen fighters streaking in. Am I the *only* man in the Group who sees these planes? I keep my eyes glued to the fighters, increasing in size with every second, trailing thin streaks of black exhaust smoke as they rush toward us under full power.

"Sixteen bandits, six o'clock, coming in fast—this is Keyworth Blue 4—*Over!*" Now I see the enemy fighters clearly—Focke-Wulfs, still closing the gap. Again I call in—I'm nearly frantic now. My entire body seems to quiver. I'm shaking; I want to rip the Thunderbolt around and tear directly into the teeth of the German formation. It's the only thing to do; break into them. For a moment, a second of indecision, I lift the P-47 up on one wing and start the turn—no, dammit! I swore I wouldn't break formation; I would act only on orders and not on my own. I jab down again on the button, this time fairly shouting the warning of enemy fighters.

What the hell's the matter with them? I glance quickly at the other Thunderbolts, expecting the leader's big fighter to swing around and meet the attack. The P-47 drones on, unconcerned, her pilot apparently oblivious to the enemy. My finger goes down on the button and I call, again: "Sixteen bandits, six o'clock, coming in f——"

A terrific explosion! A split second later, another. And yet another! Crashing, thundering sounds. WHAM! WHAM! WHAM! One after the other, an avalanche smashing into my fighter, heavy boulders hurtling out of nowhere and plunging with dev-astating force into the airplane. A blinding flash. Before my eyes the canopy glass erupts in an explosion, dissolves in a gleaming shower. Tiny particles of glass rip through the air. The Thunder-bolt shudders through her length, bucks wildly as explosions flip her out of control. Still the boulders rain against the fighter, a continuing series of crashing explosions, each roaring, each terrifying. My first instinct is to bail out; I have a frantic urge to leave the airplane.

Concussion smashes my ears, loud, pounding; the blasts dig into my brain. A new sound now, barely noticed over the crashing explosions. A sound of hail, rapid, light, unceasing. Thirty-caliber bullets, pouring in a stream against and into the Thunderbolt. Barely noticed as they tear through metal, flash brilliantly as tracers. The Thunderbolt goes berserk, jarring heavily every time another 20-mm. cannon shell shears metal, tears open the skin, races inside and explodes with steel-ripping force.

Each explosion is a personal blow, a fist thudding into my body. My head rings, my muscles protest as the explosions snap my body into the restraining straps, whip my head back against the rest. I am through! This is it! I'm absolutely help-less, at the mercy of the fighters pouring fire and steel into the Thunderbolt. Squeezed back in my seat against the armor plat-ing—my head snaps right and left as I see the disintegration of my '47. A blow spins my head to the left as a bullet creases my nose. Behind me I can feel the steel being flayed apart by the unending rain of cannon shells.

I notice no pain. I have only a frantic feeling—an explosive urge to get out!

I am not frightened; I am beyond any such gentle emotion. I am terrified, clutched in a constricting terror that engulfs me. Without conscious volition my finger stabs down the radio button and I hear a voice, loud and piercing, screaming, "May-day! Mayday! Mayday!" The words blur into a continuous stream. The voice goes on and on, shouting the distress call, and not until I have shrieked for help six times or more do I recognize my own voice.

I have no time to think, almost no time to act. Moving by sheer force of habit, by practice become instinct, my hands fly over my body. Without conscious thought, without even realizing what I am doing, I wriggle free of the shoulder harness and jerk open the seat belt.

Another explosion. A hand smashes me against the side of the cockpit; for a moment acceleration pins me helplessly. The Thunderbolt breaks away completely from my control. Earth and sky whirl crazily. I'm suddenly aware that the fighter has been thrown nose down, plunging out of control. The smashing explosions, the staccato beating of the bullets, blurs into a continuous din. A sudden lunge, the fighter snaps to the right, nose almost vertical. The Thunderbolt's wild motions flip me back and forth in the cockpit. . . .

Fire! A gleaming tongue of flame licks my forehead. It flickers, disappears. Instantly it is here again, this time a searing fire sheet, erupting into the cockpit. The fire dances and swirls, disappears within a thick, choking cloud of smoke. Intense, blinding, sucked through the shattered canopy. The draft is terror. The draft of air is Death, carrying the fire from the bottom of the cockpit, over me, crackling before my face, leaping up and out through the smashed canopy.

The terror is eternity. Burn to death!

GET OUT!

I grab the canopy bar, gasping for breath, jerk it back with maniacal strength. The canopy jerks open, slides back six inches, and jams.

Trapped! The fire blossoms, roars ominously. Frantic, I reach up with both hands, pulling with every bit of strength I can command. The canopy won't budge.

Realization. The fighter burning. Flames and smoke in the cockpit. Oxygen flow cut off. Out of control, plunging. Fighters behind. Helpless.

New sounds. Grinding, rumbling noises. In front of me, the engine. Thumping, banging. Bullets, cannon shells in the engine; maybe it's on fire!

I can't see. I rub my eyes. No good. Then I notice the oil, spraying out from the damaged engine, a sheet of oil robbing me of sight, covering the front windscreen, cutting off my vision. I look to the side, barely able to look out.

Great, dark shapes. Reeling, rushing past me. No! The Thunderbolt plunges, flips crazily earthward. The shapes—the bombers! The bomber formations, unable to evade my hurtling fighter. How did I miss them? The shapes disappear as the Thunderbolt, trailing flame and smoke, tumbles through the bombers, escaping total disaster by scant feet. Maybe less!

GET OUT!

I try, oh God, how I try! Both feet against the instrument panel, brace myself, grasp the canopy bar with both hands. Pull—pull harder! Useless. It won't budge.

Still falling. Got to pull out of the dive. I drop my hands to the stick, my feet to the rudders. Left rudder to level the wings, back pressure on the stick to bring her out of the dive. There is still wind bursting with explosive force through the shattered canopy, but it is less demoniacal with the fighter level, flying at less speed.

Still the flame. Now the fire touches, sears. I have become snared in a trap hurtling through space, a trap of vicious flames and choking smoke! I release the controls. Feet firmly against the instruments, both hands grasping the canopy bar. It won't move. *Pull harder!*

The Thunderbolt rears wildly, engine thumping. Smoke inside, oil spewing from the battered engine, a spray whipping back, almost blinding me to the outside world. It doesn't matter. The world is nothingness, only space, forever and ever down to the earth below. Up here, fire, smoke.

I've got to get out! Terror and choking increases, becomes frenzied desperation. Several times I jerk the Thunderbolt from her careening drops toward the earth, several more times I kick against the panel, pull with both hands. The canopy will not move. Six inches. Not a fraction more. I can't get out!

A miracle. Somehow, incredibly, flame disappears. The fire . . . *the fire's out!* Smoke boils into the cockpit, swirls around before it answers the shrieking call of wind through the shattered glass. But there is no flame to knife into flesh, no flame. . . . Settle down! *Think!* I'm *still* alive!

The terror ebbs, then vanishes. At one moment I am beset
with fear and frenzy, with the uncontrollable urge to hurl my
body through the restraining metal, anything, just to escape
the fire. Terror grips me, chokes my breathing and thinking
and, in an instant, a moment of wonder, it is banished. I no
longer think of other aircraft—enemy or friendly. My mind
races over my predicament; what I must do. I begin to relax.

The cessation of struggle, physically and within the mind, is
so incredibly absolute that for long seconds I ponder. I do not
comprehend this amazing self-control. It may be simply that I
am overwhelmed by the miracle of still being alive. Perhaps it
is the loss of oxygen at five miles above the earth. The precious
seconds of relief flee all too quickly. I must still get out of
the stricken airplane if I am to live.

Feet on the instrument panel, hands on the bar. Pull. I pull
with all my strength until I am fairly blue in the face. I feel
my muscles knotting with the strength of desperation, my body
quivers with the effort. Not even this renewed struggle avails
me. Cannon shells have burst against the canopy, twisted and
curled metal.

The fighter heels sickeningly over on her side, skids through
the air, flips for earth. I barely pay attention to the controls; my
feet and hands move almost of their own accord, co-ordinating
smoothly, easing the airplane from her plunge. Out of the dive
again, the desire to survive becoming more intense.

I *must* get out. I hunch up in the cockpit, desperation once
again rising about me like a flood. The canopy, the canopy. Life
or death imbedded within that blackened, twisted metal. I
hunch my shoulder, lunge at the metal. Again, and again! Hard
blows that hurt. Steel slams into my shoulder, hard, unyielding.
I cry out in frustration, a wordless profanity. My hands ball into
fists and I beat at the canopy, throwing punches, hard, strong
blows. But I am not in the ring, not striking at flesh and bone.
The steel mocks me, unyielding, triumphant. I sit back for a
moment, level the P-47 and wonder.

There is another way out. The canopy is shattered, atop me,
to both sides. I stand up in the seat, poke my head and shoulders
through the broken canopy. I hardly notice the heavy force

of the wind and cold. I ignore it. My shoulders are through. I stand to my waist—I can get out!

Despair floods my mind. The parachute snags against the ripped canopy. It can't clear; there's not enough space between the shattered cockpit for both my body and the chute. I'm not going without it! I crawl back to the seat, right the spiraling airplane, and think.

All through the struggle to escape the fighter, I have been talking to myself. Over and over again I have been repeating, "You can get out, you can. If you have to, you can get out!" Again and again the words formed, until finally reality ruled. And after each attempt: "You just must not have to."

I settle back in the seat, the terror and desperation vanished, caught by the wind shrieking through the cockpit, whisked away and scattered forever. I relax, a deliberate move to enable me to think clearly, to study my problem and to seek the solutions. My mind is clear, my thoughts spinning through my brain. I think of everything, a torrent of thoughts that refuse to be clouded, thoughts of everything imaginable.

I am absolutely unconcerned at the moment about enemy aircraft. I know the sky about me is filled with the black-crossed fighters, with pilots eager to find so helpless a target as a crippled Thunderbolt, trailing a greasy plume of smoke at it struggles through the sky, descending. There is no fear of death or of capture. The terror and desperation which so recently assailed me have been born of fire, of the horror of being burned alive. Now the fire is gone, the terror flung away with its disappearance. Solve the problems, Johnson, find the answers. You can't bail out.

A sound of danger snaps me back to full awareness. The engine is running very rough. Any moment, it seems, the giant power plant will tear itself free of its mounts to tumble through space, trapping me in an airplane unbalanced and uncontrollable. I turn my attention fully to flying, realizing that the Thunderbolt is badly crippled, almost on the verge of falling out of my control. Oil still bursts from the holes and tears in the cowling, a thin spray smearing itself against the windscreen, making vision forward almost impossible.

I cannot get out; I must ride this potential bomb to the very ground. My left hand moves almost automatically, easing the throttle back, a move made to keep the engine from exploding. Again—good fortune! The grinding, throbbing noise subsides; much smoother now. My chances are getting better.

The Thunderbolt is still true, still responsive. She obeys my commands. I head for England, a goal, a place to fly, a home to return to.

I stare at the instrument panel. A shambles. Smashed glass, many of the instruments broken. The Thunderbolt descends, nose slightly down, settling gradually, at about 170 miles per hour. I have no airspeed indicator, but I know this fighter, know her feel.

My mask seems to choke me. Strapped to my face, it had been, unknown to me, useless, unable to supply oxygen from a source shot away. I bank the fighter, stare down. At a height I estimate to be ten thousand feet, I unhook the mask from one side of my face, suck deeply the good clean air, air now richer with oxygen, oxygen to clear my head, to return to me my full senses.

With the newly returned clarity comes soberness, a critical evaluation of my predicament. I am in trouble, in serious, dangerous difficulty. Not until this moment do I realize that I have been flying almost blinded. My eyes burn, a stinging sensation that increases every moment in pain.

I touch my face with my hands. No goggles, and memory comes to me. Yesterday I broke a lens, I turned the goggles in for repair. This morning I took off on the only combat mission I ever flew or was to fly without goggles. It was a foolish move, and now, over occupied France in a crippled, smoking fighter, I am paying the penalty for my own stupidity.

In the opening moments of attack a 20-mm. cannon shell had ripped through the left side of the cockpit, exploded with a deafening roar near my left hand, and wreaked havoc with the hydraulic system. The blast sheared the flap handle and severed the hydraulic lines. Since that moment the fluid had poured into the cockpit. Then several more shells exploded, blasted apart the canopy. Wind entered at tremendous speed and, without respite, whipped the fluid into a fine, stinging spray.

Now the wind continues its devastating work. The fluid sprays into my eyes, burning and stinging. I fail to realize during the flight through thin air the effect on my eyes of the fluid.

My hand raises to my face, and I flinch. The pain is real, the source is evident. My eyes are swollen, puffed. Around them the skin is raised, almost as if I have been beaten with fists. It's hard to see. Not until now, not until this moment, do I realize that I am seeing through slits, that if my face swells any more, the skin will close over my eyes.

The moment this happens, I am finished. Half the time I fly with my eyes closed, feeling out the struggling, crippled fighter. It is now that my sense of balance, my sense of flight, comes to my aid. I can *feel* the Thunderbolt when she begins to skid, to slip through the air. I can feel a wing lowering, feel the sudden change of wind draft in the cockpit. I listen carefully, strain with eyes closed to note labor in the engine, to hear the increase in propeller revolutions, in engine tone, when the nose drops. This is how I fly, half blinded, eyes burning.

When I open my eyes to see, I must stick my head through the hole in the cockpit in order to look ahead. For the windscreen is obscured by oil. I do this several times. The wind stabs my eyes with ice picks, and the pain soars.

My attempts to clean my face, to rub away the fluid from my eyes, are pitifully hopeless. I pull a handkerchief from a pocket, wipe at my burning eyes. The first time I find relief. But the cockpit is filled with spray. My hands, my face, my clothes, are bathed, soaked in hydraulic fluid. In a moment the handkerchief too is drenched. Each time I rub my eyes I rub blood from my nose and the fluid deeper into my skin, irritating the eyes.

And yet, incredibly, I am calm and resolved. A succession of miracles has kept me alive, and I am not about to fret anxiously when only calmness will continue my survival. The pain in my eyes is nothing to the pain I have felt; certainly nothing against the past few minutes. Each time I open my eyes to check my flight, I scan the entire sky. My head swivels, I stare through burning eyes all about me. I am over enemy territory, heavily defended country, alone, in a crippled, smoking airplane, half blind. I have no company, and I do not savor the sight of other aircraft. I wish only to be left alone, to continue my slow, plodding pace through the air. I've got to get as far out over that Channel as possible.

Again I look around. My head freezes, I stare. My heart again is in my throat. A fighter, alone. I am close to the Channel, so close, as I stare at the approaching machine. Slightly behind the Thunderbolt, closing from four o'clock at about 8000 feet, the fighter closes in. I squint my eyes, trying to make out details. The fighter slides still closer.

Never have I seen so beautiful an airplane. A rich, dappled blue, from a dark, threatening thunderstorm to a light sky blue. The cowling is a brilliant, gleaming yellow. Beautiful, and Death on the wing. A Focke-Wulf 190, one of Goering's Boys on the prowl after the raging air battle from which I have been blasted, and slicing through the air—at me. I stare at the airplane, noting the wax coating gleaming on the wings and body.

What can I do? I think of waving my handkerchief at him, then realize the absurdity of such a move. That's silly! I'll rock my wings. But what good will this do? I'm at a loss as to my next move—for I don't dare to fight in the disabled Thunderbolt. I've got to get out over the Channel, continue my flight toward the water and a chance at safety and survival.

I simply stare at the Focke-Wulf. My eyes follow the yellow nose as it closes the distance. The moment the nose swings on a line that points ahead of the Thunderbolt—all hell will break loose. That can only be the German's move to lead my fighter with his guns—the moment before he fires.

All I can do is to sit, and watch. Closer and closer slides the sleek fighter. I begin to fidget, waiting for the yellow flashes to appear from his guns and cannon. Nothing. The guns remain silent, dark. The Focke-Wulf nose is glued on a line to the Thunderbolt. Damn—I'll bet he's taking pictures of me! Rare photographs of a crippled American fighter completely at his mercy.

The yellow-and-blue fighter glides in, still closer. I wonder what he has in mind, even as the Focke-Wulf comes to barely 50 yards away. I think of what I have always wanted to do, to close in to point-blank range, to stick my four right guns almost

in his cockpit and the four left guns against his tail—and fire. That would really scatter him! And that's just what this joker wants to do—to *me!*

He's too close. I shove the stick forward and to the right, swerving the Thunderbolt beneath the Focke-Wulf. I've got to get to the Channel; every move, every maneuver leads to that destination—the Channel water. As the fighter drops earthward, I bank and turn back to my left, heading directly out toward the coast. I glance up as the Focke-Wulf passes over me to my left, swings beautifully in an easy curve, and slides on my tail.

Thoughts race through my mind. I know he's going to work me over, just the second he feels he is in perfect position. I can't stop him, I can't fight in the crippled Thunderbolt; I don't

even know if the airplane will stay together through any maneuvers. Every moment of flight since I was shot up has been
in a long and gradual descent, a glide, easy enough even for a
disabled airplane. But now . . . I can't slug it out with this
Focke-Wulf.

I look the Thunderbolt over. For the first time I realize just
how severe a battering the airplane has sustained. The fighter
is a flying wreck, a sieve. Let him shoot! He can't hurt me any
more than I've been hurt!

I push back in the seat, hunching my shoulders, bringing my
arms in close to my body. I pull the seat adjustor, dropping the
seat to the full protection of the armor plate. And here I wait.

The German takes his time. He's having a ball, with a helpless pigeon lined up before his guns. When will he shoot?
C'mon, let's have it! He waits. I don't dare move away from the
armor plating. The solid metal behind me is my only chance for
life.

Pellets stinging against the wings, the fuselage, thudding into
the armor plate. A steady, pelting rain of hailstones. *And* he's
not missing! The .30-caliber bullets pour out in a stream, a rain
of lead splashing all over the Thunderbolt. And all I can do is to
sit there, crouched behind the armor plating, helpless, taking
everything the Kraut has to dish out.

For several seconds the incredible turkey shoot continues,
my Thunderbolt droning sluggishly through the air, a sitting
duck for the Focke-Wulf. How the P-47 stays together is a
mystery, for the bullets continue to pour into it.

I don't move an inch. I sit, anger building up. The bullets tear
metal, rip into spars, grinding away, chopping up the Thunderbolt. My nerves grate as if both hands hold a charge of electricity.
Sharp jolts against my back. Less than an inch away, bullets
crash against the armor.

To hell with this! My feet kick right and left on the rudder
pedals, yawing the P-47 from side to side. The sudden movement
slows the fighter to a crawl, and in that second the Focke-Wulf
overruns me and bursts ahead.

My turn. I may be almost helpless, but there are bullets in
the guns! Damn him—I can't see the Focke-Wulf. I stick my

head out of the window, wince from the pain of wind stabbing my swollen eyes. There he is, banking away. I kick right rudder, skid the Thunderbolt, squeeze the trigger in anguish. Eight heavy guns roar; my ship shudders as steel spits through the air. The moment of firing is more gesture than battle, for I cannot use my sights, I can barely see. The bullets flash in his direction, but I hold no hope that the Focke-Wulf will falter.

It doesn't. The sleek fighter circles lazily to the right, out of range. I watch him closely. Blue wings flash, the FW-190 swoops up, sweeps down in a wide turn. He's boss of the situation, and I simply fly straight and level as the German fighter slides into a perfect, tight formation with me! This is ridiculous, but I'm happier with the Jerry playing tag off my wing than sitting behind me and blazing away at the Thunderbolt.

The Focke-Wulf inches in closer, gleaming blue wing sitting over mine, the top so close that I can almost lean out of the cockpit and touch the waxed metal. I stare across the scant feet separating our two planes. Our eyes lock, then his gaze travels over the Thunderbolt, studying the fighter from nose to tail. No need to wonder what he is thinking. He is amazed that my airplane still flies; I know his astonishment that I am in the air. Each time his gaze scans the Thunderbolt he shakes his head, mystified. For at such close range he can see the tears and holes, the blackened and scorched metal from the fire, the oily film covering the nose and windscreen, the shattered canopy.

The Kraut stares directly at me, and lifts his left hand. He waves, his eyes expressionless. A wing lifts, the Focke-Wulf slides away. A long-held breath explodes from my lungs, and relief floods my mind. I watch the yellow-nosed fighter as he turns to fly away. But . . . he doesn't! The German plane keeps turning . . . he's on my tail again!

I cower again behind the armor plate. The Focke-Wulf is directly behind me, .30-caliber guns hammering. Still the bullets come, perfectly aimed. He doesn't miss, not a single bullet misses. I *know* they don't! Frantic, I kick rudder, jerk the heavy Thunderbolt from side to side, cutting my speed. The German waits for the maneuver; this time he's not sucked in. He holds back as the P-47 skids from side to side, and then I see the yellow nose drawing closer to me.

He pulls alongside tight to the P-47. Perfect formation, one battered, shot-up Thunderbolt and the gleaming new Focke-Wulf. By now we are down to 4000 feet, passing directly over Dieppe, our speed still 170 miles per hour. Over Dieppe! The realization makes me shudder, for below my wings lie the most intense antiaircraft concentrations along the entire coast.

They don't fire! Of course! The Focke-Wulf pilot is saving my life! *He* doesn't see Dieppe as a horror of flack. This is, to him, friendly territory, an area over which to fly with impunity. Unknowingly, he gives me yet another lease on life, is the un-witting party to the succession of miracles which, through one cumulative disaster after the other, are keeping me alive. Even his presence, his attacks, are in a way miraculous. For the German has laced me over with his .30-caliber guns, and it is only the smile of fortune that he found me after his four heavy cannon had expended their explosive shells.

Water below . . . the Channel beneath my wings! Still in perfect formation, the dappled blue FW-190 glides slowly down-ward with me. Then we are at 3000 feet. The coast two miles from me, and hope flares anew. There is a chance now, an ex-cellent chance to make it into the Channel where I can be rescued! I stare at the German pilot. His left hand raises slowly to his forehead in an informal salute; he waves, and his fighter lifts a wing as he slides off to the right.

Relief, the gasp of pent-up breath. Oh, no! Here he comes again! Nothing to do but to crouch within that armor plating. The enemy fighter sits behind me, perfectly in the slot. He's extra careful this time. A series of sharp bursts ripple from his guns. Again the hailstones pelting the tin roof, the bullets smashing into the fighter. Shuddering and helpless, the P-47 takes the punishment, absorbs the terrible beating. I have long given up hope of understanding why this machine continues to stay in the air. The German is whipsawing his bursts, kicking rudder gently as he fires. A stream of bullets, swinging from left to right, from right to left, a buzzsaw flinging bullets from one wingtip across the plane, into the armor plate, straight across. The firing stops.

Here he comes again. The yellow nose inching alongside, the gleaming Focke-Wulf. The German pilot again slides into formation, undesired company in the sky. For several minutes he remains alongside, staring at the wreck I am flying. He shakes his head in wonder. Below my wings the Channel is only a thousand feet away. A blue wing lifts, snaps down. I watch the salute, the rocking of wings. The sleek fighter accelerates suddenly and turns, flying away in a long climbing turn back to the coast.

Free! England ahead, the Channel lifting to meet the crippled P-47. How far, how far can I drag the Thunderbolt with her smashed and laboring engine before she drops into the waves?

All this time I have been so tense that my hand gripped the throttle and held down the mike button, transmitting all the things I had called the Jerry pilot, as well as the gunfire and the smashing of bullets into the Thunderbolt. And again, an inadvertent move comes to my aid. The moment the Focke-Wulf disappears, I release the throttle knob and begin my preparations for ditching. My plan is to belly into the Channel, nose high, tail down. As the fighter slews to a stop in the water, I will crawl out through the shattered canopy, dragging my folded dinghy life raft with me. Then, inflate the raft, move away from the sinking plane, and pray that Air-Sea Rescue will find me before the Jerries do, or before I drift long enough to starve. I am ready for all this, calm and prepared for the impact into the water.

And then . . . a voice! The moment my finger lifts from the mike button, I hear a voice calling urgently. "Climb if you can, you're getting very faint, climb if you can, you're getting very faint!" It's the Air-Sea Rescue radio—homing on me and giving instructions. At this instant I realize that it really is true—I'm still alive! The rugged old 'bolt, she'll *fly*, she'll bring me home yet!

I call back, exultation and laughter in my voice, nearly shouting. "Okay, out there! I'll try. I'll do everything I can, but I'm not sure what I can do. I'm down to less than a thousand feet now." And finally I discover that the battered and crippled Thunderbolt really *can* fly! I have been in a steady glide, convinced all this time the fighter is on the verge of falling out of control and now—only now—I discover that she'll fly. It is too good to be true, and I shout with glee.

I ease back on the stick. The Thunderbolt answers at once, nose lifting, and hauls upward in a zoom climb. I hold the fighter with her nose high until the speed drops to just above stalling.

Now, level out. Hold it, increase speed to at least 170 miles per hour, back on the stick again. And climb! Again I repeat the maneuver, a crippled series of upward zooms, each bringing me higher and higher. Each zoom—a terrific boost to my morale. Clouds above me, a scattered overcast at 5000 feet. Just below the cloud deck, nose level, more speed, and back on the stick. She goes! The big fighter rears upward into the clouds. Another levelling out, another zoom, and I'm on top. From less than 1000 feet to more than 8000! I'm shouting happily to myself, so cocky and confident and joyous that I'm nearly drunk from the sensation. Everything is wonderful! *Nothing* is going to stop me now! I nurse the fighter, baby the controls, and the crippled airplane responds, slides through the air, closer and closer to safety.

"Blue 4, Blue 4." The voice is clearer, sharper. "We have you loud and clear, Blue 4. Steer three-four-five degrees, Blue 4, steer three-four-five degrees."

"Hello Control, hello Control, this is Blue 4. I can't steer your heading. Most of my instruments are shot out. I have a general idea of my direction, but I cannot follow your exact heading. Direct me either left or right. Direct me either left or right. I will correct in this manner. Over."

Mayday Control stays with me every moment, sending flight corrections. I think the Channel is only forty miles across, but I am far south, and long miles stretch ahead of me. At my laboring speed, it seems I'll never get across the water! The minutes drag. How long can this airplane keep flying? I listen for any change in engine sound, for a faltering of the thunder ahead of me. But the engine sings true, maintaining power, and at 170 miles per hour we drone our way above the clouds, guided by an invisible voice through space, drawn inexorably toward home.

Time drags. Thirty minutes. Below the clouds, only the Channel. Thirty-five minutes, forty minutes. And then, a break in the clouds, the overcast becomes broken white cumulus and there . . . directly below me, the stark white cliffs of Dover! I'm too happy to keep radio silence, I whoop joyously. "Control, this is Blue 4. Those white cliffs sure look wonderful from up here!" No one can imagine just how wonderful they look!

The Controller seems to share my joy. In the next several minutes he guides me unerringly through the clouds and steers me to the Hawkinge air base. I can't find the field. The Controller tells me I am directly over the base, but this doesn't help. My eyes are too swollen, the field too well camouflaged. I pass directly over the hidden airfield, circle the field under the direction of the Mayday Controller, but cannot see a thing.

I check the fuel gauges: about a hundred gallons left. I call the Controller. "Hello, Mayday Control; hello, Mayday Control, this is Keyworth Blue 4. I'm okay now. I'm going to fly to Manston. I'd like to land back at my outfit. Blue 4, Out."

Immediately a call comes back. "Roger, Blue 4. If you're sure you can make it, go to B Channel and give them a call. Mayday Control, Out." He signs off. I switch radio control, and call Manston. The field is less than forty miles away, almost in sight. The Thunderbolt chews up the miles, and soon I begin to descend, heading directly for the field.

"Hello, Manston Tower, this is Keyworth Blue 4, Pancake, Over." The reply comes at once. "Hello, Blue 4, Hello Blue 4, this is Manston, Pancake Number One, zero-six-zero, Over."

"Hello, Manston. Blue 4 here. I'm shot up. I will have to make a belly landing. I do not know the condition of my landing gear. I have no hydraulics for flaps or brakes. Over."

"Blue 4 from Manston. Make a wheels down landing if you possibly can. Repeat, make a wheels down landing if you possibly can. We are very crowded, and have other crippled airplanes coming in. Over."

"Okay, Manston, from Blue 4. I'll try it. Check my wheels as I come over the tower. I cannot bail out, repeat, I cannot bail out. I have no hydraulic system to pull the wheels back up, no brakes, no flaps. Over."

I move the landing gear control to "Down" position. Fate still smiles on me. The wheels drop down, lock into position. With all the holes and gaping tears in the Thunderbolt, the wheels and tires have come through unscathed. I circle the field with my eyes almost closed, at 500 feet and less than 150 miles per hour.

This is it; now or never. I descend, turn into a long gliding turn for the runway so that I can see my point of touchdown. I cannot see through the oil-covered windscreen. Carefully, carefully, not enough power for an emergency go-around. I fly every inch toward the runway, nursing the Thunderbolt down. Over the very end of the field, just above stalling speed, I chop the throttle, drop the heavy fighter to the grass. It is one of the best landings I have ever made!

The fighter rolls down the hill to the center of the Manston field. On the rough, grassy landing strip I fight to keep her headed straight. Without flaps or brakes the big fighter rolls freely, barely losing speed. In the center of the field the strip slopes upward and the Thunderbolt charges along the grass. Ahead of me is a line of parked Spitfires and Typhoons; if I don't stop I'm going to slam into them!

At the last moment I kick left rudder, letting the ship turn freely with the wind. The wing tilts, the heavy machine slews violently about, slides backward into a slot between two Typhoons almost as if I'd planned it that way.

The Thunderbolt has brought me home. Battered into a flying, wrecked cripple, she fought her way back, brought me home. It's almost too much to believe! I feel a great wonder settling about me. My hand moves of its own accord. Engine off, switches off. My hands move over my body. Chute harness undone, straps free.

I crawl out through the hole in the canopy, dragging my parachute behind me. A grin stretches from ear to ear as I stand on the wing, stretch gratefully.

I jump to the ground, kneel down, and plant a great big kiss on Terra Firma. Oh, how good that solid earth feels!

FROM
Serenade to the Big Bird

BERT STILES

There were nine in the crew of the B-17, all of them in their early twenties. The pilot was First Lieutenant Samuel Newton. First Lieutenant Bert Stiles was the copilot. The crew had arrived in England with a new plane in March 1944. Their first mission over German-held Europe was on April 19.

Bert Stiles would complete thirty-five bomber missions. Then, instead of returning to the United States, he would transfer to fighters. On November 26, 1944, he would be shot down in a P-51 on an escort mission to Hanover. He would die at the age of twenty-three.

First Mission

WE went on our first one on the nineteenth of April. We had a practice mission the afternoon before, the first time we'd flown in a month, and we weren't bad, so the colonel said we could go.

Some major gave us a little talk about how we might as well start sometime, and were there any questions, and just fly that baby in close and you'll come home every time.

The squadron was short on crews or we would have had some more practice missions.

After the major let us go, Sam got the crew over in the corner and told us we'd have to be on the ball from here on in.

"And you've got to fly in close," he told me. "I'm not going to do all the work."

He had slept most of the way across the Atlantic, but now he was feeling serious.

I'd only flown formation in a 17 twice, once in the phases and once on the practice mission. I wasn't very hot.

"This is the big league now," Sam said.

Everybody said so. We'd been in the Bomb Group for four days and everyone in the Group knew he was in the big league.

After Sam let the crew go I asked him, "Are you scared?"

"I'm Sam," he said.

He was all right. He was ready to go.

We went over to the club then. It didn't seem any different. Nobody seemed to care that there was an alert on, and a raid tomorrow. Nobody went off in the corner to brood.

We had pork chops for dinner, and I sat next to a guy in our squadron named La something. I called him La French, because I could never remember the last part. He was big and acted half-drunk most of the time and he looked like a pirate.

"So you've joined our noble band," he said.

"We'll probably go tomorrow," I said.

"A joy ride," he said. "Lucky boy!"

"Where to?"

"What does it matter?" He waved his hands. "The Luftwaffe is beat. Haven't you heard?"

That was fine with me. I wanted to see a Focke-Wulf some time, but I didn't care about seeing one tomorrow.

After chow La French and I went out to say good night to his airplane. The dispersal area is way down past the skeet range and a turnip field. We took our bikes and rode through a world of blue and green and soft through the haze.

We saw that the plane was chocked in good for the night, and then hung around waiting for the sun to go down.

"Sort of pretty," La French said.

I thought he was talking to himself, so I didn't say anything.

I was well established in the sack when a bunch of guys came into the room and turned the lights on. A bombardier and a navigator were putting their copilot to bed, but he'd broken away into my room.

He was pretty drunk, and he really had the bright stare of death in his eyes.

"So you made the team?" this copilot said.

I said, "I guess so." I was about half-asleep.

All he did was laugh, just stand there and laugh, until the whole room was full of it, and shaking from it.

The bombardier and navigator got him under control then and took him away to bed. The bombardier came back after they put him away.

"That baby's got it bad," he said. "He won't last much longer. He's seen too many guys go down."

When the lights were out again I lay there for a while, not ready to go to sleep.

I wasn't scared. I was just wondering what I was doing here at all. I'd been building up to that night for a long time. I used to dream about it at school, sitting there drinking Cokes with some girl, reading the airplane magazines. I used to think about it all the time in the cadets. And now we were really here, ready to go to war in the morning. We were going out to knock off the Germans.

I knew right then that I didn't know much about killing.

I didn't feel like the Polish Spitfire pilots we met in Iceland, coming over. They had it bad. They wanted to kill every German in the world. But it was different with me, I'd never been shot at, or bombed. My folks live on York Street in Denver, which is a long way from this war.

All I knew about war I got through books and movies and magazine articles, and listening to a few big wheels who came through the cadet schools to give us the low-down. It wasn't in my blood, it was all in my mind.

The whole idea was to blow up just as much Germany to-morrow as possible. From way up high, it wouldn't mean a thing to me. I wouldn't know if any women or little kids got in the way. I'd thought about it before, but that night it was close. The more I thought of it, the uglier it seemed.

What I wanted to do tomorrow was ski down Baldy up at Sun Valley, or wade out into the surf at Santa Monica, and get all knocked out in the waves, and come in and lie in the sun all afternoon.

Instead I was going on a trip, a long trip, to help some other guys beat up a town, or an oil plant, or a steel mill. It seemed like a pretty futile way to live.

Then I thought a while about the eight guys who had slept in my bed in the last four months. They were all dead or down in some German Stalag, or getting drunk in Sweden, or hiding in a French ditch somewhere. They hadn't hurt the bed much. It was a nice sack, the only good one in England up to then.

Some joker dragged me out of it at two in the morning.

"Come on," he said, "breakfast at two-thirty, briefing at three-thirty." It was Lieutenant Porada.

Somebody upstairs who wasn't on the list was shouting, "Drag the Luftwaffe up and give 'em a blow for me."

I walked over to the mess hall through the dark. The stars were out and it was pretty cold.

Before missions we used to eat at the big dogs' mess hall, Number 1, with the colonels and the majors, and the ground-grippers like weathermen and intelligence. I was the first one in there, and I had to eat eggs and toast for a whole hour before we went to briefing.

The briefing was in a big overgrown Nissen hut. Some major got up first and told us we were going down south to Kassel to a place called Eschwege, where the Germans had a fighter park, a sort of shipping point and comfort station for ships clearing to the forward bases. They showed us where it was on the big wall map, and how it looked to the recco cameras the last time they were over there. The weatherman showed us where the clouds would be, and the guy in charge of traffic told us how to taxi out.

The formation was all drawn up on the blackboard and I copied down all the ship numbers and where they flew. We were flying right wing off the lead ship of the high squadron.

The navigators went somewhere else for some more briefing. Sam went off to change his pants, and I queued up in the co-pilots' line for kits. The gunners were somewhere else getting the same thing. There wasn't room for them in our briefing hut.

Standing there in line, I could tell this was going to be the bad time. We were supposed to have a record escort, 47's and 51's all over, all the way. But we were going in deep, and the Germans didn't want us over there at all.

The equipment hut was a mess with everyone trying to dress in the same place at the same time. I decided to wear an electric suit because I hate long-johns. I put on my O.D.'s over that, and a summer flying suit over that, and a leather jacket on top. A Mae West comes last.

I was sweating before I got into all my clothes, and by the time I had heaved my flak suit and parachute on the truck I could feel the sweat rolling down my knees and pooling up in my insteps.

The rest of the crew was still struggling in the equipment room, so Crone and I lay down among the parachutes and looked at the stars. It was time to think again.

I said hello to Lady Luck up there somewhere in the blue. As long as she went along too I knew I'd be all right. I told her where we were going, but I think she knew already.

The others came out in time and the truck took us out to the plane. Everybody was talking fast and laughing, and I felt sort of ready, like I'd been waiting for a long time for this to happen.

Lewis was trying to put his guns in the turret, while I tried to stow my flak suit under the seat where I could reach for it fast.

"Goddamn it," I said, "there ought to be more room in these goddamned things."

"Take it easy," he said.

I couldn't find my helmet, and one of my gloves was missing. Bird and Benson were all tangled up in the nose getting their guns in. Sam was the only smart one. He stayed outside talking to the crew chief until everyone else got set.

We were flying somebody else's plane, the *Keystone Mama.* I turned my flashlight on the brown lady with no brassière, painted on the side, and decided they were short of artists at this base.

Spaugh and I went up to look at the bombs, and I tore the whole back end out of my flying suit crawling through the bomb bay. We were hauling ten 500's, big and blunt-nosed and ugly things. I patted one a couple of times and it felt cold and dead.

When all the guns were in we huddled up back by the tail. It was sort of like the locker room in high school before a ball game, only not so tense.

Crone said, "I hope they come in on my side."

Sharpe said, "I hope they all stay in the sack."

Beach didn't have anything to say at all. He was a sleepy guy, and older than the rest of us. For a minute he seemed closer than the others, just because he came from Denver, and we were so far from there.

I passed out the candy bars and the gum and the kits, and Sam cleared his throat.

"Okay," he said, "this is our first one. We might as well make it good."

Everyone looked all right, just a little tense, and tired of stalling around.

We started our engines at six o'clock. They kicked over right on down the line . . . start one, mesh one . . . start two . . . mesh two . . . good engines.

There was plenty of daylight when we got to take-off position. There were Forts stacked up there for blocks. They didn't look very eager, just sitting there on their tail wheels. There were a lot of new silver ones, but the majority still had the old dirty brown-green paint on, like the *Keystone Mama.*

Then we moved out on the runway, everything set, and got the green light. I watched the instruments and called off the air speed and Sam herded her down the runway. We were bouncing all over before the needle hit 120. Then Sam pulled her off, and we were airborne.

Grant gave me the heading over the interphone and we started climbing on course, away from the blood-colored dawn.

Sam and I had decided to trade off every fifteen minutes until we got used to going to war, but he flew most of the assembly, and I just changed the RPM when he called for it and sweated.

I thought the eighteen planes would never get together. We just flew around and around, getting nowhere, and then miraculously we were all in, flying off the right leaders, trying to look pretty.

We formed at seventeen thousand and my oxygen mask was bothering me, and my hair was soupy with sweat, and I couldn't move my shoulders in my electric suit. It was too late to do anything though.

Our group got lined up in the wing formation, but someone was off somewhere, or some other wings were way out of line, because just as I was about to sit back and look around, we went driving through into another wing on a collision course. For a few seconds there were airplanes everywhere, and we were flopping around in prop wash. Sam was screaming inside his oxygen mask, and then they were gone.

I hadn't even stopped breathing hard before it happened again.

Bird yelled over interphone, "Here they come!" I ducked, and he said, "I don't wanna die this way."

Nobody got it head on, but nobody missed very far.

The air looked clear then, so Sam let me take it awhile.

I held it in for a while and then started thinking about something or other, and when I came to we were way back out of formation. Sam grabbed the throttles, and I could hear him swearing into his oxygen mask.

"Get on the ball," he said a minute later. "You gotta stay in there."

Somewhere down in the formation the lead navigator was sweating out his checkpoints, and the various squadron leaders were sweating out keeping their boys out of prop wash and in the right position, and all we had to do was hang onto that wing. But that was plenty. I was hot, and my oxygen mask was trying to gag me, and I overcontrolled the throttles, too much, then too little, trying to fly that big bird close.

Sam could sit there and move the throttles a quarter of an inch once in a while and keep us in tight, unless he got careless. But I just didn't have the touch. I made labor out of it. I heaved that big lady all over the sky, jockeying for position, eating up gas.

We flew up across the Channel and cut in at the Dutch coast. The navigator was on the ball, and we didn't see any flak until we were out in the Zuider Zee. Some other wing navigator was asleep and they caught it right in the middle of the formation. Nobody went down. Pretty black puffs in a blue sky . . . harmless-looking stuff.

We were flying into the sun, and our top window was so dirty I couldn't see out of it at all. The front sheet of bulletproof wasn't any too clean and it was rough trying to see anything into the sun.

Bird called for the oxygen check every ten minutes. We were numbered off from the tail.

"One okay."

"Two okay," and so on up through ten in the nose. We sounded like a hot outfit.

"Fighters, three o'clock, high," came over interphone.

"They look like 47's," Bird said from the nose.

They were 47's and they hustled on by into the sun.

"We're over the Third Reich," Benson announced.

The land was all chopped up into little fields and little towns. The fields were just as green as England, greener than Illinois when we crossed it last. They used the same sun down there, and the same moon. The sky was just as blue to them as to anyone at home probably. But for some reason the people down there were Nazis.

Sam signaled me to take the throttles for a while. The wing on our left was swinging in front of us, and it threw a wrench in the collective works. Everyone started chopping throttles back. I overran the lead and stayed throttles clear back too long. When I hit the power again we were faded.

I looked up into the sun and knew right then we were meat for the Luftwaffe. I could feel them up there waiting for a chance like this. I jacked up the RPM and poured on the gas and we moved back in slowly.

There were Forts everywhere, grouped into wings, winged into

Air Divisions. The whole works was the 8th, Jimmy Doolittle's Air Force.

Sharpe called off some flak at seven o'clock. "Look at that stuff," he yelled. "It's all over hell."

"Take it easy on interphone," Sam yelled at him.

Maybe our wing was off, maybe everyone was off a little. Anyway, wings started swinging in for their targets in front of us, behind us, and a couple of them tried to go through our formation while we were lining up for our bomb run.

I didn't have any idea we were near the target until I saw the lead ship's bomb bays swing open.

Benson said, "We're at the I.P."

"Why didn't you tell me?" Bird said excitedly.

I thought we'd probably get left with a bomb load, but it turned out we had plenty of time for Bird to get ready to operate.

I crouched down, waiting for the flak to start. By all the rules there was supposed to be flak around us, right in our laps.

The bombs fell out of the lead ship, and Bird yelled ours were gone.

"Radioman, see if all the bombs went," Sam said.

"Wahoooooooooo," somebody yelled from the back end. "Look at that smoke."

Everyone was talking at once. We had the RPM jacked up, swinging off the target. Still no flak.

"We missed it all to hell," Bird said. "I couldn't even see the target."

All he had to do was toggle the bombs out when the leader let his go. Soft life.

Everyone was letting down a thousand feet so we could get out of the country a little sooner. A couple of wings off to the left were catching some flak and somebody had wiped out most of a town down to our right. We seemed to be out on the edge of the show.

"We're in France now," Benson called up. "We're out of their goddamn country."

I couldn't tell the difference. From that high I couldn't see that the people were all good guys. I did see a barn where I

"Every direction up or down or sideways there were airplanes, big birds and little friends."
—*First Mission*

could hide if we had to bail out. Maybe there was a hayloft where some dark-eyed French girl was waiting with a couple of jugs of wine. Maybe there was a storm trooper with big boots and a bayonet to comb through the hay.

I decided to stay up high as long as possible.

There were quite a few airplanes in sight when we came in, but on the way out we saw thousands. Every direction up or down or sideways there were airplanes, big birds and little friends. There was one beat-up old B-24 straggling along down low with a couple of P-38's hanging around for company.

"We're over Belgium," Benson called up after a while. "That big town is Brussels."

It looked peaceful down there.

Then I remembered my flak suit stowed under the seat. It was a little late, but I put it on. Sam had climbed into his, way back over the Channel, coming in. It was heavy on my neck. I flew for a while until my neck began to bend in. My neck began to ache and my shoulder was sending in sympathy pains from time to time. Then I decided it wasn't worth it and dumped the thing down in the catwalk.

Two P-51's came jazzing by, looking for game.

I traded with Sam for a while and he went on the interphone. There was nothing but shrieks with static.

Then I heard this guy call in to the wing leader, "I'm going down. Our oxygen's gone. Can you get us some escort?" He was breathing like a horse. "My navigator's shot to hell. I got to go down." There was terror in his voice.

Up there somewhere in that soft blue sky a navigator was dying. It was pretty hard to believe.

The coast came in sight. Sometimes Crone or Sharpe would call off flak to the left or right, but we didn't come even close.

There were three straggling 17's down with the Liberators by then, but the fighters were herding them home.

"There's a war on down there," Sharpe said as we crossed the coast. "Look at all the blood."

He couldn't believe it and neither could I, but somewhere down there in that crazy patchwork of farms and towns and beaches there were some hard-eyed jokers who would have liked to get at us.

Sam was back on VHF. "Somebody's dying," he said to me. "Some navigator. This guy keeps calling up that his navigator is dying. What the hell good does that do?"

We started letting down when we crossed the coast. The formation began to loosen up a little. We'd heard a lot of stories about the old days, eight months ago, when the Abbeville Kids were waiting at the coast for loose formations. We stayed in.

At sixteen thousand I took off my helmet. There was a puddle of drool in my oxygen mask. I rubbed my face but it felt like a piece of fish. The candy bar tasted wonderful.

When we hit the English coast I was flying.

"Tighten it up a little," Sam said. "They said to tighten it up." He waved me in closer. "That navigator is still dying," he said thoughtfully. "That guy keeps calling in."

We were supposed to look sharp when we flew over some field at the coast, because Doolittle and Spaatz were down there watching, and maybe Mr. Stettinius and Mr. Churchill were along as guests.

I don't know how we looked. I know I didn't care much. I'd never been so tired.

The navigator found the way home, and we circled the field while the low squadron peeled off.

I put the wheels down, and Sam came in high and plunked us in halfway down the runway.

"We been to the war," Sharpe said.

"We're back now," Bird said.

Back on that big wide runway. We put the *Keystone Mama* back where we got her and threw all the stuff out on the ground.

"Wonder if we killed anybody?" Lewis said.

"Wonder if we hit the fighter park?" Sam said.

I was so shot I didn't want to move. My flying had been lousy. My hair was spongy with sweat and my eyes felt like they'd been sanded down and wrapped in a dry sack.

While I sat there a plane taxied by with half its tail blown off. It was one of ours. I didn't believe it.

Lewis got his guns out, and I carried one of them over and put it on the truck for him.

Sharpe said, "Well, we're not virgins any more."

"I still feel like one," Crone said. "I didn't see nothing."

We'd been there and we were home. I lay back in a pile of flak suits and closed my eyes. There weren't any holes in us, our tail wasn't blown off. Right then I didn't want to be anywhere else in the world, and these were the people I wanted to be with, these guys on this crew.

The equipment hut was jammed with guys and it smelled like a stable.

"How was it?" somebody said.

I turned around and there was the chaplain, the Catholic one.

"Milk run," I said. "A joy ride."

He smiled at me. He knew I was new. Then the smile went away.

"They got two," he said. "Two whole crews are gone."

He moved on to the next guy, but I heard someone else say they were out of the high composite.

We had put up part of another group and those guys were in the other one.

"They made a 360 at the target," somebody said, "and the 109's were up there in those clouds."

Nobody saw the fighters. They came out of the sun, and they only made one pass. One Fort blew up and one went down burning. La French was one of them and the drunk copilot that woke me up the night before was in the other.

"That poor guy could see it coming," somebody said.

"He knew it was his turn."

They were talking about that copilot.

But La French wasn't like that. He was all alive the last time I saw him. He rode that bike of his like it was Seabiscuit. And now he was just blood and little chunks of bones and meat, blown all over the sky. Or he was cooked, burned into nothing.

I thought about him all through the interrogation. I drank three cups of coffee, but I couldn't get him out of my mind.

A G.I. brought around a shot of scotch for each man on the

crew. Lewis was sick, and Beach was too tired, and Spaugh didn't want any.

"I don't like this goddamn English scotch," Crone said. "It don't taste like American scotch."

"I'm not in the mood." Bird pushed his away.

In the end I had a tall glass full of scotch and part of another one. I knew what was going to happen, but I drank it and chased it with coffee.

The room got warm and the sunlight turned deep gold. La French was gone, but it was no good thinking about him any more. I was there and I was alive.

Billy Behrend came along on his bike when I went outside.

"It's early," he said. "Let's go for a ride."

I didn't know him very well. He lived in the room across the hall, and he was always smiling.

We went down a road till it turned, and then we went the other way. There was a church with old gray walls and houses with thatched roofs and some little kids pulling a wagon full of milk bottles, and a muddy pond with dirty ducks in it.

There isn't any way to tell how good it was to be there. Just to be moving, just to be riding down a road on a bicycle, and breathing and laughing once in a while, not knowing where the road led to and not caring. The world was endlessly big, and so green and soft and endlessly green.

We didn't come back until late.

FROM

Under My Wings

BASIL L. ROWE

Routine is the mark of an airline pilot's life. But in forty years of flying, including twenty-five with Pan American Airways, Captain Basil Rowe logged many flights that were far from routine. The adventure he relates here occurred over the Pacific Ocean one day in the early 1950s.

Pacific Airlift

ONE time during my hitch with the Pacific Airlift, which was a co-operative project operated by several air lines, I was captain of a DC-4 from Honolulu to San Francisco. We were carrying ambulatory cases from the Korean battles. Four hours out of Honolulu I noticed a slight tremor in the rhythm of the engines. I had dimmed the cockpit lights for better forward vision. I turned them up just as Starke, my flight engineer, six foot four of straw blond, sunburned, perpetually peeling Scotsman, untangled his big body from a dozing position. He was all concentration. On the other side of him Masson, my copilot, a dark, square-shaped man built like a small bulldozer, was studying the engine instruments with the same intensity, his cap coming just above level with Starke's ear. I flipped the switch on my jack box to intercom, the only way a crew can talk comfortably above the cockpit roar of four 1500 horsepower engines.

I said, "Which one is it?"

"I don't know." Starke kept his eyes on his instruments. "It happened so quick I didn't catch it."

At first we couldn't find the trouble. Finally we traced it to number four engine, the farthest to the crew's right. We still didn't know what was wrong. The individual magnetos checked O.K. But the cylinder head temperature showed that number four was running a fever. Starke suspected that it might be a sticking intake valve. We cracked the cowls a little to let more air circulate around the engines' cylinders.

We were still concentrating on the instruments when Cora, the stewardess, leaned over me and motioned for me to lift my earpiece. She told me that a GI had noticed oil streaming back over the wing. I sent Starke to take a look. When he came back, he said, "I told him the oil tanks were too full, but it's bad, Cap. She's pouring oil all over the wing and vibrating badly. It seems to be coming out around the nose section. I think she's swallowed a valve. We'd better feather before she blows a jug."

Feathering a motor is the only way to kill it. You can't stop an airplane engine the way you can stop the motor of your car. You can cut the gas and the switch, but that big prop, being pulled along at well over two hundred miles an hour, just keeps on going and turning the motor with it. The only way to stop it is to change the pitch of the blades. To understand the term pitch, the propeller should be thought of as a giant screw that bites into the air the way a screw bites into a piece of wood. Whether the propeller is a coarse-threaded screw, taking deep bites of air, or a fine-threaded screw, turning more easily because it's taking shallower bites, depends on the pitch of the blades—the amount of bite they try to take out of the air with each revolution. This pitch can be governed from the cockpit. Obviously there's a maximum pitch, beyond which the blades of the propeller are parallel to the line of flight, knifing straight through the air. In this feathered position, of course, they would provide no traction at all, but it is the only position in which a dead propeller with an air blast against it will stop revolving. If Starke and I did this, we could stop the propeller windmilling, kill the motor, and prevent what might result in an exploding cylinder.

I didn't want to feather if I could avoid it because it meant that we would be forced by regulations to head for the nearest airport, which for us meant back to Honolulu. But even out there over the broad Pacific there just wasn't room enough for flying cylinders and a DC-4 at the same time. I agreed with Starke and gave him the order.

"O.K., Starke. Feather."

Starke reached up to the cockpit ceiling and jabbed his thumb on one of the four big red feathering buttons. He had enough arm left over to reach another foot. Then he reached down and cut the gas and the switch on number four. The propeller wouldn't feather because of insufficient oil pressure to actuate the feathering mechanism. Instead it went into low pitch, running wild with the air blast and against it. Starke whacked the feathering button again. The prop went on spinning, completely out of control. He yanked at the pitch-control lever. Nothing we could do would stop it.

I started to reverse course, hauling the nose up to gain as much free altitude as I could. I slowed the ship to minimum flying speed to reduce the speed of the freewheeling prop.

"Where are we, Hap?" I spoke to the navigator, who occupied a position behind the copilot.

"We're about three hundred knots from the point of no return and three hundred and eighty knots to Jones's Corner."

Jones's Corner is the intersection of the thirtieth parallel of latitude and the hundred and fortieth meridian. Nobody knows where the name Jones's Corner came from, but it's as real a corner to Pacific pilots as if there were a drugstore there instead of sweeping miles of open Pacific. A weather ship was stationed there, equipped with every modern device for weather observation, and with radar for tracking everything in the vicinity, including the upper-air balloons used to determine wind direction and velocity. It stood guard on all emergency frequencies, ready to dash to the aid of any plane or surface craft in distress.

"Ask Jones to track us with his radar if he can reach us," I told Hap.

We normally cruise with the engines revving about two thousand. The tachometer only registers up to three thousand. Now the needle for number four had hit the top end of the gauge and was trying to shove past it. There was imminent danger of the prop's flying apart and ripping through the cockpit. I'd seen fuselages that had been sliced like salami by thrown blades. There is a lot of bursting energy in a twelve-inch steel blade with a reach of twelve feet turning at 3000 rpm's plus. It's a big butcher blade that would make the giants' swords of our boyhood stories look as lethal as toothpicks. On top of this the windmilling blades were creating a terrific drag. It had pulled our speed down by fifty miles an hour. The ship began to lose altitude. We had been cruising at ten thousand, a bit too high for the heavily loaded DC-4, but we had gone up to catch the skirt of a low-pressure area. We had been able to hold the altitude by maintaining a slight climb. What we lost by this mushing we had more than picked up from the tail wind that had increased our speed by twenty-four knots.

But now every foot of altitude we lost from the slightest air current or roll of the ship we lost for good. We couldn't climb back. We were like a fish getting reeled in bit by bit, only instead of being pulled out of the ocean we were being reeled into it.

I checked with Starke to find out how much gas we'd had when we'd taken off.

"Twenty-nine hundred and fifty gallons."

I used a short, round, vulgar word. "I don't want the gas you've got on paper. I want the amount we have in our tanks. How much did you have for your wife?"

I saw a faint grin crease Starke's pink face. "Gas for your wife" is a term that has an important meaning to air crews. On a plane the first thing anyone in the crew thinks of if trouble starts is, how much gas have we got? It's basic, an automatic reflex. It's called fuel fever, and nobody likes it. For long hops the pilot is always trying to wangle enough gas out of Operations to make sure he doesn't contract fuel fever on the trip. Sometimes he's about as popular with Operations as a skunk at a corn roast when he arrives happily at his destination with enough fuel for another four hours after off-loading a couple of paying passengers to carry the extra weight. Not that it bothers him too much. But it bothers Operations, who try to get the maximum safe pay load on a ship. You don't make money flying gas from continent to continent. On top of all this the pilot knows that he's going to have even more than the extra gas he wangled because his engineer will load a bit extra into each tank. This is known as his "wife's gas," because he puts it in for her sake—to make sure she still has a husband.

"O.K., Cap," Starke said. "I put another twenty-five in each tank. That gives us a hundred gallons in the pocket."

"How much can I dump?"

My navigator, Hap Lee, a boy from Brooklyn with a cheerful, boyish face and a bald head, cut in on us. "I've already figured it out, Cap. Bucking this wind with a dragging prop, you'll be lucky if you make it on dry tanks."

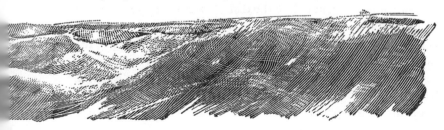

I was crabbing around, sweeping the nose of the plane through the points of the compass to pick up the return course of two hundred and forty-two degrees. By banking toward the good engines I could keep them pulling uphill, which lessened the pressure on my left leg from the unbalanced power. I was fighting the controls to avoid wallowing, but we were still slowly losing altitude. I knew we couldn't hold ten thousand feet on three engines even with full power when about thirty percent of that power was consumed by the windmilling prop. But I'd made up my mind I wasn't going to give up a foot of altitude without a fight. I hoped the ship would eventually find a level that it could hold.

My leg was nearly paralyzed trying to keep the ship from yawing to the right. I had the copilot take it. "Stand hard on that port rudder," I told him.

Masson got both feet on the left rudder pedal, but in spite of his having legs like fireplugs the power of the pull took him by surprise. We lost another precious two hundred feet before he could straighten out. I got up and went through the usual gavotte with Starke as he tried to squeeze enough of himself aside to let me out of my seat. I went back and started things going with the radio operator, Louis Niosi. I told him to keep me posted on our ground speed and mileage out every fifteen minutes and to alert Honolulu. Not that they could do anything for me now, but I wanted to let Honolulu know exactly where I was in case I would need a rescue ship.

"Call Search and Rescue at Pearl Harbor," I told him. "Ask them to send out one of the biggest flying boats to sit patrol. Tell them we have a runaway prop and that we're slowly losing altitude. It looks doubtful."

"I have everybody from here to New York standing by."

"Declare an emergency. Use the distress frequency so we won't have any interference."

We got a signal from a Spanish boat, the *Hernando*. "He's got a peculiar fist," Niosi said, frowning. "I can hardly read him."

He handed me a note. It read: *Envié su mensaje en español.*

"He wants you to transmit in Spanish." I started to write on the bottom of the paper: *¿Cuál es su posición, velocidad y des-*

tino? I intended to set the automatic direction finder on his frequency and home in on his signal. My plan was to line up enough boats so that if we had to ditch we could do it beside one of them. I was going to try to make Honolulu something like the way a kid plays musical chairs, with our tail always hovering not too far from a place to sit down.

I heard Cora say behind me, "Any instructions, sir?"

I hadn't heard her enter the cockpit. I had no idea how long she'd been there or how much she had overheard. I motioned her back to the cabin and followed her. She was a big, slow-moving redhead. Six hours earlier I'd been watching her give half a dozen anguished males an eyeful at Waikiki Beach, and I I remembered wondering at the time if a girl with all that glamour would have enough room left over for what it takes when things get rough. Now I wondered again as I followed her into the cabin.

It's probably because I'm small, wiry, fast on my feet and play a lot of tennis, but I've always had a struggle to assume that stately stroll expected in the captain of an air liner especially when, like me, he is bald, full of years and, presumably, of quiet dignity. I'd rather run, and when I'm on the ground often do. I get kidded about it by my friends. But maybe it has nothing to do with my build. Perhaps it's because I started flying when dignity had nothing to do with it. You were satisfied if you had a tail wind, a railway track to navigate by, and a chance to barnstorm enough passengers to pay for your breakfast.

But I managed to be all dignified captain when I entered the cabin. The GIs still had no idea what was going on. The sound level of four engines is too high for anybody to detect a rogue motor except the crew members, who are as sensitive to the sound of the engines as a fiddler to a fugue. The overhead lights were off. Most of the GIs were over on the moonlit side of the cabin watching the tops of the cumulus clouds drift beneath the plane and, between the clouds, the big patches of silver Pacific that, without their knowing it, was reeling us in foot by foot. For everyone's benefit I leaned over casually and looked out at the moon, trying hard not to look at that mad runaway prop on number four. I strolled after Cora toward her galley.

"Keep everybody out of line of that number four prop," I told her. "Get all your passengers in life jackets and assign them to lifeboats. Prepare to ditch. Minimize the emergency. Just because we're making all preparations doesn't mean we'll have to ditch. If we do, it will be at least a half hour. Give each passenger a slip of paper with his boat number on it. The copilot will be in command of number one lifeboat, and the navigator his assistant. The engineer will be in command of number two lifeboat, and Sparks will be his assistant. Assign fifteen passengers to each boat. That will account for all souls on board except you two and myself. We'll take the ten-passenger life raft. Take only your first-aid kits, water and valuables. We haven't space for anything else."

It would be up to me to supervise the abandonment of the ship and to stay with it until the last person was safely in a raft. Apart from its being the captain's responsibility to see that all hands are rescued or else to go down with his ship, the batteries on a plane, even though it's immersed in salt water, will sometimes continue to work for some time, and additional radio communications can be maintained until the ocean seeps into the batteries. If he is down with a flying boat, the captain will usually stay with his ship as long as there is any chance of being rescued or the ship saved. The minute all life has abandoned an airplane it becomes salvage, and the first rescue ship that puts a line on the salvage can claim it as such. Some captains used to carry cats or dogs as pets. The captain left the animal aboard in case of abandoning ship so that the ship couldn't be claimed for salvage. Usually a captain will not allow a rescue craft to put a line on the ship without an arrangement beforehand. Otherwise the rescuing captain will exert his salvage claim.

One look at Cora back in the lights of her galley, and I knew I had no worries about her. Although this was on the Airlift, I knew she would follow by second nature the training she had received on passenger lines. The cabin attendants on passenger liners get a good, thorough drilling when they go through training school. They get the actual works when they are taken out in a boat and thrown overboard with a life raft. It is up to them to inflate the raft and get everyone aboard the twenty-man lifesaver that is bobbing about in the water. They get this check at six-month intervals, and in between they get additional checks by the different captains with whom they fly. In the crew's ready room at the airport there is a large diagram of each ship with plastic placards on which are printed the many items that make up the emergency equipment. The captain checks out each crew member by having the person being tested place each placard at its proper place on the diagram to give a thorough knowledge of where each piece of emergency equipment is located. The entire crew go through this so frequently that it becomes second nature to locate the equipment without even thinking where it might be.

Cora was as calm and steady as when she'd juiced us only an hour earlier. There was a lot of Cora in every way. Those girls never cease to amaze me. In the tightest spots they can be as nonchalant as if they were going to a party. I don't know whether it's courage or some sort of feminine fatalism, but whatever it is, I admire it. It was a bit different with her assistant, a Mexican kid from Ybor City, near Tampa, Florida, who was on her first flight, looking spick-and-span in her new uniform and plenty scared when I started giving Cora ditching orders.

Each rubber raft, which would inflate as soon as it was unzipped from its cover and kicked out into the water, carried a full complement of emergency supplies and equipment, including fishing outfit, shark repellent, flare pistols and cartridges, flares for day and night, a sail, oars, knife, emergency rations, a kite to carry antennae, a kite balloon complete with gas generator, spray cover and briquettes to distill sea water.

"I don't think you'll have to break out your emergency supplies," I said, chiefly for the Mexican kid's benefit. "We'll have a patrol over us all the time we're down until we're picked up. Don't let anyone inflate his life jacket until he's in the water. If anyone jumps into the water with it inflated, he can be pretty sure of a broken neck. Any questions?"

"Not now, sir." Cora picked up her passenger list.

"Any riders who might go off their rocker or who can't make it because of wounds?"

"I don't think so. I don't expect any trouble."

"If you need me, just ring or come forward."

Back in the cockpit I stepped to the copilot's window and flashed my light back on number four engine out on the big, gleaming metal wing. It seemed to be trying to tear itself to pieces. It was just a matter of time until the prop and engine would begin to disintegrate from the centrifugal force of the runaway mass. Once the breakup started it would be anyone's guess which way the pieces would go and how many of the chunks of metal would blast holes through the fuselage or nose of the plane. Some of the pieces might fly into the next propeller. That would be the end of another engine. We couldn't afford to lose any more.

"Do you think we can hold this critical speed when we hit the low road?" Masson yelled over his shoulder. "It looks pretty turbulent."

"We'll see how badly she wallows when we hit the clouds."

I delayed a decision because I could see the many holes in the road below me. We'd both have our hands full of airplane as soon as we reached the level of the cloud tops. They mark the upper limit of the syphoning thermal air currents, which are really winds created by difference in temperatures but blow straight up or down instead of horizontally. We would be off the city pavement and onto the dirt lanes. Those clouds aren't always as soft as they look from a porch hammock. They can be full of ditches, bumps, ruts, rocks and vertical currents that have lifted me a lot higher than the Empire State Building in seconds and dropped me the same distance at the same speed. When you hit the bottom of a draft like that, it's like ramming a stone wall.

The crew now started a lot of elaborate jokes about signaling Honolulu to call out the tourists to watch us come in on the deck. I've found out one thing in close to forty years of flying that has included hauling men to and from battle in two wars: whenever men are in a tight spot they'll start joking. I don't know why. It's kind of whistling in the dark. It's usually not good humor but nobody cares. It's humor and it sounds mighty good at the time. I told them that we were going to have to jettison everything that wasn't nailed down, and Masson put on a big show of breaking down because he had to toss out a silk robe he'd bought for his girl in San Francisco.

"Control yourself, man," Starke told him. "You won't have to dump it. You just might have to wrap it around another girl—in Honolulu."

"Honolulu?" I forced a smile. "Just what kind of miracle do you guys expect me to pull off?"

"You'll think of something," Starke said. He sounded as if he really believed it. I let it go.

I took another look out the cockpit window. I knew a heavy sea was running down there, and ditching into it would be like running into Diamond Head. I told Masson I was going to take another look in the cabin. I saw Cora and her assistant on their knees near the entrance wrapping emergency supplies in strips cut from a plastic raincoat. The GIs were in their life jackets. Everyone looked plenty worried, but there was no sign of panic. I went back and sat on one of the bunks that had been fitted into the crew room. I wanted time to think.

I leaned my elbows on my knees, squeezed my hands together and swore. The chances of an accident in flying nowadays are far less than in driving a car to the local supermarket. I cursed the rare fluke that had put us on this spot. I was a fine guy for it to happen to. Under the emergency conditions of World War II I'd flown transports with no brakes. I had taken up crocks that were fluttering with inspectors' red tags stating that they were grounded because of wrinkles in their belly, a sign of excessive age. I'd taken a plane off the ground that, due to a loader's mistake, carried more than twice the load I was supposed to have. I had flown with a wartime navigator who, when I asked him where we were, said, "Off with your hat, we're right over St. Paul's Cathedral," when we were over the south of Ireland. Now, with a highly trained crew and a constantly serviced modern air liner, I was going to dunk thirty-seven people and a two-and-a-half million dollar investment in the Pacific.

While I was getting madder and madder I was abstractedly watching the drip, drip, drip of oil from a leaking gauge on the auxiliary tank under the bunk. There was a greasy patch on the floor by my feet. I slid my shoe over it, and my thoughts took an abrupt right-angle turn.

I started to think. Oil. What would happen if I starved that crazy number four engine for lubrication? It would seize up. It would stop. I got up suddenly. Was that the answer to the fix we were in? Or was it connected to a gimmick of some kind? Did I really want to chance cutting off the oil and deliberately freezing that racing power plant? The engine would be ruined but that was a minor point. The main thing was, what would the engine do? I tried my best to visualize what would take place. Would it freeze so suddenly that the terrific force of the heavy prop would twist the engine out of the frame—or tear the wing to pieces? On the optimistic side, if it froze gradually we might not have any damage at all. And I was inclined to be an optimist. I'd been through a lot of tight spots in my life, both before and after aviation became respectable. I was still alive and healthy. I decided to ride my luck a bit longer.

I went back to the cockpit, took one last thoughtful look at that big, roaring renegade engine, squeezed past Starke into my seat, and said, "Cut off the oil to number four."

Starke's eyebrows went up around the visor of his cap. "You mean engine oil?"

"I don't mean hair oil." I kept my eyes on my instruments.

"But, Cap . . . It'll tear itself to pieces."

"Better than tearing us to pieces."

Starke reached up across the control pedestal and hesitated for one last look at me, his hand poised on the oil shutoff. Then he grabbed it. "Roger! Here she goes!"

I don't think any of us did much breathing while we waited, although we knew holding our breath wasn't going to help hold the plane together. We knew it wouldn't take long. With no lubrication the molten pistons would soon start running out the exhaust stacks.

"Drag that wing so the pieces have to throw uphill," I ordered Masson.

That was the last thing said before number four let go. It came even sooner than I'd figured. There was a mighty shock athwartships. Then I saw something that, looking back on it now, I'm glad I didn't miss, but I hope I never see it again. The propeller from number four passed the cockpit window in the moonlight all by itself, making better time than the plane. We watched it in bug-eyed wonder while it gradually arced down toward the ocean with the velocity of a meteor. The engine had seized up so suddenly that the heavy metal prop had twisted the steel shaft in two like a bread roll.

As the plane, freed from the dragging propeller, began to climb like a kite, Starke was the first to speak. "I'd call that little trick very non-habit-forming."

"If it had been one of the port engines, we would have had to hitch a ride with an angel." Hap was still staring unbelievingly through his navigator's porthole at the stub-nosed engine.

We all let go a bit then. Niosi picked up a coffee cup and held it to show that he was still steady enough not to spill a drop. He lifted it high, hoping that none of us would see that it was empty. I saw Masson looking down at the surface of the ocean. He gave a shudder. I didn't blame him.

We had no trouble maintaining altitude on the three good engines. I went back to the cabin and made one of the easiest announcements I've ever had to make. I told the boys they could take off their life jackets, that they wouldn't need them in Honolulu. The chatter that started as they reacted to the tension sounded like the last stages of a cocktail party. We homed in over the Spanish boat, even though it was somewhat south of our course, to express our gratitude for the all-out assistance of its crew. From there on we set a course almost due west to Makapuu Point on the southeast tip of Oahu and coasted around Diamond Head, which never shone so brightly as it did that day.

FROM

Stranger to the Ground

RICHARD BACH

In this description of his encounter with a storm over France in 1961, Richard Bach evokes the special world of the jet pilot— remote from the ground, insulated even from the air around him by his marvelous machine and the myriad instruments by which he maneuvers it, inexpressibly solitary. How different from—yet how essentially alike—the world of Saint Exupéry, whose fragile ship was caught in a similar storm nearly thirty years before!

Courier

THE wind tonight is from the west, down runway two eight. It pushes gently at my polka-dot scarf and makes the steel buckles of my parachute harness tinkle in the darkness. It is a cold wind, and because of it my takeoff roll will be shorter than usual and my airplane will climb more quickly than it usually does when it lifts into the sky.

Two ground crewmen work together to lift a heavy padlocked canvas bag of Top Secret documents into the nose of the airplane. It sags awkwardly into space normally occupied by contoured ammunition cans, above four oiled black machine guns, and forward of the bomb release computers. Tonight I am not a fighter pilot. I am a courier for thirty-nine pounds of paper that is of sudden urgent interest to my wing commander, and though the weather this night over Europe is already freakish and violent, I have been asked to move these pounds of paper from England into the heart of France.

In the bright beam of my flashlight, the Form One, with its inked boxes and penciled initials, tells me that the airplane is ready, that it carries only minor shortcomings of which I already know: a dent in one drop tank, an inspection of the command radio antenna is due, the ATO system is disconnected. It is hard to turn the thin pages of the Form One with gloves on, but the cold wind helps me turn them.

Form signed, gun bay door locked over the mysterious canvas bag, I climb the narrow yellow ladder to my dark cockpit, like a high-booted mountain climber pulling himself to a peak from whose snows he can stand and look down upon the world. My peak is the small cockpit of a Republic F-84F *Thunderstreak*.

The safety belt of the yellow-handled ejection seat is wide nylon web, heavy and olive-drab; into its explosive buckle fits the nylon harness from over my shoulders and the amber steel link that automatically opens my parachute if I should have to bail out tonight. I surround myself with the universal quiet metallic noises of a pilot joining himself to his airplane. The two straps to the seat cushion survival kit, after their usual struggle, are captured and clink softly to my parachute harness. The green oxygen mask fits into its regulator hose with a muffled rubbery snap. The steel D-ring lanyard clanks as it fastens to the curved bar of the parachute ripcord handle. The red-streamered ejection seat safety pin scrapes out of its hole drilled in the trigger of the right armrest and rustles in the darkness into the small pocket on the leg of my tight-laced G-suit. The elastic leg strap of my scratched aluminum kneeboard cinches around my left thigh, latching itself with a hollow clank. My hard white fiberglass crash helmet, dark-visored, gold-lettered 1/LT. BACH, fits stiffly down to cover my head, its soft sponge-rubber earphones waiting a long cold moment before they begin to warm against my ears. The chamois chinstrap snaps at the left side, microphone cable connects with its own frosty click into the aircraft radio cord, and at last the wind-chilled green rubber oxygen mask snugs over my nose and mouth, fitting with a tight click-click of the smooth chromed fastener at the right side of the helmet. When the little family of noises is still, by tubes and wires and snaps and buckles, my body is attached to the larger, sleeping body of my airplane.

Outside, in the dark moving blanket of cold, a ghostly yellow auxiliary power unit roars into life, controlled by a man in a heavy issue parka who is hoping that I will be quick to start my engine and taxi away. Despite the parka, he is cold. The clatter and roar of the big gasoline engine under his hands settles a bit, and on its voltage dials, white needles spring into their green arcs.

From the engine of the power unit, through the spinning generator, through the black rubber snake into the cold silver wing of my airplane, through the marked wires of the DC electrical system, the power explodes in my dark cockpit as six brilliant red and yellow warning lights, and as quick tremblings of a few instrument pointers.

My leather gloves, stamped with the white wings and star of Air Force property, go through a familiar little act for the interested audience that watches from behind my eyes. From left to right around the cockpit they travel; checking left console circuit breakers in, gun heater switch *off*, engine screen switch *extend*, drop tank pressure switches *off*, speed brake switch *extend*, throttle *off*, altimeter, drag chute handle, sight caging lever, radiocompass, TACAN, oxygen, generator, IFF, inverter selector. The gloves dance, the eyes watch. The right glove flourishes into the air at the end of its act and spins a little circle of information to the man waiting in the wind below: checks are finished, engine is starting in two seconds. Now it is throttle on, down with the glove, and starter switch to *start*.

There is no time to take a breath or blink the eye. There is one tiny tenth-second hiss before concussion shatters icy air. Suddenly, instantly, air and sparks and Jet Propellant Four. My airplane is designed to start its engine with an explosion. It can be started in no other way. But the sound is a keg of black powder under the match, a cannon firing, the burst of a hand grenade. The man outside blinks, painfully.

With the blast, as though with suddenly-opened eyes, my airplane is alive. Instantly awake. The thunderclap is gone as quickly as it came, replaced by a quiet rising whine that peaks quickly, very high, and slides back down the scale into nothingness. But before the whine is gone, deep inside the engine, combustion chambers have earned their name. The luminous white pointer of the gage marked *exhaust gas temperature* pivots upward, lifting as thermocouples taste a swirling flood of yellow fire that twists from fourteen stainless steel chambers. The fire spins a turbine. The turbine spins a compressor. The compressor crushes fuel and air for the fire. Weak yellow flames change to businesslike blue torches held in their separate round offices, and the ghostly power unit is needed no more.

Flourish with the right glove, finger pointing away; away the power, I'm on my own.

Tailpipe temperature is settled and at home with 450 degrees of centigrade, tachometer steadies to note that the engine is turning at 45 percent of its possible rpm. The rush of air to the insatiable steel engine is a constant rasping scream at the oval intake, a chained banshee shrieking in the icy black air and the searing blue fire.

Hydraulic pressure shows on a dial, under a pointer. Speed brake switch to *retract,* and the pressure pulls two great slabs of steel to disappear into the smooth sides of my airplane. Rainbow lights go dark as pressure rises in systems for fuel and oil. I have just been born, with the press of wind at my scarf. With the wind keening along the tall swept silver of my rudder. With the rush of wind to the torches of my engine.

There is one light left on, stubbornly glowing over a placard marked *canopy unlocked.* My left glove moves a steel handle aft. With the right I reach high overhead to grasp the frame of the counterbalanced section of double-walled plexiglass. A gentle pull downward, and the smooth-hinged canopy settles over my little world. I move the handle forward in my left glove, I hear a muffled sound of latches engaging, I see the light wink out. The wind at my scarf is gone.

I am held by my straps and my buckles and my wires in a deep pool of dim red light. In the pool is all that I must know about my airplane and my position and my altitude until I pull the throttle back to *off,* one hour and 29 minutes and 579 airway miles from Wethersfield Air Base, England.

On the heavy black throttle under my left glove there is a microphone button, and I press it with my thumb. "Wethersfield Tower," I say to the microphone buried in the snug green rubber of my oxygen mask. I hear my own voice in the earphones of my helmet, and know that in the high glass cube of the control tower the same voice and the same words are this moment speaking. "Air Force Jet Two Niner Four Zero Five; taxi information and standing by for ATC clearance."

"Roger, Zero Five," comes a new voice in the earphones. "Taxi runway two eight; wind is two seven zero degrees at one five knots, altimeter is two niner niner five, tower time is two one two five, clearance is on request. Type aircraft, please."

I twist the small knurled knob near the altimeter to set 29.95 in a red-lit window. The hands of the altimeter move slightly. My gloved thumb is down again on the microphone button. "Roger, tower, Zero Five is a Fox Eight Four, courier: returning to Chaumont Air Base, France."

Forward goes the thick black throttle and in the quickening roar of startled, very hot thunder, my Republic F-84F, slightly dented, slightly old-fashioned, governed by my left glove, begins to move. A touch of boot on left brake and the airplane turns. Back with the throttle to keep from blasting the man and his power unit with a 600-degree hurricane from the tailpipe. Tactical Air Navigation selector to *transmit and receive*.

The sleeping silver silhouettes of the F-100's of Wethersfield Air Base sweep by in the dark as I taxi, and I am engulfed in comfort. The endless crackle of light static in my earphones, the intimate weight of my helmet, the tremble of my airplane, rocking and slowly pitching as it rolls on hard tires and oil-filled struts over the bumps and ridges of the taxiway. Like an animal. Like a trusted and trusting eager heavy swift animal of prey, the airplane that I control from its birth to its sleep trundles toward the two-mile runway lulled by the murmur of the cold wind.

The filtered voice of the tower operator shatters the serene static in the earphones. "Air Force Jet Two Niner Four Zero Five, clearance received. Ready to copy?"

My pencil springs from flight jacket sleeve to poise itself over the folded flight plan trapped in the jaws of the clipboard on my left leg. "Ready to copy."

"ATC clears; Air Force Jet Two Niner Four Zero Five to the Chaumont Airport . . ." I mark the words in scrawled shorthand. I have been cleared to fly the route I have planned. ". . . via direct Abbeville, direct Laon, direct Spangdahlem, direct Wiesbaden, direct Strasbourg, direct Chaumont." A route detoured before it begins; planned to avoid the mass of storms and severe weather that the forecaster has marked in red squares across the direct route to my home base. "Climb in radar control to flight level three three zero, contact Anglia control . . ." The clearance comes in through the earphones and out through the sharp point of the pencil; whom to contact and when and on which frequency, one hour and 29 minutes of flying pressed onto a four-inch square of penciled paper bathed in dim red light. I read the shorthand back to the tower operator, and tap the brakes to stop short of the runway.

"Roger, Zero Five, readback is correct. Cleared for take-off; no reported traffic in the local area."

Throttle forward again and the airplane swings into take-off position on runway two eight. The concrete is wide and long. The painted white stripe along its center is held at one end by my nosewheel, at the invisible other end by the tough nylon webbing of the overrun barrier. A twin row of white edge lights converges in the black distance ahead, pointing the way. The throttle moves now, under my left glove, all the way forward; until the radium-caked tachometer needle covers the line marked 100 *percent*, until the tailpipe temperature is up by the short red arc on the dial that means 642 degrees centigrade, until each pointer on each dial of the red-soaked instrument panel agrees with what we are to do, until I say to myself, as I say every time, Here we go. I release the brakes.

There is no instant rush of speed, no head forced against the headrest. I feel only a gentle push at my back. The stripe of the runway unrolls, lazily at first, beneath the nosewheel. Crackling thunder twists and blasts and tumbles behind me, and, slowly, I see the runway lights begin to blur at the side of the concrete and the airspeed needle lifts to cover 50 knots, to cover 80 knots, to cover 120 knots (go-no-go speed checks OK) and between the two white rows of blur I see the barrier waiting in the darkness at the end of the runway and the control stick tilts easily back in my right glove and the airspeed needle is covering 160 knots and the nosewheel lifts from the concrete and the main wheels follow a half-second later and there is nothing in the world but me and an airplane alive and together and the cool wind lifts us to its heart and we are one with the wind and one with the dark sky and the stars ahead and the barrier is a forgotten dwindling blur behind and the wheels swing up to tuck themselves away in my seamless aluminum skin and the airspeed is up to one nine zero and flap lever forward and airspeed two two zero and I am in my element and I am flying. I am flying.

The voice that I hear in the soft earphones is unlike my own. It is the voice of a man concerned only with business; a man speaking while he has yet many things to do. Still it is my thumb down on the microphone button and my words screened through the receiver in the tower. "Wethersfield Tower, Air Force Jet Two Niner Four Zero Five departing on course, leaving your station and frequency."

My airplane climbs easily through the strange clear air over southern England, and my gloves, not content to accept idleness, move across the cockpit and complete the little tasks that have been assigned to them. The needles of my altimeter swing quickly through the 5000-foot mark, and while my gloves work at the task of retracting the engine screens, pressurizing the drop tanks, loosing the D-ring lanyard from the ripcord, setting the pneumatic compressor into life, I notice suddenly that there is no moon. I had hoped for a moon.

My eyes, at the command of the audience behind them, check once again that all the small-dialed engine instruments have pointers properly under their arcs of green paint on the glass. The right glove, conscientious, pushes the oxygen lever from 100 *percent* to *normal*, and sets the four white numbers of the departure control frequency in the four black windows of the command ultra-high frequency transmitter.

The strange voice that is mine speaks to the radar control

center guiding my departure. The voice is capable of doing the necessary talking, the gloves are capable of moving throttle and control stick to guide the slanting climb of my airplane into the night. Ahead of me, through the heavy angled glass of the windscreen, through a shrinking wall of clear air, is the weather. I can see that it hugs the ground at first, low and thin, as if uncertain that it is over the land that it has been assigned to cover.

The three white hands of the altimeter swing through 10,-000 feet, sending my right glove into another, shorter, series of menial tasks in the cockpit. It dials now the numbers 387 into the pie-slice of window on the radiocompass control panel. In the soft earphones are the faint Morse letters A-B: the Abbeville radiobeacon.

"France Control, Air Force Jet Two Niner Four Zero Five, Abbeville." Empty static for a moment in the soft earphones, and I see, very clearly, a man in a large square room cluttered with teletypes and speakers and frequency dials and round gray radar screens. At an upholstered swivel chair, the man leans forward to his microphone, setting aside a glass of red wine.

"Four Zero Five, France Control, go ahead." The accent in his English is barely noticeable. That is rare. He reaches for a pencil, from a jar bristling with pencils.

The microphone button is down again under my left thumb, and I hear again the sidetone, just as the man on the ground is hearing it. The engine in the sidetone is a quiet and businesslike roar, a waterfall of purposeful sound that is a background for my message. My words are filtered through the tubed body of the transmitter to become impersonal and faraway, the voice of someone I know only as a casual acquaintance. "France Control, Zero Five is over Alpha Bravo on the hour, flight level three three zero assigned instrument flight rules, estimating Lima Charlie at zero niner, Spangdahlem." Good old France. The only country in Europe where you never say the name of a reporting point, but only its initials, with a little air of mystery as you do. The familiar pattern of the position report is rhythmic and poetic; it is a pattern of pure efficiency that is beautiful to speak. There are thousands of position reports spoken and heard every hour across the earth; they are as basic a part of instrument flying as the calls for landing information are a basic part of fair-weather flight. Position reports are part of a way of life.

"Roger, Zero Five, on your position. Report Lima Charlie." The pencil stops, the wine is lifted.

With his last word, the man at France Control has ceased to exist. I am left alone again with the night and the stars and the sounds of my airplane.

As I fly tonight, navigating with the TACAN locked firmly onto the Laon transmitter, there is plenty of time for thought, and obligingly, events telescope themselves so that seven minutes will pass in the moment between the haunted land of Abbeville and the TACAN transmitter at Laon, France. I do not pass time as I fly, time passes me.

The hills slip away. There is a solid layer of black cloud from the ground to within a thousand feet of my airplane. The ground is buried, but in my chariot of steel and aluminum and plexiglass I am carried above, and the stars are bright.

In the red light, on the windowed face of the radiocompass, are four selector knobs, one switch, and one coffee-grinder tuning crank. I turn the crank. It is as old-fashioned in the cockpit of a fighter plane as would be a hand-wound telephone in an atomic research center. If it was much more quiet and if I wore no helmet, perhaps I could hear the crank squeak as it turned. I turn the handle, imagining the squeaks, until the frequency needle comes to rest over the number 344, the frequency of the Laon radiobeacon.

Turn up the volume. Listen. Crank the handle a little to the left, a little to the right. Static static crank dih-dih. Pause. Static. Listen for L-C. Dah-dih-dah-dih. . . . Dih-dah-dih-dih. . . . That is it. My right glove turns the selector from *antenna* to *compass*, while the left has the unnatural task of holding the control stick grip. The slim luminous green radiocompass needle spins majestically from the bottom of its dial to the top—a crosscheck on the TACAN—Laon radiobeacon is ahead. A little adjustment with the crank, an eighth of an inch, and the radiocompass is locked strong on Laon. Turn down the volume.

"France Control, Air Force Jet Two Niner Four Zero Five, Laon." There is quiet static in the soft earphones. I wait. Perhaps my call went unnoticed.

"France Control, France Control, Jet Two Niner Four Zero Five, how do you read on frequency three one seven point eight." There is no answer.

It is not at all unusual for a radio to break down in flight, for radios are temperamental things. But it is never a comfortable feeling to fly at night above weather without some way of talking to the people on the ground. My glove moves to the right, to the frequency selector of the UHF command radio. I do not bother to watch it work, for it is simply changing a sliding square knob one click, from *manual* to *preset*. An indicator on the instrument panel juggles numbers in small windows, and finally decides to present the number 18, in small red-lit figures. In that one click I am aligned with a different set of people, away from the busy hub of the France Control Center to the quiet and pastoral surroundings of Calva Radar. I know that the stereotype is not a valid one, for radar stations are only smaller places than traffic control centers, and are often far more rushed and busy. Yet whenever I call a radar site, I feel a little more at ease, and imagine a small red brick building set in a field of brilliant green grass, with a cow grazing not far away.

"Calva Radar, Calva Radar, Air Force Jet Two Niner Four Zero Five, how do you read channel one eight." There is perhaps one chance in three that the UHF will work on this frequency when it did not work on the frequency for France Control. The cow outside the brick building is asleep, a sculptured boulder in the dark of the grass. A light is in the window of the building, and a man's shadow moves across the glass as he reaches for his microphone.

". . . ero five. . . . d you. . . . . arbled. . . . . Calva?"

The UHF is definitely on its way out of commission. But even if it goes completely out, I am still cleared to maintain flight level 330 all the way to the Chaumont TACAN holding pattern. There are occasional moments like this when I wish that the airplane had just one more communication radio installed. But the F-84F was built for fighting, not for talking, and I must make do with what I have.

"Calva Radar, Four Zero Five unable to contact France Control, was Laon at one zero, flight level three three zero assigned instrument flight rules, estimating Spangdahlem at two eight, Wiesbaden." A wild try. A shot in the dark. But at least the information was said, and I have made the required report. I hear Calva's microphone button go down.

". . . ive . . . ort . . . . . mly garb . . . . come up . . . point zero . . ."

Calva is suggesting another frequency, but by the time I can understand all of his message I will be too far away for it to matter. Trying to send a position report with a radio in this condition is like trying to shout a message across a deep and windy chasm; difficult and frustrating. I give my report once again to comply with the rules, click back to *manual* and forget the matter. Too bad. It would have been good to hear the latest weather report along my route, but simply getting my request understood would have been a major problem, to say nothing of receiving a reply. The weather is of only academic interest anyway, for there would have to be a pilot report of a squall line with severe turbulence and heavy icing to 40,000 feet before I would consider turning back.

I look back over my left shoulder as I turn to the heading that will take me to Spangdahlem.

I am pulling a contrail.

In a sweeping turn behind me, following like a narrow wake of a high-speed racing boat, is a twisting tunnel of glowing gray mist in the starlight that is the path that I have followed. Clearly and precisely in texts on atmospheric physics, contrails are explained by the men who spend their time with radio balloons and diagrams of the upper air.

Contrails are like fireflies. If I desire, I can find pages of explanation about them in books and in specialized magazines. But when I see one close at hand, it is alive and mystic and grayly luminous. Watching the con as I turn, I can see the rise and fall of it where I made small changes to keep my airplane at flight level 330. It looks like a very gentle roller-coaster, one for people who do not like excitement. That is where I have been. No air aside from the rolling tunnel of mist can say that it has felt my passage. If I desire, I can turn now and fly through exactly the same air that I flew before. And I am alone. As far as I can see, and that is a long distance about me, there is no other contrail in the sky. I am the only person in all the world to fly above the clouds in the hundreds of cubic miles that make the world of high altitude between Abbeville and Spangdahlem this evening. It is a solitary feeling.

But there is work to be done. Back to the coffee grinder. Squeak squeak to frequency 428. Volume up. Static. And no second thoughts, no mistaking this one. An S and a P and an A. A city with its thousands of people, with the cares and the joys that they share, people, with me. I am alone and six miles above their earth, and their city is not even a light gray glow in the black cloud. Their city is an S and a P and an A in the soft earphones. Their city is the needlepoint at the top of the dial.

The frequency selector knob of the TACAN set clicks under my right glove to channel 100, and after a moment of indecision, the modern, smoothworking mileage drum spins to show 110 miles to the Spangdahlem beacon. Except for the failure of the UHF radio, my flight has gone very smoothly. There is a faint flicker in the rising hills of cloud far ahead to my right, as if someone is having difficulty striking an arc with a gigantic welding rod. But distances at night are deceiving, and the flash of light could be over any one of four countries.

"Air Force Jet Two Niner Four Zero Five, France Control with an advisory." Like a telephone ringing. My radio. There is not the slightest flaw in its operation. How can that be when only a minute ago . . . but it is working now and that is all that matters. Microphone button down. Professional voice.

"Roger, France; Four Zero Five, go."

"Four Zero Five, Flight Service advised multiengine aircraft reports severe turbulence, hail and heavy icing in vicinity of Phalsbourg. Also T-33 reported moderate turbulence at flight level three zero zero, light clear icing."

Button down. What about that. Sounds as if there might be a thunderstorm or two in the stratus ahead. That was in the textbook, too. But still it is rare to have very large thunderstorms in France. "Roger, France, thank you for the advisory. What is the current weather at Chaumont?"

"Stand by one."

I stand by, waiting while another man in a white shirt and loose tie riffles through his teletyped weather reports looking for the one out of hundreds that is coded LFQU. With one hand he sorts and moves the weather from the Continent over; he shuffles through rain and haze and fog and high cloud and winds and ice and blowing dust. He is at this moment touching the sheet of yellow paper that tells him, if he wants to read it, that Wheelus Air Base, Libya, has clear skies with visibilities to 20 miles and a 10-knot wind from the southwest. If he wants to know, a line on the paper tells him that Nouasseur, Morocco, is calling high broken cirrus, visibility 15 miles, wind west southwest at 15 knots. He thumbs through weather from Hamburg (measured 1200-foot overcast, visibility three miles in rain showers, wind from the northwest at ten knots) from Wiesbaden Air Base (900-foot overcast, visibility two miles, wind from the south at seven knots), from Chaumont Air Base.

"Jet Two Niner Four Zero Five, Chaumont is calling a measured one thousand one hundred foot overcast, visibility four miles in rain, winds from the southwest at one zero gusting one seven." The weather at Chaumont is neither good nor bad.

"Thank you very much, France." The man clicks his microphone button in reply. He lets the thick sheaf of yellow paper pile upon itself again, covering with its weight the weather of hundreds of airports across the Continent. And cover the report from Phalsbourg Air Base (measured ceiling 200 feet, visibility one half mile in heavy rain showers, wind from the west at 25 gusting 35 knots. Cloud-to-cloud, cloud-to-ground lightning all quadrants, one-half-inch hail).

Suddenly, in my dark cockpit, the thin luminous needle of the radiocompass swings wildly from its grip on the Spangdahlem radiobeacon and snaps me from my idle thoughts to the business of flying.

The needle should not move. When it begins to swing over Spangdahlem, it will first make very small leftright quivers on its card to warn me. The leftrights will become wider and wider, and the needle will finally turn to point at the bottom of the dial, as it did passing Laon.

But the distance-measuring drum shows that I am still 40 miles from my first German checkpoint. The radiocompass has just warned me that it is a radiocompass like all the others. It was designed to point the way to centers of low-frequency radio activity, and there is no more powerful center of low-frequency radio activity than a fully-grown thunderstorm. For years I have heard the rule of thumb and applied it: stratus clouds mean stable air and smooth flying. In an aside to itself, the rule adds (except when there are thunderstorms hidden in the stratus).

Now, like a boxer pulling on his gloves before a fight, I reach to my left and push the switch marked *pitot heat*. On the right console is a switch with a placard *windscreen defrost* and my right glove flicks it to the *on* position, lighted in red by hidden bulbs. I check that the safety belt is as tight as I can pull it, and I cinch the shoulder harness straps a quarter of an inch tighter. I have no intention of deliberately flying into a thunderstorm tonight, but the padlocked canvas sack in the gun bay ahead of my boots reminds me that my mission is not a trifling one, and is worth a calculated risk against the weather.

The radiocompass needle swings again, wildly. I look for the flicker of lightning, but the cloud is still and dark. I have met a little rough weather in my hours as a pilot, why should the contorted warning feel so different and so ominous and so final? I note my heading indicator needle steady on my course of 084 degrees, and, from habit, check it against the standby magnetic compass. The gyro-held needle is within a degree of the incorruptible mag compass. In a few minutes the cloud will reach up to swallow my airplane, and I shall be on instruments, and alone.

The wide luminous needle of the TACAN swings serenely as I pass over Spangdahlem at 2218, and one more leg of the flight is complete.

As if it recognized that Spangdahlem is a checkpoint and time for things to be happening, the thick dark cloud puts an end to its toying and abruptly lifts to swallow my airplane in blackness. For a second it is uncomfortable, and I sit tall in my seat to see over the top of the cloud. But the second quickly passes, and I am on instruments.

For just a moment, though, I look up through the top of my canopy. Above, the last bright star fades and the sky above is as dark and faceless as it is about me. The stars are gone, and I am indeed on instruments.

"Rhein Control, Air Force Jet Two Niner Four Zero Five, Spangdahlem, over." From my capricious radio I do not know whether or not to expect an answer. The "over," which I rarely use, is a wistful sort of hope. I am doubtful.

"Jet Four Zero Five, Rhein Control, go ahead."

Someday I will give up trying to predict the performance of a UHF radio. "Roger, Rhein, Zero Five was Spangdahlem at two niner, flight level three three zero assigned instrument flight rules, Wiesbaden at three seven, Phalsbourg next. Latest weather at Chaumont Air Base, please." A long pause of faint flowing static. My thumb is beginning to be heavy on the microphone button.

"Roger your position, Zero Five. Latest Chaumont weather is one thousand overcast, visibility five miles in rain, winds from the west at one zero knots."

"Thank you, Rhein. How about the Phalsbourg weather?" The static is suddenly louder and there is a light blue glow across the windscreen. St. Elmo's fire. Harmless and pretty to watch, but it turns low-frequency radio navigation into a patchwork of guesses and estimates. The radiocompass needle is wobbling in an aimless arc. It is good to have a TACAN set.

"Zero Five, Phalsbourg weather is garbled on our machine. Strasbourg is calling eight hundred overcast, visibility one-half mile in heavy rain showers, winds variable two zero gusting three zero knots, isolated thunderstorms all quadrants." Strasbourg is to the left of course, but I could catch the edge of their thunderstorms. Too bad that Phalsbourg is out. Always seems to happen when you need it most.

"What is the last weather you had from Phalsbourg, Rhein?" A garbled teletype weather report is really garbled. It is either a meaningless mass of consonants or a black jumble where one weather sequence has been typed on top of another.

"Latest we have, sir, is two hours old. They were calling five hundred overcast, visibility one-quarter mile in . . ." he pauses, and his thumb comes off the microphone button. It comes on again ". . . hail—that might be a misprint—scattered thunderstorms all quadrants." Quarter-mile visibility in hail. I have heard that nocturnal thunderstorms can be violent, but this is the first time that I have heard the direct report as I fly on instruments in the weather. But the sequence is two hours old, and the storms are isolated. It is rare for storms to hold their violence for a long time, and I can get a radar vector from a ground station around active storm cells.

"Thank you, Rhein." The air is very smooth in the stratus, and it is not difficult to hold the new heading at 093 degrees. But I am beginning to think that perhaps my detour did not take me far enough around the severe weather.

"Rhein Control, Air Force Jet Two Niner Four Zero Five, Wiesbaden." The City That Was Not Bombed.

Silence. Here we go again. "Rhein Control, Rhein Control; Air Force Jet . . ." I try once. Twice. Three times. There is no answer. I am alone with my instruments, and suddenly aware of my aloneness.

Click around with the radio channel selector under my right glove; perhaps I can talk to Barber Radar. "Barber Radar, Air Force Jet Two Niner Four Zero Five, over." Once. Twice. Three times. Nothing.

A flash in the clouds ahead. The air is still smooth, paving the way. Hold the heading. Hold the altitude.

A decision in my mind. If I were flying this crosscountry just to get myself home tonight, I would turn back now. I still have enough fuel to return to the clear air over Wethersfield. With my transmitter out, I cannot ask for a radar vector through the storms ahead. If it was not for the sack above the machine guns, I would turn back. But it is there, and at Chaumont there is a wing commander who is trusting me to complete my mission. I will continue.

I can use the radiocompass needle to point out the storms, if worst comes to worst I can dodge them by flying between the flashes. But still it is much more comfortable to be a spot of light on someone's radar screen, listening for sure direction about the white blurs that are the most severe cells of a thunderstorm. One more try, although I am certain now that my UHF radio is completely dead. Click click click to 317.5 megacycles. "Moselle Control, Moselle Control, Jet Zero Five." I have no hope. The feeling is justified, for there is no answer from the many-screened room that is Moselle Radar.

Turn back. Forget the wing commander. You will be killed in the storms.

Fear again, and it is exaggerating, as usual. I will not be killed in any storm. Someone else, perhaps, but not me. I have too much flying experience and I fly too strong an airplane to be killed by the weather.

Flash to the right, small flash to the left. A tiny tongue of turbulence licks at my airplane, making the wings rock slightly. No problem. Forty minutes from now I shall be walking across the ramp through the rain to Squadron Operations, Chaumont Air Base. The TACAN is working well, Phalsbourg is 80 miles ahead.

The flashes in the dark clouds north of Phalsbourg are more frequent and flicker now from behind my airplane as well as in front of it. They are good indicators of thunderstorm cells, and they do not exactly fit my definition of "scattered." Directly ahead, on course, are three quick bright flashes in a row. Correct 30 degrees left. Alone. Time for twisted thoughts in the back of the mind. "You have to be crazy or just plain stupid to fly into a thunderstorm in an eighty-four F." The words are my words, agreed and illustrated by other pilots who had circumstance force them to fly this airplane through an active storm cell.

The airplane, they say, goes almost completely out of control, and despite the soothing words of the flight handbook, the pilot is relying only on his airplane's inertia to hurl it through and into smooth air beyond the storm.

But still I have no intention of penetrating one of the flickering monsters ahead. And I see that my words were wrong. I face the storms on my course now through a chain of logic that any pilot would have followed. The report called them "scattered," not numerous or continuous. I flew on. There are at least four separate radar-equipped facilities below me capable of calling vectors through the worst cells. I fly on. A single-engine pilot does not predicate his action on what-shall-I-do-if-the-radio-goes-out. The risk of the mission is worth the result of delivering the heavy canvas sack in the gun bay.

Now, neither crazy nor stupid, I am at the last link of the chain: I dodge the storms by the swerving radiocompass needle and the flashes of lightning that I see from the cockpit. The TACAN is not in the least disturbed by my uneasy state of mind. The only thing that matters in the world of its transistorized brain is that we are 061 miles from Phalsbourg, slightly to the left of course. The radiocompass has gone wild, pointing left and right and ahead and behind. Its panic is disconcerting among the level-headed coolness of the other instruments, and my right glove moves its function switch to *off*. Gratefully accepting the sedative, the needle slows, and stops.

Flash to the left, alter course 10 degrees right. Flash behind the right wing, forget about it. Flash-FLASH directly brilliantly ahead and the instrument panel goes featureless and white. There is no dodging this one. Scattered.

The storm, in quick sudden hard cold fury, grips my airplane in its jaws and shakes it as a furious terrier shakes a rat. Right glove is tight on the stick. Instrument panel, shock-mounted, slams into blur. The tin horizon whips from an instant 30-degree left bank to an instant 60-degree right bank. That is not possible. A storm is only air.

Left glove, throttle full forward. My airplane, in slow motion, yaws dully to the left. Right rudder, hard. Like a crash landing on a deep-rutted rock trail. Yaw to the right. My airplane has been drugged, she will not respond. Vicious left rudder.

The power, where is the power? Left glove back, forward again, as far as it will go, as hard as it will go. A shimmering

blurred line where the tachometer needle should be. Less than 90 percent rpm at full throttle.

I hear the airplane shaking. I cannot hear the engine. Stick and rudders are useless moving pieces of metal. I cannot control my airplane. But throttle, I need the throttle. What is wrong?

Ice. The intake guide vanes are icing, and the engine is not getting air. I see intake clogged in gray ice. Flash and FLASH the bolt is a brilliant snake of incandescent noonwhite sun in the dark. I cannot see. Everything has gone red and I cannot even see the blurred panel. I feel the stick I feel the throttle I cannot see. I have suddenly a ship in the sky, and the storm is breaking it. So quickly. This cannot last. Thunderstorms cannot hurt fighters. I am on my way to Chaumont. Important mission.

Slowly, through the bone-jarring shake of the storm, I can see again. The windscreen is caked with gray ice and bright blue fire. I have never seen the fire so brightly blue. My wings are white. I am heavy with ice and I am falling and the worst part of a thunderstorm is at the lowest altitudes. I cannot take much more of this pounding. White wings, covered in shroud. Right glove grips the stick, for that is what has kept my airplane in the sky for six years. But tonight the airplane is very slow and does not respond, as if she were suddenly very tired and did not care to live. As if her engine had been shut down.

The storm is a wild horse of the desert that has suddenly discovered a monster on its back. It is in a frenzy to rid itself of me, and it strikes with shocks so fast they cannot be seen. I learn a new fact. The ejection seat is not always an escape. Bailout into the storm will be just as fatal as the meeting of earth and airplane, for in the churning air my parachute would be a tangled nylon rag. My airplane and I have been together for a long time, we will stay together now. The decision bolts the ejection seat to the cockpit floor, the *Thunderstreak* and I smash down through the jagged sky as a single dying soul. My arm is heavy on the stick, and tired. It will be good to rest. There is a roaring in my ears, and I feel the hard ground widening about me, falling up to me.

So this is the way it will end. With a violent shuddering of airplane and an unreadable instrument panel; with a smothered engine and heavy white wings. Again the feeling: I am not really ready to end the game. I have told myself that this day would come to meet me, as inevitably as the ground which rushes to meet me now, and yet I think, quickly, of a future lost. It cannot be helped. I am falling through a hard splintering storm with a control stick that is not a control stick. I am a chip in a hurricane a raindrop in a typhoon about to become one with the sea a mass of pieces-to-be a concern of air traffic controllers and air police and gendarmerie and coroners and accident investigators and statisticians and newspaper reporters and a board of officers and a theater commander and a wing commander and a squadron commander and a little circle of friends. I am a knight smashed from his square and thrown to the side of the chessboard.

Tomorrow morning there will be no storm, and the sun will be shining on the quiet bits of metal that used to be Air Force Jet Two Niner Four Zero Five.

But at this instant there is a great heavy steel-bladed storm that is battering and crushing me down, out of the sky, and the thing that follows this instant is another just like it.

Altimeter is a blur, airspeed is a blur, vertical speed is a blur, attitude indicator is a quick-rocking blurred luminous line that does not respond to my orders. Any second now, as before, I am tense and waiting. There will be an impact, and blackness and quiet. Far in the back of my mind, behind the calm fear, is curiosity and a patient waiting. And a pride. I am a pilot. I would be a pilot again.

The terrier flings the rat free.

The air is instantly smooth, and soft as layered smoke. Altimeter three thousand feet airspeed one-ninety knots vertical speed four thousand feet per minute down attitude indicator steep right bank heading indicator one seven zero degrees tachometer eighty-three percent rpm at full throttle. Level the white wings. Air is warm. Thudthudthud from the engine as ice tears from guide vanes and splinters into compressor blades. Wide slabs of ice rip from the wings. Half the windscreen is suddenly clear. Faint blue fire on the glass. Power is taking hold: 90 percent on the tachometer . . . thud . . . 91 percent . . . thudthud . . .

96 percent. Airspeed coming up through 240 knots, left turn, climb. Five hundred feet per minute, 700 feet per minute altimeter showing 3000 feet and climbing I am 50 degrees off course and I don't care attitude indicator showing steady left climbing turn I'm alive the oil pressure is good utility and power hydraulic pressure are good I don't believe it voltmeter and loadmeter showing normal control stick is smooth and steady how strange it is to be alive windscreen is clear thud 99 percent rpm tailpipe temperature is in the green. Flash-FLASH look out to the left look out! Hard turn right I'll never make it through another storm tonight forget the flight plan go north of Phalsbourg 15,-000 feet 320 knots flash to the left and behind, faint.

And strangely, the words of an old pilot's song: ". . . for I, am, too young, to die . . ." It is a good feeling, this being alive. Something I haven't appreciated. I have learned again.

Rpm is up to 100 percent. I am climbing, and 20,000 feet is below flash 21,000 feet is below. Blue fire washes across the windscreen as if it did not know that a windscreen is just a collection of broken bits of glass.

What a ridiculous thought. A windscreen is a windscreen, a solid piece of six-ply plate glass, for keeping out the wind and the rain and the ice and a place to look through and a place to shine the gunsight. I will be looking through windscreens for a long time to come.

Why didn't I bail out? Because the seat was bolted to the cockpit floor. No. Because I decided not to bail out into the storm. I should have bailed out. I definitely should have left the airplane. Better to take my chances with a rough descent in a torn chute than certain death in a crash. I should have dropped the external tanks, at least. Would have made the airplane lighter and easier to control. Now, at 32,000 feet, I think of dropping the tanks. Quick thinking.

Flash.

I flew out of the storm, and that is what I wanted to do. I am glad now that I did not drop the tanks; there would have been reports to write and reasons to give. When I walk away from my airplane tonight I will have only one comment to make on the Form One: UHF transmitter and receiver failed during flight. I will be the only person to know that the United States Air Force in Europe came within a few seconds of losing an airplane.

Flashflash. Ahead.

I have had enough storm-flying for one night. Throttle to 100 percent and climb. I will fly over the weather for the rest of the way home; there will be one cog slipping tonight in the European Air Traffic Control System, above the weather near Phalsbourg. The cog has earned it.

FROM

The Lonely Sky

WILLIAM BRIDGEMAN AND JACQUELINE HAZARD

They called it the Skyrocket. Officially it was the D-558-II, one of six or seven high-speed research airplanes ordered by the government after World War II to study supersonic flight. Built for the Navy by the Douglas Aircraft Company, it was a sleek, narrow, needle-nosed ship, dead-white, with thin, swept-back wings. Its first version had combined a turbo-jet and a rocket engine. Now a modified version, with a rocket engine only, was being tested at Edwards Air Force Base in California. The Douglas engineers were confident that, air-launched from the belly of a B-29 at 35,000 feet, the all-rocket Skyrocket could reach Mach 2 (twice the speed of sound) at 70,000 feet. But it was not the engineers who flew it. That was the job of test pilot William Bridgeman, a former navy pilot now employed by Douglas. He alone would someday ride that ship higher and faster than any airplane had ever flown before—but only after many failures and at least one near disaster.

Skyrocket

Tᴇsᴛ Flight Number 24 Navy D-558-II. April 5, 1951. Two years with the Skyrocket, two springs in the desert. This morning would be the seventh time that we'd try to ram our way into the unknown—beyond the sound barrier. Only we moved toward the flight like streetcar conductors making the same tedious run.

A sight that once seemed an enormity to me now seemed ordinary. The Skyrocket half borne from the superfortress did not appear out of order, and the equipment I wore no longer seemed a curious costume to me or the rest of the crew. It looked as if we would be able to take off this morning. The wind was holding steady, the sky was clear, the 29's engines were functioning. Once more I had to manufacture the tension that I would need for the flight ahead.

George's volunteer crew dressed in Air Force surplus had learned to handle their oxygen masks well, the uncertainty they first displayed was gone. In three months they were veterans of an unfulfilled mission. The line tenders on the long, cold climb were like men riding a subway—they looked out the window, at me, at the pilots, and back out the window.

On the long path up I review the flight to assure myself that it is still securely locked in my mind, still ready to be put into effect if this time I drop. The navigator's altimeter above my head to the right reads 25,000 feet. In the drafty forward compartment of the vibrating, roaring bomber boring her way up through the minus-50-degree-below-zero sky the cold penetrates the cloth of the pressure suit that is tightly bound to my legs. I slap my thighs and fold my arms over my chest. The exertion of the movement has forced me to let the air in faster from the helmet. The water should be beginning to warm up at Hermosa now.

I cannot allow myself to sit here leisurely thinking of the weekend ahead of me. There is the flight. Twenty minutes from now I may need all the help I can get. I force myself to go over the emergency procedures and my mind wanders back to the weekend.

Twenty-eight thousand feet! Here's where I get off. This is my street. I get to my feet—thump Jansen on the shoulder to let him know I'm vacating his ship for the seventh time. George bends around and without inspiration lifts his hand in a ribald gesture and shouts over the roar, rattling through the compartment, "Gentlemen," and in a precise imitation of Hal Bellew he recites, "I don't think you'll have a bit of trouble. Not a bit."

How the hell did he get a hold of that? It is with great amusement that George watches my face as he repeats the familiar and faraway imitation of "Buzz" Miller's nostalgic salutation before a difficult strike. But the line tenders are beside me, ready to convoy me back to the Skyrocket, and I turn away without asking where he heard the line. As I do, Jansen drops the rest of it: "Go get 'em, Tiger."

Today we are going to drop. I know it. I am ready for it. My hands run over the familiar knobs, levers, and buttons. I follow the 26 steps necessary for a cockpit check. Test the fire warning circuit . . . circuit breakers down . . . set the oxygen system . . . call the chase planes . . . check with Carder . . . check with Jansen. I move the switch that will set the stabilizer to 1.5 degrees, nose down, and I open and close my dive brakes. Performing the familiar tasks that set things in order, I prepare the plane for the flight.

"*Five minutes.*" Change over oxygen to the Skyrocket's limited supply. Apply full pressure into the helmet. I'm under water now, breathing laboriously. Instrumentation power switch on. Okay. I release the valve that pressurizes the cabin for 35,000 feet.

"*Four minutes.*" Here is where we can meet trouble if there is to be any. Turn rocket master switch to on. Pressurize rocket system.

The rocket pressure gauges are all in the green. The 12 dials are in an even line and appear to be holding. Catalyst temperature okay. *Maybe this is it!* This is as far as we have ever come. I am expectant and alert and the tension automatically increases and without any effort now I am on the edge.

"Fifty seconds!"

The stream of practiced steps continues to flow ahead without interruption, building in momentum, and I hurry along before them. Prime the rocket system, twist the knobs, turn the levers, read the dials, twelve of them—the pulse of the pressures wrapped up aft of me in the bullet fuselage. This must be it. This is the time!

In the twilight of the B-29's belly the black faces on the pressure gauges command my attention. The white, quivering needles are holding, and I watch them intently as a fakir with a cobra weaving in front of his flute.

Then the white sliver on the middle gauge slips out of line! Number Three system pressure is weakening, and as the needle drops a plug has been pulled and I am suddenly drained. Again we must abort!

"No drop. This is an abort." That's that. I yank the circuit breakers up, shut off the valve beside me that puts the rocket system back to sleep, and begin to secure the plane. As I do I hear, with disbelief, George starting his ten-second countdown as if he had not heard my order to cancel the flight.

"Ten, nine . . . ," slowly he calls off the seconds.

I shout through my throat-mike, "Don't drop me, George." But his voice doesn't stop and the count continues in my ears as I frantically repeat, "Aren't you receiving me? Don't drop me; the pressure on Number Three system has failed." No response.

". . . eight, seven," the steady count moves on unperturbed. I can't break through. George has his thumb on the key. He does not hear my frantic protestings. Now as I futilely shout into the helmet in the hope that he takes his thumb off the mike key between seconds, I work furiously to reinstate the ship for flight.

It is an accelerated, precise scramble. With both fists I pound the board of circuit breaker buttons down into their holes, move the stick to neutral.

The hollow voice of the pilot drones on, ticking off the seconds, ". . . five, four . . ." And still I try to get through, to break the count.

"Don't drop." There is no doubt. No getting out now. He is going to let me go.

Am I forgetting anything; God, am I forgetting anything? I force myself to retrace the steps I performed to inactivate the Skyrocket—although I know there is not enough time, before I am dropped, to thoroughly retrace the steps, to see if I have opened all the right doors that a minute ago I closed. Swiftly I start at the beginning to go over the movements that will bring her back to life. There are some big decisions to be made in

three seconds . . . whether or not to hit the first rocket switch and take a chance on her blowing all over the sky or whether to jettison the load of fuel that will allow me a longer chance at gliding home. To jettison the fuel is bad: if only one tank empties she will lose her balance. *Make up your mind quick.*

"Three . . . two . . . one . . . *drop!*"

Time's up. The bright light of the world bursts over my eyes as I plunge through the trap door from the protective, dark gut of the sheltering bomber and the traffic is moving. I'm thrown into the middle of the sky-sea without a life belt. It's a living, moving world, where the Skyrocket must be alive. She is dropping fast with her heavy load—15,650 pounds of pure rocket, silent as a bird dropped by a hunter, straight down with no control of her own yet.

A living thing! I think of my father. I remember what he said the day he came down to see me off to Pensacola, when he offered me the armament of his thirty years in the air. He told me about airplanes.

"You can't think of an airplane solely as a piece of machinery, Bill; she isn't. She's a living thing. Her world's the sky and when you get her up there she wants to fly, she wants to live. Thousands of man-hours have created an intricate nervous system that makes her want to fly, that compels her to; the man who controls her can keep her from her function, the pilot's the villain. Now if the pilot doesn't panic, if he trusts her and presses all the right buttons, she'll fly!"

The airman—my father, whom I barely knew, who had spent his life in a plane—finished his offering to me, "Go ahead. Go ahead and be a pilot . . . only remember someday it's going to get real deep . . . maybe you won't meet it for a long time, but just keep flying and it'll happen." It was pretty deep right now, so deep so fast that it was almost a joke.

I reach for the first rocket switch! Six seconds pass before the explosion, before the rocket blasts on with a giant reassertion. She lives! And hopefully and thankfully I click on the rest of the tubes as fast as possible. The force slams in . . . Number Two, *slam* . . . Number Three, *slam* . . . Number Four . . . she is accelerating with all the power in the world blasting her on. She's a living thing! A big hunk of energy that wants to go somewhere. Twenty-five seconds and 3000 feet down from where George spewed me helplessly into the sky, she begins to shallow out. The rockets have lit miraculously enough, but I don't expect them to last long with the pressure low in Number Three. But as long as they are burning I will follow the flight pattern.

Tentatively and timidly I point the long bayonet nose upward. It quivers. Too much! She's on the edge of stall according to the vibrating pole that I use as a stall indicator. If I feel around too long for the correct angle she'll burn up her fuel before I reach the pushover altitude of 45,000 feet—the altitude, planned to keep her Mach number down to 1.5, where I will begin the speed run.

Forty-five degrees. We are around the corner, sucked up through a hole in the sky, accelerating fantastically, and it requires a great deal of attention to hold her at her climbing speed that will eventually run into Mach .85, the number I will hold on the Machmeter until the indicated air speed falls to stalling speed. In the thin, sheer air, shooting for the top, the air speed falls off now as the Mach .85 holds steadily on the Machmeter. My eyes move back and forth between the indicated air speed and Machmeter. When the indicated air speed drops to 230, I hold the speed on the gauge and let the Mach number move up on its own. And as it does the thrust grabs hold positive and powerfully. This is complete freedom and detachment. This is the world and I'm the only living thing in it, running away from pain, boredom, desire, and fear.

And then I remember, as if they were people I left a long time ago, the crew. No more than thirty-five seconds have passed since George dropped me. There is a second to call now that the steps are successfully and wondrously following the pattern. It seems an enormously long time since I have opened my mouth to speak.

"Goddam it, George, I *told* you not to drop me." The words are ridiculously inadequate and without purpose.

Pete Everest, up for the first time in months, laughs somewhere in the sky in his F-86 and his is the first voice I hear, "You got keen friends, Bridgeman . . ."

Then Carder's shaky voice: "How's he doing, Pete?"

"He's accelerating away from me in a climb. Looks like he's doing all right . . . all four rockets appear to have lit off."

The patient is rallying. Carder is relieved, but he will have to wait approximately ten minutes before he will get any news from me. I am busy. He doesn't call to me.

The radio is silent and the altimeter hand is a whirring pin-wheel as I hang on to the Skyrocket on her way out of this world. Mach 1 . . . she doesn't react as she does at a lower altitude and the sky is still as she runs away from the speed of sound, a rocket ripping through space, carrying a pilot that is audaciously put there to control the trip. She feels like she is never going to quit, like she is going clear out the top.

I follow the plan that I have carried in my head these last three months. She is to pick up five tenths of a Mach number, almost a third faster than she has ever demonstrated. Up until this minute I have crossed into the shallow end of the super-sonic region and then backed out quick. Now I am all the way in and I will be here until the fuel burns up. I can barely read my altitude with the altimeter 100-foot hand a revolving blur obscuring the 1000-foot and 10,000-foot hands.

I move the stick forward to control the angle of climb. The control stick moves loosely forward without effort. It's as if the cables have been cut. There is no response! She won't be con-trolled at this speed by ordinary means; the elevators are use-less, completely ineffective. I have anticipated this reaction at sustained supersonic speed, but the helpless feeling of holding a stick in your hands that can be moved back and forth forcibly with no effect at all on the ship is a sickening surprise at 800 miles an hour.

It has been by feel that I have flown an airplane. By putting the right amount of pressure on the stick I've produced a de-sired amount of G. It has become a matter of conditioning. It is like being part of the ship—one of its reflexes. By feel I have prevented my plane from stalling out—it comes through my fin-gers, I can sense it. Now all this conditioning is no good to me;

the feel isn't there. In order to direct her a more rigid control is needed to stand up to the terrific forces at supersonic speed. I must fly her with the stabilizer that I move electrically by means of a small switch. I must fly by a switch, trust a switch that gives you no feel, no warning. If I move it too far I can instantly put enough c on the plane to black myself out. Subsonically, movement of the control column brings a gentle response—there is a big displacement and little action. But not here. The little switch I fly by has a subtle displacement and a gigantic reaction.

A ghost control takes over the silent ship. It is a matter now of moving a tiny switch and reading the 86 dials and lights before me that register the functions, the automatic warnings, temperatures, and myriad reactions imposed upon the Skyrocket as she is shoved off the edge of the cliff.

The rocket-cylinder seconds are running out. Twenty seconds remain for the push over the top. I watch the fire warning devices, and I listen. If I detect the buzz of flutter on the controls immediately I will cut off the rockets.

We are at the top, 45,000 feet, or close to it.

Beneath the blurring altimeter needle I try to figure the altitude. Z-zz-zut, zut, zut, I move the electric switch to direct the plane over into her run at three tenths of a c, and as she begins the long arc over the top I am lifted up from my seat and my body grows lighter by the second as I approach zero c. A white, blazing bullet in the bright blue around her, the Skyrocket shoots through the lonely, silent sky, accelerating over the rim of the pushover, blasting toward the shallow dive. All the black dials before me are shifting, changing, and whirling. I fly by only one now—the accelerometer that is measuring the degree of c I am putting on the ship. The c hand holds steady on .3 and briefly I move my eyes from the gauge to see the Machmeter dial moving up 1.2 . . . 1.25 . . . *what the hell is this?* She is rocking gently and rapidly back and forth like a cradle. The action is unreal, incomprehensible. A helpless feeling; my body, light as a balloon, oscillates from side to side with the ship. I grab the stick to dampen the gyration, but the ailerons have little effect, and the ominous rocking continues.

Before fear has a chance to set in solidly the Skyrocket is in the sloping dive and steady once again. The Mach needle reaches toward 1.3 and I hang on and wait for the rockets to quit . . . 1.32 . . . 1.38 . . . 1.4 . . . *plowie* . . . she decelerates in the brick wall as one rocket cuts off and *slam, slam, slam,* the other tubes follow, pulling me violently into the instrument panel. One by one I hear them sputter off as I lay jammed tight against the wall of whirling dials, and then she is silent and powerless once more, pointing her way across the sky following the path she was directed along.

My recovery has to be quick; every second is an important one. The steps must be followed, to delay can be awkward. I pick myself off of the panel and move her into a 3-g climbing turn, as scheduled on my map, toward the south end of the lake, using four degrees of horizontal stabilizer until I reach a set air speed. There is no time to experience any relief at completing the important mission of the day's flight. Ahead of me waits the dead-stick landing and on the way home I am to pick up added data—side-slips and constant-speed runs. I have planned to pick them up in a box pattern over the lake as I glide down.

Data! Oh God, no! None of the flight has been recorded. Under pressure of the unexpected drop I have neglected to turn on the data switch. The flight has brought home no information for the men who wait on the ground. It is as if she hadn't dropped again.

The radio speaks. "Fifteen thousand." Mabry prompts me. "Dump the cockpit."

Fifteen thousand feet and I pull the plug. In an instant the cockpit pressure equalizes to that surrounding the airplane; it is like an explosive decompression, as it was in the tank at Wright-Patterson Aero Medical Laboratory. A heavy blow in the chest that forces a loud gasp deep out of my insides and at the same time the pod is filled with a white fog that evaporates at once.

Now it is safe to take away the face-plate. After 20 minutes of confinement in the big helmet, the pressure squeezing my head in a tight grip, I have the delicious relief of a man coming up to the surface after being under water too long. I drink in a long gulp of air and savor the experience of breathing normally.

There is no time to just sit and breathe luxuriously the pure air. Already Mabry is checking the steps to be taken in preparation for the dead-stick, 175-mile-an-hour landing three minutes away from me.

The air splits by the canopy like a river raging around a rock in its path. It whistles mournfully at the seams that seal the cockpit, and there is not another sound in the world. Silently the hushed rocket eats through 7000 feet in a gradual descent toward the position I have, months before, plotted on the map that is now clipped to my knee. The spot marked is three miles out from the lake and 7000 feet above it. This is where I will move out on the downwind leg of my landing. There is no alternative now. Only one way. Down.

Okay, junior. There it is! Below me is the bean-shaped lake bed, the sanctuary that I aim for. Between me and the rest of the world lie 7000 feet of booby traps where a slight miscalculation can be embarrassingly fatal. I talk to myself. The sound of my voice helps to break the tension. *You're three miles out from the lake bed. You're at 310 miles per hour. Slow it up, get the gear down.* A detached "other" mind begins to direct the show.

The chase pilot is beside me and he calls, "Gear shows. Appears to be locked down." Reluctantly I head away from home on the long downwind leg of my approach. It must be just the right length—not too far, not too close. The altitude is gradually being used up and she is dropping closer to the ground. There is an uncomfortable tightness in my chest as I leave behind me the only island I can safely land on. Perhaps I am going too far. *Don't be a kid.* My judgment remains firm despite the little panicky wave. *Simmer down. You're doing all right.* Behind me the lake has melted away in the flat, nubby-textured desert bottom. I can no longer see it.

Okay. This is far enough, stupid. Where are you going to land—Palmdale? Steadily she is using up the protective altitude and the color of the spring desert is now clearly defined: the cactus stands out like warning figures waving their arms. It is with some relief that I move her into the turn for the base leg. By the way she reacts to the wind that she is now nosed into I

can gauge the distance home. It gives little resistance. The wind
is weak today. My turn is a wide one.

"Don't forget the data switch on the landing, Bill," Mabry
interrupts me. The radio links me with the control tower,
the chase planes, and the little knot of men on the lake bed.
All other radio traffic on the base and in the sky was halted
when Douglas' 558-II left the 29. Every plane in the area will
have to wait until she is back on the ground before receiving
their landing or take-off instructions. Everest reserves any advice
on how to handle the dead-stick landing. He sits quietly by off
my right wing, waiting.

Forty-five hundred feet. One mile straight ahead sprawls the
big, safe, empty lake. I am committed. I've got to be right the
first time. I cannot change my mind now and go around again.
How big an S turn will put me on? Damn little wind. *Make up
your mind quick. Take it out a little, bright boy. Widen it up!*
Eight hundred feet below, the scrubby hard bottom rushes by
in a blur. There is the runway. I "S" back on to it. *Not bad, not
bad. Looks pretty damn good, Bridge.* Two hundred feet and I
am over the edge of the lake, looking ahead at the mile marker
coming at me. Pete keeps me company; he is right at my side.
He moves in and reads off the distance that separates the silent
rocket shell from the runway.

"A good attitude, Bill. You got about ten feet. Let her down
a little more. Now a little more, on down . . . five feet . . .
one. Hold what you got. That's a boy!" And he proclaims the
reassuring fact, "You got seven long miles of runway ahead of
you, boy."

A great, big beautiful margin. She touches the bumpy, hard
surface at 175 miles an hour. She's down! I have made all the
right decisions and adjustments and I got the right answer.
There is no time to congratulate myself. I've got to guide this
thing along the lake bed. Far ahead of me, dragging rows of
dust behind them, the fire trucks and ambulance turn in to meet
me. And, as always, instead of continuing along a straight path,
I point the Skyrocket's needle-nose directly at them. They veer
wildly from their course, scattering like chickens in a barnyard.
The sight of the scurrying fire trucks is enormously funny.

"Thanks, Pete."

"My pleasure," Everest sweeps out the words. He skims across the deck over the bewildered group of trucks, points up, and heads north to the Air Force runway. Radio traffic resumes. Life begins again around me.

"The D-558-II is on the lake bed," the control tower announces, and at once the radio crackles with calls.

"Nine-ten to control tower requests landing instructions . . ."

"Control tower to 558, the fire chief would like you to release the trucks as soon as you can. We've got a project ready to go on the north side of the lake that needs them."

Mabry manages to break through the jam-up of calls; "Bill, cut the data switch off."

Three miles of runway behind her. She is rolling at 20 miles an hour to a stop and I open the canopy. The hot, clean desert air washes over my face and the white flash-bulb brightness of the lake bed bursts into my eyes. Now she is motionless. It is over. Everything is done; the chain of steps is completed. There is no emergency to anticipate, no race to keep the steps moving. I have nothing to remember. Remembering and anticipating are no longer tools needed to stay alive and to keep my ship in its original state. The muscles in my legs and arms begin to slack, the thing that has gripped me begins to let go a little but it will take a day to get rid of the whole armament.

The seventh time—a mistake—and she did it. The tension was put to use at last. Sitting alone, motionless, slumped in the cockpit with the placid, now-comforting desert holding me on all sides, it is a rich and full moment.

FROM

We Seven

JOHN H. GLENN, JR.

Americans were startled in 1957 when the Soviet Union launched the first artificial satellite. That was the start of the "space race." The Soviets were also first to put men into space; Cosmonauts Yuri Gagarin and Gherman Titov accomplished orbital flights in 1961. That same year, two U.S. astronauts, Alan Shepard and the late Virgil Grissom, completed suborbital flights down the Atlantic testing range. But it was not until February 1962, that the United States was ready to put a man into orbit. The astronaut selected for the flight was Marine Lieutenant Colonel John H. Glenn, Jr., a former fighter pilot in the Pacific and Korea and later a navy test pilot. The pride and hope of an entire nation rode with Glenn that day. Lift-off was at Cape Canaveral, Florida, at 9:47 A.M. on February 20. Glenn made three orbits in his spacecraft, Friendship 7, *before his splashdown at 2:43 P.M. in the Atlantic near Grand Turk Island. Here is Glenn's own story of the first American-manned orbital flight.*

The Flight of Friendship 7

THE Atlas is an interesting thing to sit on top of when the gantry is gone. You are seventy-four feet above the ground, and the booster is so tall that it sways slightly in a heavy gust of wind. In fact, I could set the whole structure to rocking a bit myself, just by moving back and forth in the couch. I could look at the whole sky now as it was filling with bigger patches

of blue. Through a mirror which was mounted near the window
—like the rear-view mirror on a car—I could see the blockhouse
where the technicians were monitoring the countdown and on
across the Cape to other installations where we had prepared
for the flight. Through the periscope I looked out at the Atlantic and eastward along the track that I would soon follow.
I took only a few brief glances outside, however, for I was still
checking switches and monitoring the systems on the instrument panel in front of me. If the oxygen-pressure or fuel-supply
gauges should suddenly drop, indicating a failure somewhere in
the system, I wanted to know about it instantly. Everything
was proceeding normally, however. I could also hear some of
the telltale sounds over the noises in my headset. I could hear
the pipes whining and crackling below me as the liquid oxygen
flowed into the booster tanks, and I could hear a vibrant hissing
noise as the tanks were supercooled by the cold lox. The metal
walls of the tanks set up a high-frequency resonance and buzzing as they shivered from contact with the oxygen. When the
technicians gimbaled the engines for a moment to make sure
they were working, I could hear a faint shaking and thumping
coming up through the booster. These were all sounds that I
had been briefed about, and it was reassuring that each new
sound indicated that we had reached another stage in the countdown. I talked over the hard line with Paul Donnelly, the NASA
test conductor who was in charge of preparing the capsule
system for launch, and with Tom O'Malley of General Dynam-
ics, the firm that made the Atlas, who was in the blockhouse
as the over-all test conductor. I also made radio checks with Al
Shepard, who would be communicating with me from the Mercury Control Center during the flight and was keeping me
posted on the latest status of the weather, the tracking range
and the emergency recovery vehicles stationed on the Cape.
There was a real feeling of excitement in many of the voices—
"Go" fever, some people have termed it—and this was height-
ened at T minus 35 minutes when the decision was made to
start putting in the final load of lox. This was one of the landmarks on the countdown, and when I heard that this procedure
was beginning I knew that we were almost on our way.

I had to wait through two more brief holds, however. One came at T minus 22 minutes when one of the loxing valves stuck and the technicians had to shift to a smaller valve to complete the loading process. This was a minor problem and it took about 25 minutes. Then, at T minus 6 minutes and 30 seconds, there was a 2-minute hold to check on a power failure in the computer system at the Bermuda tracking station. Bermuda was a key station in the network because it lay close to the area where I would actually be going into orbit and served as a backup control center for Cape Canaveral. I knew that I would not be launched unless this station was in perfect shape. I was greatly relieved, therefore, when the power was restored and the count was resumed.

We were getting down to the short rows now. Over the radio I could hear the people responsible for each of the systems reporting in to the test conductor. "Communications, 'Go,'" "ASCS, 'Go,'" "Aeromed, 'Go,'" "Range, 'Go.'" The Astronaut was one of the last items on the list, and when my turn came I said, "Ready." I was.

About a minute and a half before lift-off, I did a few quick exercises to make sure that my body was toned and ready for the launch. The aeromed people asked for one final blood-pressure check before lift-off. They had been asking for this all through the count, and pushed a button which started the recording instrument and I pumped up the bulb, took the blood-pressure reading automatically from a cuff on my left arm and sent it along by telemetry to the Control Center. Then, I put my left hand on the abort handle, as procedure requires. At T minus 35 seconds, a special countdown started for dropping the umbilical cord which had been providing external power and cooling for the capsule up until now. This was the last physical link between the capsule and the ground, and I watched through the periscope as the umbilical fell away and I heard it fall with a loud plop. The periscope retracted automatically, and this shut off my view from that direction. The land lines to the blockhouse and Control Center were cut off now and we communicated from now on only by radio. I could detect a tone of excitement in the voices in my headset, and as the countdown

we had practiced so often ran down for this final time, I shared the feeling. At T minus 18 seconds there was a planned momentary hold of 2 or 3 seconds while the automatic engine starter was switched on. I did not hear it at the time, but just as the engine sequence started and he knew this was it, Scott spoke into his microphone in the blockhouse. "Godspeed, John Glenn," he said. I heard it later on a recording of the transmissions; it was a very impressive moment. No one would push any more buttons or take any further positive action now—except to stop the show at the last second in case of an emergency. Then Al Shepard's voice gave me the final 10 seconds of the count. He reached zero and the engines started.

I could feel the engines light off as the capsule vibrated from their ignition, and I could hear a faint roar inside the capsule. The booster stood fast on the pad for 2 or 3 seconds while the engines built up to their proper thrust. Then the big hold-down clamps dropped away and I could feel us start to go. I had always thought from watching Atlas launches that it would seem slow and a little sluggish, like an elevator rising. I was wrong; it was not like that at all. It was a solid and exhilarating surge of up and away. Al Shepard received a signal that I was lifting off and confirmed it for me over the radio. The capsule clock started right on time and I reported this.

"The clock is operating," I said. "We're under way."

It was 9:47:39 A.M. (E.S.T.) when the Atlas left the ground. Al rogered for the message and told me to stand by for the 20-second count to start up the stop watch I had on my right wrist as a backup timer. It was already preset at 20 seconds; all I had to do was take my left hand off the abort handle for a second or two to push in the stem. The personnel down in the Control Center had a lot of fast figuring to do now as the tracking instruments and telemetry circuits started sending in data which had to be analyzed in a hurry to determine exactly how well the launch was progressing.

The launch itself was the first of four hurdles that I had to jump to get properly into space, and it was a big one. The booster had to function perfectly, and it had some maneuvers to start executing immediately. Pad 14, where we took off, is lined up with the Atlantic Missile Range which lies to the southeast of the Cape—at an azimuth, in fact, of 105 degrees. In order to get into the correct orbit, however, the booster and the capsule had to start off almost immediately on an azimuth of approximately 75 degrees. For the first 2 seconds, the Atlas went straight up. Then, for the next 13 seconds, the automatic guidance system which was built into the booster made it roll gradually to a northeast heading. Eight seconds after lift-off I reported that this was taking place.

"We're programing in roll O.K.," I said. I could feel the motion and see it happening by glancing out the window through the mirror.

Five seconds later, I reported that the flight was getting "bumpy along about here." This was something that we had predicted by studying the pattern of previous Atlas launches, and it was nothing to worry about. It was just that I could feel a little resonance or roughness and wanted the Control Center to know for the record what was happening. I found out later that my voice was also vibrating slightly over the radio as I called in.

We went over that first hurdle in good shape. I started the backup clock on my wrist at T plus 20 seconds. Then I started ticking off a list of items—oxygen and fuel supply and the ampere reading on the batteries. Everything read off just as it should; the capsule was functioning perfectly. Al Shepard came on the radio to assure me that from the telemetry indication in the Control Center the flight path looked good.

The second hurdle came when I started into what we call the "maximum q" area, or the portion of the flight where we knew we would encounter the highest aerodynamic forces against the capsule and the booster. This comes at an altitude of about 35,000 feet and is an area where we had had some difficulties earlier in the Mercury program. We entered the area about 45 seconds after launch. I reported to Al that I could feel the vibration building. This phase lasted about 30 seconds. The shaking was more pronounced at this point. I did not expect any trouble, but we knew there were certain limits beyond which the Atlas and capsule should not be allowed to go. One

Mercury flight with an empty capsule had ended here when the Atlas blew up. The abort system had worked fine, however, and the capsule came down in such good condition that the engineers were able to use it later on another test flight. Structural changes had been made in the Atlas and tested on later flights, and, in any event, automatic sensors in the ASIS system would abort the mission and break me loose from the Atlas if the vibrations got too high. Nevertheless, it is difficult for the human body to judge the exact frequency and amplitude of vibrations like this, and I was not sure whether we were approaching the top limits that ASIS was set for or not. As it turned out, the capsule was under aerodynamic pressure of 982 pounds per square foot during this phase of flight. This was well within limits, and we made this hurdle, too. I saw what looked like a contrail float by the window. I reported again on the supplies of consumables that we had stocked in the capsule—fuel, oxygen and battery power. At 1 minute and 16 seconds after launch, Al confirmed that I had passed through "maximum q," and I answered that I felt good and that the flight was "smoothing out real fine." The G forces were building up to about 6 now. I strained against them to make sure that I was in good shape. I was.

At 2 minutes and 11 seconds after launch we jumped the third hurdle right on schedule when the two big outboard booster engines shut down and dropped away. We were out of the atmosphere by now, and had built up enough speed so that all we needed was the long, final push from the sustainer engine to drive us into orbit. There was no sensation of speed, however, because my window was not aligned so I could see anything and use it as a reference point. The only time I took my left hand off the abort handle during this period was to be ready to jettison the escape tower at 2 minutes and 34 seconds after lift-off in case it failed to leave automatically. Now that we were out of the atmosphere where the drag forces were high, we no longer needed the escape rocket to force us free of the booster; and since the tower's extra weight would just waste fuel that we needed for getting into orbit, it was supposed to jettison and drop away. I thought I saw it go about 20 seconds early, and I reported this to Al. I did not actually see the tower, but I did see smoke go by the window and I assumed it was from the escape rocket firing. I was wrong, however. The smoke had apparently been deflected around the capsule during booster engine shutdown and staging. The tower went on schedule a little later and shot out a momentary cloud of flame and smoke. I could feel a slight bump as it took off, and I watched it going straight away from me, accelerating at a tremendous clip. It disappeared quickly. The G forces on me had dropped at staging to about 1.5.

The sustainer engine was being guided now from the ground, and the Atlas was completing another precise maneuver. It had been turning a corner in the sky and programing over on its pitch axis at the rate of about 2 degrees per second until at one point—just before the tower fired—the capsule was actually riding lower than the engine section of the booster. The booster-capsule combination was still climbing, but it was changing course through space at this point so that it would thread itself through the keyhole and not keep going straight up. I caught a quick glimpse of the ocean through the window as we pitched down. I knew we would pitch up again and make the approach to the fourth hurdle, the insertion into orbit.

The insertion was perfect. Al and I had been talking during the corner-turning stage. He said that the Cape was "Go" and was standing by for me. "Roger," I said. "Cape is 'Go' and I am 'Go.' Capsule is in good shape." Then I read off the instrument readings again and said that all systems were "Go." Al said we had "twenty seconds to SECO"—or sustainer engine cutoff. At 5 minutes, 1.4 seconds after lift-off, the sustainer engine shut down. Then the bolts which held the booster and the capsule together exploded, and the posigrade rockets fired to push the capsule away from the booster. I could hear and feel each of these explosions take place. There seemed to be a barely noticeable sensation of tumbling forward when the capsule separated; it was only momentary, and I did not feel disoriented at any time as we turned around.

This was it. We were 100 miles up and going at a velocity of 25,730 feet per second. I went weightless as the G forces dropped from 6 to zero; it was a very pleasant sensation. The periscope extended, and the capsule began to turn around automatically to orbital attitude—blunt end forward—which it would hold throughout the three orbits. The automatic system accomplished this maneuver by activating the nozzles which then turned the capsule. Now, for the first time, I could look out the window and see back along the flight path. I could not help exclaiming over the radio about what I saw. "Oh," I said, "that view is tremendous!" It really was. I could see for hundreds of miles in every direction—the sun on white clouds, patches of blue water beneath and great chunks of Florida and the southeastern U.S. Much nearer, I could see the Atlas drifting along by itself, about 200 yards behind me and slightly above. But these were only quick glances, for I had to concentrate on monitoring the capsule and preparing to start on the flight plan items. I was still not sure about our insertion conditions. Then Al Shepard called with the message that I had been waiting for. "You have a 'Go,'" he said "for at least seven orbits." I was really jubilant. Al meant that the computers at the Cape had run through all of the data and had indicated that the insertion of the capsule was good enough for a minimum of seven orbits. This is more or less a standard computer figure. The factors would probably have been good enough for seventeen or seventy orbits if we had been able to carry enough fuel and oxygen for such a long mission.

I loosened my chest strap now and went to work. Until this moment, every sequence and event had been extremely time-critical. That is, the successful jumping of each hurdle had depended on split-second timing. Now that I was in orbit and at zero G, however, we did not have to be quite so conscious of each fleeting second until it was time for firing the retro-rockets at the start of re-entry. I had a lot of work to do, and in order to get it all done I would have to adhere to the schedule as closely as possible.

The plan called for me to spend most of the first orbit getting used to the new environment and helping the ground stations establish an accurate pattern of radar tracking so they could pin down an exact orbital path early in the mission. I was also scheduled to test out the various systems on the capsule before we got too far along, so that we would know if we had any problems before we committed ourselves to a second orbit. Eight minutes after launch, as soon as Gus Grissom finished relaying to me the correct times for retro-firing from his Cap Com desk at the Bermuda tracking station, I started checking out the attitude control systems—automatic, manual and fly-by-wire. I tried each system on all three axes—yaw, pitch, and roll—and in all directions—up, down, left and right. This took about two minutes, and by the time I was finished with it I was almost across the Atlantic and was in communication with the tracking station in the Canary Islands. All of the controls had responded perfectly, just like clockwork. The stick handled very well. I was happy to see this, for there is always some doubt whether such complicated controls will work as well under actual conditions as they do on the procedure trainers—and whether I would be able to work as well, also. I could see no difference—at least not yet.

Inside the spacecraft, I could hear a number of muffled sounds. There was some noise from the gyros which gave us our attitude references, another noise caused by the inverters which were converting D.C. power into A.C., the hiss of the oxygen flow as it ran through the hose in my helmet, and sounds from the nozzles which were spitting out hydrogen peroxide to correct the attitude of the capsule.

In addition to closely monitoring all the systems, I started making a few observations out the window. Since I was facing backward, everything came out from underneath me, similar to the way things look when you ride backwards in a car, and it seemed to move more rapidly than I had thought it would. The sense of speed was similar to what you normally experience in a jet airliner at about 30,000 feet when you are looking down on a cloud bank at low altitudes. I think our training devices had been a little inadequate on this score; they had given us less sensation of motion and speed than I could feel in actual flight. Just before I finished crossing the Atlantic, I had my last glimpses of the Atlas. It was still in orbit, about 2 miles behind me and a mile beneath me. It was bright enough so that I could see it even against the bright background of the earth.

I saw the Canary Islands through the periscope and then saw them through the window. They were partially hidden by clouds. While I was reporting in by radio to the Canary Island tracking station I had my first glimpse of the coast of Africa. The Atlas Mountains were clearly visible through the window. Inland, I could see huge dust storms blowing across the desert, as well as clouds of smoke from brush fires raging along the edge of the desert. One of the things that surprised me most about the flight was the percentage of the earth which was covered by clouds. They were nearly solid over Central Africa and extended out over most of the Indian Ocean and clear across the Pacific. I could not establish the exact altitude of all of the various layers, but I could easily determine where one layer ended and another layer began by the shadows, and I believe that with better optical instruments we can contribute a good deal to the art of weather forecasting from this orbital altitude.

Four seconds after I lost radio contact with the Canary Island station, I could hear the Cap Com at the Kano station in Nigeria calling me. I read off the figures on fuel, oxygen and cabin pressure, and then I opened up the faceplate on the helmet for a few seconds to take a xylose pill. This is a special sugar tablet which allows the doctors to determine some things about how well the digestive system is functioning.

Zanzibar was the next tracking station, and here the flight surgeon who was on duty came on the air to discuss how I was doing physically. I gave him a blood-pressure reading, but before I pushed the button and pumped up the bulb I pulled thirty times at the bungee cord which permitted me to exercise with a known workload that could be compared with the same exercise taken on the ground. The cord was attached under the instrument panel, and I gave it one full pull per second for 30 seconds to see what effect exercise would have on my system under a condition of weightlessness. The only real effect it had on me at the time was the same effect it had had on the ground. It made me tired. My pulse went up from 80 beats per minute to 124 beats in 30 seconds, but it returned to 84 beats per minute within a couple of minutes. My blood pressure read 120 over 76 before the exercise period and 129 over 74 afterwards. This was the sort of mild reaction we had expected from doing similar tests on the procedures trainer. The doctor also asked me what physical reactions, if any, I had experienced so far from weightlessness. I was able to tell him that there had been none at all; I assured him that I felt fine. I had had no trouble reaching accurately for the controls and switches. There had been no tendency to get awkward and overreach them, as some people had thought there might be. I could hit directly any spot that I wanted to hit. I had an eye chart on board, a small version of the kind you find in doctors' offices, and I had no trouble reading the same line of type each time. After making a few slow movements with my head to see if this brought on a feeling of disorientation, I even tried to induce a little dizziness by nodding my head up and down and moving it from side to side. I experienced no disturbances, however. I felt no sense of vertigo, astigmatism, or nausea whatever.

In fact, I found weightlessness to be extremely pleasant. I must say it is convenient for a space pilot. I was busy at one moment, for example, taking pictures, and suddenly I had to free my hands to attend to something else. Without even thinking about it, I simply left the camera in mid-air, and it stayed there as if I had laid it on a table until I was ready to pick it up again. The fact that this strange phenomenon seemed so natural at the time indicates how rapidly man can adapt to a new environment. I am sure that I could have gone for a much longer period in a weightless condition without being bothered by it at all. Being suspended in a state of zero G is much more comfortable than lying down under the pressure of 1 G on the ground, for you are not subject to any pressure points. You feel absolutely free. The state is so pleasant, as a matter of fact, that we joked that a person could probably become addicted to it without any trouble. I know that I could. The only catch that I can think of on a space flight is that you would have to be careful about the kind of food you carried along. Cookies or crackers or anything crumbly could be a nuisance, for the pieces would float around and get in your way. But I think that an Astronaut could easily take a plain old ham sandwich up with him, complete with mustard, and not have to rely on tubes of vegetable purée and applesauce—although most of them taste good, too.

By the time I had completed various medical tests for the flight surgeon at Zanzibar, I had also completed preparations for the coming of darkness. We had hoped to make some observations of the moon and stars from orbital altitude during the three 40-minute nights which I would experience on the flight, in order to determine how visible the horizon would be at night and how useful it might be for maintaining the capsule's attitude. This meant that I had to be prepared for night vision —or "dark adapted"—well before night came. I placed red covers over the lights in the cockpit and turned off the special photo-lights which helped us make pictures of my reactions during the flight. I turned on the tiny bulbs which we had had installed at the ends of the index and middle fingers on each glove. These served as miniature flashlights and were very useful. I also tried to install the special eyepatch which had been molded to fit the left side of my face. The patch did not work very well, however. My face was moist and the special tape we had brought along failed to keep the patch in place.

I witnessed my first sunset over the Indian Ocean, and it was a beautiful display of vivid colors. The sun is perfectly round and it gives off an intense, clear light which is more bluish-white than yellow, and which reminded me in color and intensity of the huge arc lights we used at the Cape. It was so bright that I had to use filters to look directly at it. Then, just as the sun starts to sink into the bright horizon, it seems to flatten out a little. As the sun gets lower and lower, a black shadow moves across the earth until the entire surface that you can see is dark except for the bright band of light along the horizon. At the beginning, this band is almost white in color. But as the sun sinks deeper the bottom layer of light turns to bright orange. The next layers are red, then purple, then light blue, then darker blue and finally the blackness of space. They are all brilliant colors, more brilliant than in a rainbow, and the band extends out about 60 degrees on either side of the sun. It is a fabulous display. I watched the first sunset through an instrument we call a photometer, which has a polarizing filter mounted on the front of it so you can look directly at the sun without hurting your eyes. I discovered later that it was possible to look directly at the sun without the photometer, just by squinting my eyes, the same as we have always done from here on the surface of the earth. We had thought that perhaps it would be too bright for that above the atmosphere.

I saw a total of four sunsets before the day was over—three during the flight and a final one after I had landed and been picked up by the destroyer. Each time I saw it set, the sun was slightly to my left, and I turned the spacecraft around a little on its yaw axis to get a better view. One thing that interested me was the length of the twilight. The brilliant band of light along the horizon was visible for up to five minutes after the sun went down, which is a long time considering the fact that I was moving away from the sunset and watching it occur at eighteen times the speed at which we normally watch sunsets from down here on earth.

Then the earth was dark; looking down at it was like gazing into a black pit. It was bright again, however, as soon as the moon came up. The moon was almost full. The clouds below

showed up clearly in the moonlight, and I was able to estimate my angle of drift by looking down at the formations far below me.

I was able to see the horizon at night, and this enabled me to correct the attitude of my spacecraft against the horizontal plane of the earth below. I noticed an unexpected effect along the horizon on the nightside. There seemed to be a layer of haze about 2 degrees thick, which hung about 6 to 8 degrees above the real horizon and lay parallel to it. I first noticed this phenomenon over the Indian Ocean as I was watching the stars set. They became dim for a few seconds as they approached the horizon and then they brightened again before they finally went out of sight. I looked carefully, and there seemed to be a definite band of some kind where they dimmed. It was not white like the moonlit clouds, but more tan or buff in color. And it did not have a definite configuration. The only real sign that a layer of some kind was there was that the stars dimmed as they passed through this area and then brightened again. The same phenomenon occurred on all three orbits, and it was most noticeable when the moon was up.

I had thought that I might be able to see more stars than I did. I was prepared to study the various constellations and groupings and count the number of stars in each one to see if I could spot any that we do not normally see clearly from beneath the atmosphere. I did see a whole sky full of stars, and it was a beautiful sight. The effect was much the same as you would have if you went out into a desert on a clear night and looked up. It was not much more than that, however. Laboratory tests of the window made before the flight were correct. The heavy glass in the window provided about the same attenuation that the atmosphere does, and though I saw the stars clearly—and they did not twinkle—I saw about the same number as you would on a clear night from earth. We will probably have to have a new kind of window before we can do much better. I did see a few stars during the day, shining against the black sky. But they were far more clear at night. The stars that I saw at night were of some help in delineating the horizon so I could control the attitude of the capsule. The constellations of Orion and the Pleiades were especially bright, and on one pass over the Indian Ocean I focused on Orion through the center of the window and used it as my only reference for maintaining attitude. All in all, a night in space is a beautiful sight. You see the moon shining bright on the clouds far below you and fields of stars silhouetting the horizon for hundreds of miles in each direction. Just like the sun, the moon and the stars declined and finally set at a speed eighteen times faster from my fast-moving, orbital vantage point than they do for us here on earth.

I saw my first and only signs of man-made light as I came over Australia on my first pass. Looking through the window, I could see several great patches of brightness down below. Gordon Cooper, who was on duty as the Cap Com at the tracking station in Muchea, Australia, had alerted me to look off to the right. He knew that the citizens of Perth and several other cities and towns along the coast had turned on all of the lights they had as a greeting, and when I spotted them I asked him to thank everyone for being so thoughtful. I gave Gordon a reading on fuel, oxygen and amps and told him that the control system was operating in fine shape. I also told him about the haze layer that I had seen, and said that I had the Pleiades in sight as we were talking. Gordon said I should be picking up Orion and Canopus and Sirius very shortly. He also relayed to me the information that the launching had been so near perfect that the orbital velocity was only 8 feet per second under what we had predicted it would be. In other words, it was 25,730 feet per second instead of 25,738 feet per second. When you are dealing with figures like that, worrying about a difference of 8 is like quibbling over one drop of spilled milk out of a barrel.

"That was sure a short day," I said to Gordon.

He didn't hear the remark and asked me to repeat it.

"That was about the shortest day I've ever run into," I said.

He heard me that time, and then we went back to work. Cooper said the surgeons were standing by for a new blood-pressure reading, so I pushed the button and pumped up the cuff. A minute later I was in contact with the Woomera tracking station, which is about halfway across Australia. The Cap

Com there informed me that the Woomera Airport lights were on, and he asked me if I could see them.

"Negative," I said. "There's too much cloud cover in this area. Sorry."

An hour and thirteen minutes after launch I had left Australia behind and was in touch with the Canton Island tracking station, which is about halfway across the Pacific. I decided to have the first of two planned meals here. I pulled a squeeze-tube of applesauce out of its receptacle and parked it out in the air in front of me. Weightless, it stayed put while I opened up the visor on my helmet. Then I squeezed the applesauce into my mouth, and swallowed it without spilling a drop and closed up the visor again. There was no problem. I could see the brilliant blue horizon coming up behind me now; the sunrise was approaching.

The strangest sight of the entire flight came a few seconds later. I was watching the sunrise, which suddenly filled the scope with a brilliant red, and had put a filter onto the scope to cut down the glare. Then I glanced out of the window and looked back towards the dark western horizon. It was a startling sight. All around me, as far as I could see, were thousands and thousands of small, luminous particles. I thought for a minute that I must have drifted upside down and was looking up at a new field of stars. I checked my instruments to make sure that I was right side up. Then I looked again. I was in contact with the Canton Island tracking station at the time, and I tried to tell the Cap Com there what it was like.

"This is Friendship Seven," I began. "I'll try to describe what I'm in here. I am in a big mass of very small particles that are brilliantly lit up like they're luminescent. I never saw anything like it. They're coming by the capsule, and they look like little stars. A whole shower of them coming by. They swirl around the capsule and go in front of the window and they're all brilliantly lighted. They probably average seven or eight feet apart, but I can see them all down below me, also."

The Canton Island Cap Com came on the air and asked if I could hear any impact between the particles and the capsule.

"Negative," I reported. "They're very slow; they're not going away from me more than maybe three or four miles per hour. They're going at the same speed I am approximately. They're only very slightly under my speed. They do have a different motion, though, from me because they swirl around the capsule and then depart back the way I am looking."

The particles seemed to disappear in the glare as soon as the sun came up. But I saw them again under the same conditions on the next orbit. This time, although I was having a few troubles with the capsule, I turned it around 180 degrees in order to look at the particles from another direction. I wanted to see if perhaps they were emanating from the capsule itself. They did not appear to be, however. They were not centered around the capsule but were stretched out as far as I could see. I saw fewer of them this time, because I was looking against the sun. But some of them still came drifting toward me, just as they had done when I first saw them. They were yellowish green in color, and they appeared to vary in size from a pinhead to perhaps three-eighths of an inch. They had the same color, luminous quality and approximate intensity of light as fireflies, and the sensation as I slowly rode through them was like walking backwards through a pasture where someone had waved a wand and made all of the fireflies stop right where they were and glow steadily.

I saw the particles once more on the third orbit, again just as the first rays of the sun appeared over the horizon. They stayed in sight for about four minutes, some of them turning dark as they went into the shadow of the capsule, others swirling up past the window and changing direction as I moved through them. It was a fascinating spectacle, and though various scientists have assumed since that the particles were undoubtedly emanating from the capsule itself, I found this hard to believe. I thought at first that they might be a layer of tiny needles that the Air Force had sent into space on a communications experiment and had then lost. But needles would not have been luminescent— nor was I at the proper altitude. I also thought that they might be tiny snowflakes formed by the condensation of water vapor from the control nozzles. I intentionally blipped the thrusters to see if they gave off particles. They gave off steam, but no particles that I could see. The particles were a mystery at the time, and they have remained one as far as I'm concerned. Our staff psychiatrist, Dr. George Ruff, heard me describe them at one of the debriefings after the flight, and he had only one question: "What did they say, John?" I guess they were as speechless as I was.

Though there was absolutely no connection between the two, I started having trouble with the automatic control system about fifteen minutes after I saw the particles for the first time, just as I was nearing the California coast on the first orbit. The capsule started to stray off to the right on the yaw axis. It would drift about 20 degrees; then the automatic pilot would sense the error and activate the large nozzles to swing it back into line again. The capsule kept cycling back and forth like this, between error and correction, until finally I switched off the ASCS altogether and started to control the capsule manually. There was no danger that this malfunction would move the capsule off course. We were on a predetermined path which had been set when we first went into orbit. But this constant repetition of error meant that the automatic system was using up hydrogen peroxide fuel at an excessive rate as it made each big correction. This would soon deplete the fuel supply unless we took precautions. I decided to remain on fly-by-wire, the system we use to manipulate the automatic thrusters with the manual control stick. There was no question at this point about going on. We were already committed to a second orbit before the control problem cropped up, and I was satisfied that I could keep things under control with the manual and fly-by-wire systems. The problem did mean, however, that I had to cut down on many of the other activities which I planned to carry out during the second and third orbits, for much of my time from now on was spent controlling the capsule. I had to cancel several of the experiments and observations which I wanted to make, including a series of tests of the sun's corona, some measurements of the brightness of the clouds, a second meal—a tube of mashed-up roast beef—and some further tests of a pilot's ability in space to adapt himself to darkness. I was also unable to take as many pictures as I had intended. I had intended putting the capsule

held the package of retro-rockets in place under the heatshield
were attached directly to the capsule. So long as they stayed in
place, they might also help hold the shield against the capsule.
Normally, the retro-package would be jettisoned immediately
after the rockets had been fired, and the straps would go with it.
This would be done so the heatshield would be clean and
smooth and would ablate away up the re-entry heat most
efficiently. Leaving the retro-package in place would spoil this
arrangement. But it might save the shield—and John Glenn.
The Control Center decided that this was the safest course to
follow. It also decided not to burden John Glenn with such a
tremendous cause for worry until it had been able to check on
the problem in greater detail. The tracking stations were in-
formed, however, and were asked to monitor the situation
and to ask John Glenn a few calm questions about the status
of his heatshield as he entered their respective areas.

During much of the second orbit I worked over the control
system, trying to pin down a pattern of errors so I could determine what was wrong and make allowances for it. I could hear
and feel the large thrusters outside of the capsule as they popped
off their bursts of hydrogen peroxide, first in one direction and
then in the other. I could feel the slight throb of the smaller
nozzles when I cut them in. As I was crossing the Atlantic the
second time, the problem I had been having seemed to reverse
itself, and I reported this to the Cap Com on board the Atlantic
ship tracking station.

"At one time," I said, "I had no left low thrust in yaw; now
that one is working and I now have no low right thrust in
yaw. Over."

I confirmed this report over Kano, Nigeria. All of this routine
kept me pretty busy. I had to keep my hands busy with the
controls most of the time, but I thoroughly enjoyed it. The idea
that I was flying this thing myself and proving on our first
orbital flight that a man's capabilities are needed in space was
one of the high spots of the day.

The problems had increased by the time I reached the Indian
Ocean the second time. Something had gone wrong now with

on automatic controls while I concentrated on these other
lems. I believe that we more than made up for the thing
we had to leave out, however, by the fact that the troub
had proved the validity of having a man in space. I was a
intercede and take over when the control system acted up
probable that the capsule would never have completed
orbits or might not have returned to earth at all if a ma
not been aboard to exercise human judgment and contro
the spacecraft machine.

*John Glenn did not know it at the time, but Mercury C
had picked up a much more serious problem as the c
passed over the Canaveral area and headed for its second
The Control Center received a telemetry signal from the c
which indicated that the ablative heatshield on the blun
of the capsule had come loose. The shield is designed to
loose during the final stage of descent towards the ocean
will extend a perforated skirt, designed to hang beneath th
sule as part of an impact bag that takes up some of the
of landing. The shield must remain locked to the capsule
re-entry, for it is the only means of protecting the Astr
from the tremendous heat which builds up outside as th
sule penetrates the atmosphere. John Glenn did not kn
this time that the people on the ground were concerned
of two switches mounted on the base of the capsule had
the status of the locks which hold the shield in place and
signals going directly to the ground had warned that the
was deployed. John did not have the same indicator
capsule. This caused a good deal of concern in the C
Center, to say the least. Telephone calls were put throug
mediately over open circuits to the McDonnell factory
Louis, and engineers pored over all of their wiring diagram
specifications trying to determine what might be wrong.
knew it was possible that the switch itself was faulty an
it had sent an erroneous signal. It was also possible, ho
that the signal was correct. If this was true, John Glenn
for an uncomfortable and perhaps tragic ride to earth.
was one possible way out, however. Heavy metal straps*

the ASCS indicators, and the various attitudes of yaw, pitch, and roll which the instruments presented did not jibe at all with what I could see just by looking out of the window. The Cap Com on the Indian Ocean ship asked me if I had noticed any constellations yet. I answered that I was too busy paying attention to the control system to identify any stars. He also gave me my first clue that something might be wrong with the heatshield.

"We have message from MCC" (Mercury Control Center), he said, "for you to keep your landing bag switch in OFF position, landing bag switch in OFF position. Over."

I rogered for the transmission, and I thought right away that the ground must be getting some peculiar indications. I was to get a better inkling of what was going on about seven minutes later when I checked in with Gordon Cooper in Australia.

"Will you confirm the landing bag switch is in the OFF position? Over," said Cooper.

"That is affirmative," I said. "Landing bag switch is in the center OFF position."

"You haven't had any banging noises or anything of this type at higher rates?" Cooper asked.

"Negative," I said.

It was clear to me now that the people down on the ground were really concerned or they would not be asking such leading questions. I was fairly certain, however, that everything was in good shape. It occurred to me that if the heatshield were really loose, I would almost certainly have been able to hear or feel it shaking behind me or banging against the edge of the capsule as we drifted back and forth on those large deviations in yaw. I had heard nothing. Still, there was room for concern. The heatshield is made up of a thick coating of resinous material which is designed to dissipate most of the heat and energy picked up during re-entry and get it out of the capsule's system by melting and boiling away very slowly. This was the only thing that stood between me and disaster as we came through the atmosphere. If it was not tightly in place, we could be in real trouble.

I was having a few other minor problems along about this

time. I had two warning lights shining on the panel. One showed an excess of water in the cabin environmental control system. This could mean that not all of the water was turning into steam and popping off outside through the outlet valve as it was supposed to. The danger was that the water which did not bleed off as steam could freeze up the outlet valve and clog the system. I turned down the volume of water which was running through the system, and this had the proper effect. The light would come on again every time I tried to increase the water flow substantially. The system never did clog up, however. The other warning light showed that we had used up more fuel than we should have at this point in the automatic control system. Considering all of the erratic control maneuvers which the system had been making, this was not surprising. We still had plenty of fuel left, however. The light is designed to flash on when you have 65 percent of your supply remaining in the tank, simply to make you pay attention to the problem. Another problem was that the supply of oxygen in the secondary tank started to decline even though I was not using it. The people on the ground picked this up by telemetry and asked me at one point how much of this supply I had been using. I told them I had not touched it. There must have been a leak somewhere in the system, but fortunately I did not need to draw on this supply, so it was not a serious matter. It could have been, however, and the technicians went over the system with a fine-tooth comb when they got the capsule back. It was a fault we would want to repair before any future flights.

As I passed over Canton Island on the second orbit, I saw the particles again. I tried to photograph them, but apparently there was not enough light for the color film and none of the pictures came out. The heatshield problem came up again as I was putting the camera away. The Cap Com at Canton Island put it this way: "We also have no indication that your landing bag might be deployed. Over."

I asked if someone else had reported that it could be down, and he said, "Negative. We had a request to monitor this and to ask you if you heard any flapping."

"Negative," I said. I was still not overly concerned because I had had no indication in the capsule that anything was wrong. Looking back on the whole event, I realize that the controllers were trying to keep me from being worried about the situation. I really don't think, however, that you ought to keep the pilot in the dark, especially if you believe he might be in real trouble. It is the pilot's job to be as ready for emergencies as anyone else, if not more so. And he can hardly be fully prepared if he is not being kept fully informed. On future space flights, when the spacecraft and its crew will get thousands of miles from earth, some of the apron strings will have to be cut. On this flight, of course, it was the first time that the man had been that far away from home, and the entire family was naturally concerned.

I did have some doubts along about this time as to whether we would go for a third orbit. The automatic controls were misbehaving; the manual controls that I relied on most had become a little mushy—at least, they were not as crisp as they had been. With the problems we were having, I was concerned that perhaps the people down on the ground might prefer for me to come on home. I sincerely hoped not. There was nothing to be concerned about unless the problem got significantly worse. We were still in good shape and I felt that if it was going to be necessary for me to bring the capsule back myself, I might as well have another 90 minutes of practice at the controls. The people on the ground apparently felt the same way. I was very happy when Mercury Control recommended that I go for the third orbit. We talked about it as I passed over Hawaii, and I concurred 100 percent. As I crossed California, Wally Schirra gave me the temperatures on the inverters which the ground stations had picked up by telemetry. The inverter on the fans was 215 degrees and the ASCS inverter was 198 degrees. These were both a little high, but Wally said they recommended that I not do anything about it. We had discovered in recent tests that the inverter could stand more heat than we had originally anticipated. "It looks real good," Wally said. He also informed me that my elapsed-time clock was running about a second slow. Since this would effect the sequence time for firing the retros, he gave me a new reading and told me to subtract one second from the other readings that I had already jotted down in order to compensate for the error in the clock. We would actually reset the clock in another four or five minutes, he said, when I checked in with Al Shepard over Cape Canaveral.

Al then told me to reset the clock manually so that it read 04:32:38. This meant that the retro-rockets would start firing 4 hours, 32 minutes and 38 seconds after launch. This would be in another hour and 24 minutes. As I was talking to Al I could look down and see the entire state of Florida and clear back to the delta of the Mississippi River around New Orleans. This was the best view I had had of the United States. There was a cloud deck to the north, but I could see as far north as North Carolina. To the south I spotted islands east of Cuba. I looked out over the Atlantic to check the recovery area where I would be landing the next time around. There were a few scattered clouds but no sign of a major weather system. The sea seemed to be placid, though it was so far below me I could not really tell. I had noticed the wake of a ship on a previous pass over the Atlantic, and I assumed it might have been one of the three aircraft carriers, standing by waiting to launch helicopters to pick me up.

Gus Grissom and I had a brief chat as I passed over his Bermuda station for the last time. I told him about the view I had and that it looked good in the recovery area. "Very good," Gus said. "We'll see you in Grand Turk."

"Yes, sir," I answered. This was the last lap and I felt that we had things well under control. Gus relayed a message from the Cape that they recommended I use the automatic control system during re-entry and back it up with the manual controls. I pointed out that the ASCS had been very erratic and that I had not been able to pin it down to any particular item. It had gone wrong in pitch, yaw and roll. I was going to reserve that decision until closer to retro-fire time. Gus said they had recorded this information and asked me to read off the oxygen supply. I still had 62 percent left in the primary tank and 94 percent left in the secondary tank. We had lost 6 percent from the secondary tank without even tapping it, but this was no problem since I had not needed it anyway.

The Cap Com asked me, as I passed over the Canary Island

station for the last time, if I was still seeing those particles I had talked about. Apparently everyone was fascinated by this phenomenon. I told him that I had seen a few just after I left Canaveral, and that I knew they were not coming from the capsule because they were moving toward me. The aeromed surgeon at the Canary Station came on to ask me again if I had experienced any nausea. I told him that I had not, and that I had felt perfectly normal during the entire flight. "I feel fine," I said.

A few seconds later the Atlantic Ocean tracking ship contacted me. I gave them another reading on fuel, oxygen and amps. We were down to 64 percent on the manual control system now and to 54 percent on the automatic system. The gauge showed that we still had 62 percent of the oxygen left in the primary tank and 94 percent in the secondary. The amperes stood at 23. Then I gave the ship a long message describing the status of the attitude control system and asked the Cap Com on the ship to pass it along to Cape Canaveral. I told him that I had let the capsule drift 180 degrees off center, in order to see what would happen, and was now trying to reorient it again.

"When I am all lined up with the horizon and the periscope," I explained, "my attitude indications on the instrument panel are way off. My roll indicates thirty degrees right; my yaw indicates thirty-five degrees right; and pitch indicates plus forty degrees. I repeat, plus forty when I am in orbit attitude." Roll and yaw should have been zero, and pitch should have read minus 34 degrees. This meant that the gyros in the autopilot were not keeping up with the actual attitude of the capsule and were giving me misleading information. The situation was not serious at the moment. So long as I could see the horizon outside and line the capsule up against it by myself, I knew that I could keep it properly aligned. It did mean, however, that I could not trust the ASCS to control the capsule while I attended to other matters. I would have to control it accurately myself or we might not be in the correct attitude when it came time to fire the retros. The capsule's attitude would have to be near-perfect when the rockets fired, or the angle of re-entry would be affected. If we were too far off at that moment, I might have trouble getting down.

I turned the capsule to the left a little on the yaw axis as I crossed the Atlantic in order to get a better view of my third sunset of the day. I described the sight to the Atlantic Ocean tracking ship and said that I could see a very orange band along the horizon, then a lighter yellow on top of that, followed by a very deep blue, a very light blue and then the black sky. I also reported that it was not too easy to see anything through the window when I was looking towards the sun. It appeared, I said, as if "we might have smashed some bugs on the way up off the pad. Looks like blood on the outside of the window." There was no attendant around to wash this windshield.

As I passed the tip of Africa and started over the Indian Ocean I could see a huge storm front stretching out beneath me as far as I could see. It was dark now, and the ocean itself was covered with a thick layer of clouds. But I could see bright flashes of lightning inside the clouds. The weather people had wondered whether I would be able to see lightning from such a high altitude. The flashes showed up brilliantly, like flashbulbs being popped off behind a white sheet. Each flash lit up an entire bank of clouds. I reported this to the Zanzibar tracking station as I passed near it for the last time. I did not see any of Africa on this pass; the third orbit took me further south than I had gone before and the entire area was dark and cloudy.

Three hours, 59 minutes and 15 seconds after launch, I was in contact once more with Gordon Cooper at the Muchea station in Australia. We chatted briefly about the troubles I was having—the ASCS was still not functioning properly. But I told him I was still able to correct the errors with the manual system, and I felt in fine shape. I asked him to send a message to General David Shoup, the commandant of the U.S. Marine Corps.

"This is Friendship Seven," I told Gordon over the radio. "In forty-five seconds I would like to have you send a message for me, please. I want you to send a message to the commandant, U.S. Marine Corps, Washington. Tell him I have my four hours required flight time in for the month and request flight chit be established for me. Over."

"Roger," Cooper answered. "Will do. Think they'll pay it?"

"I don't know," I said. "Gonna find out."

"Roger," said Cooper. "Is this flying time or rocket time?"

"Lighter than air," I answered.

Gordon and I then discussed the various readings on my instrument panel and the positions of all the switches. The temperature inside the suit at this point was 70 degrees Fahrenheit. The cabin temperature was 90 degrees. The pressure inside the suit was 5.8 pounds per square inch. The cabin pressure was holding at 5.5 psi. The amps stood at 24. I had 60 percent of the oxygen left in the main tank, 90 percent in the secondary tank—which meant that it was still leaking. The relative humidity in the cabin was 36 percent. The temperature on the ASCS inverter was 115 degrees. The fan inverter was 110 degrees. All of the warning lights were out except the fuel quantity light, and I had turned off the audio warning signal on this light to cut down on the noise level. I told Cooper that if the ASCS did not respond I would stay on manual control throughout the retro sequence.

I started to stow the loose equipment away as I checked in with the Canton Island station for the last time, so that nothing would get in my way during the re-entry phase. A few minutes later I was over the Hawaii tracking station and gave the gauge readings to the Cap Com there. I had 43 percent fuel remaining in the automatic system, 45 percent in the manual system. The oxygen supply was still 60 percent and 90 percent. The amps stood at 23. Then the Cap Com asked me another leading question about the heatshield.

"Friendship Seven," he said, "we have been reading an indication on the ground of segment 5-1, which is landing-bag deploy. We suspect this is an erroneous signal. However, Cape would like you to check this by putting the landing-bag switch in auto position and see if you get a light. Do you concur with this? Over." I thought that one over for a few seconds.

"O.K.," I answered, "If that's what they recommend, we'll go ahead and try it. Are you ready for it now?"

"Yes," the Cap Com said, "when you're ready."

This was a rather tricky thing to do, and I was a little reluctant to try it. The idea was that if I turned my landing-bag deploy switch to the automatic position and the light on my instrument panel turned green, this would indicate that the shield had indeed deployed on its own and that it was loose. At least, we would know. I was slightly concerned about the reverse side of this coin, however. What if the shield had not deployed but, because the system was malfunctioning, would decide to do just that when I switched it to automatic? Then we would have jumped from the frying pan into the fire. I knew that personnel at the Cape would never make such a recommendation without considering all the aspects of the problem carefully, so I went ahead and rapidly turned the switch on and off again. The light did not come on. This was a pretty good indication to me that we were in good shape. The Hawaii Cap Com seemed to think so, too, for he rogered for my message and said, "That's fine. In this case, we'll go ahead, and the re-entry sequence will be normal."

As it turned out, he was a bit premature. I received different instructions a little later on, and the re-entry sequence was not normal at all. The Hawaii Cap Com also instructed me to change the retro clock again by one second. Apparently we had gone just a wee bit faster than our original predictions, and we lopped one more second off the elapsed time to make it 4 hours, 32 minutes and 37 seconds. This was a total change of 2 seconds on the clock during the entire trip, which was not bad at all on an orbital mission which lasted 16,357 seconds from launch to retro-fire. The flight surgeon at the Hawaii station asked me if I was still comfortable. I told him that I was in very good shape. A light on my instrument panel went on to signal that I had exactly 5 minutes left before retro-fire, and the Hawaii Cap Com started to give me a time hack based on Greenwich Mean Time so that I could double-check the schedule. Our communications faded out, however, just before we could complete this important transmission, and I was a little uncertain about exactly when the retro-rockets should be fired. From what I thought I had heard, there seemed to be a small discrepancy between my time and the time they had computed on the ground, and this bothered me. The timing had to be precise, since at my orbital speed of 5 miles per second an error of a single second would mean a dispersion of 5 miles in the impact area. I tried to call Wally Schirra, who was standing by at the Point Arguello station in California, but it took about a minute and a half before we had good communication. It seemed quite a bit longer at the time. By the time I finally got through to Wally and explained the timing discrepancy to him, I had only 50 seconds left before the retro sequence was due to start. Wally worked fast and confirmed the timing. We had 45 seconds to go, he said. I told him that I was on ASCS, which was working well at this point, and backing it up with the manual system. Wally rogered for this message and said that I had 30 seconds to go before the retro sequence began. I rogered for this and told him that my 30-second retro-warning light was on. Then, for the next couple of minutes, while I went through the most critical phase of the entire flight, Wally and I kept up a fairly constant exchange of messages. They went like this:

SCHIRRA: John, leave your retro-pack on through your pass over Texas. Do you read?
GLENN: Roger.
SCHIRRA: Fifteen seconds to sequence.
GLENN: Roger.
SCHIRRA: Ten.
SCHIRRA: Five, four, three, two, one, mark.
GLENN: Roger. Retro sequence is green. (*There was a 30-second built-in delay here.*)
SCHIRRA: You have a green. You look good on attitude.
GLENN: Retro attitude is green.
SCHIRRA: Just past twenty.
GLENN: Say again.
SCHIRRA: Seconds.
GLENN: Roger.
SCHIRRA: Five, four, three, two, one, fire.
GLENN: Roger, retros are firing.
SCHIRRA: Sure, they be.

GLENN: Are they ever. It feels like I'm going back towards Hawaii.

SCHIRRA: Don't do that. You want to go to the East Coast.

GLENN: Roger. Fire retro-light is green.

SCHIRRA: All three here. (*Meaning that Schirra could see telemetry indications that all three rockets had fired on schedule.*)

GLENN: Roger. Retros have stopped.

SCHIRRA: Keep your retro-pack on until you pass Texas.

GLENN: That's affirmative.

SCHIRRA: Check.

SCHIRRA: Pretty good flight from all we've seen.

GLENN: Roger. Everything went pretty good except for all this ASCS problem.

SCHIRRA: It looked like your attitude held pretty well. Did you have to back it up at all?

GLENN: Oh, yes, quite a bit. Yeah, I had a lot of trouble with it. (*He was referring here to the general behavior of the ASCS during the flight and not just to the retro-fire sequence when the ASCS was working well.*)

SCHIRRA: Good enough for government work from down here.

GLENN: Yes, sir, it looks good, Wally. We'll see you back East.

SCHIRRA: Rog.

GLENN: All right, boy.

GLENN: Fire retro is green.

SCHIRRA: Roger.

GLENN: Jettison retro is red. I'm holding onto it.

SCHIRRA: Good head.

GLENN: I'll tell you, there is no doubt about it when the retros fire.

The three retro-rockets had fired on schedule at five-second intervals. Each one gave me a very solid push, and since I was weightless at the time and they were firing forward, against the direction of the flight, I had the distinct sensation of accelerating back in the direction I had come from. Actually, the rockets were only slowing me down by about 500 feet per second.

Both Al Shepard and Gus Grissom had experienced the same sensation when they tested out the retros on their flights, and I was prepared for it. The firing of the rockets caused some motion of the capsule, but since I was using both the automatic and manual control systems together, I maintained the proper attitude during retro-firing and then realigned Friendship 7 for its descent through the atmosphere.

Approximately 5 minutes after the retro-rockets fired, I came into radio contact with the tracking station in Texas. I had rather hoped that by this time the people on the ground could tell me to go ahead and jettison the retro-pack. We did not know exactly what effect the retro-pack might have on the even distribution of heat over the shield. It was just possible that it might cause hot spots to break out and damage the shield before we had completed re-entry. Holding onto the pack would also upset the normal chain of events which the capsule was supposed to perform automatically. The wiring was so arranged, for example, that if the retro-pack did not drop, the circuits which were normally set in motion by this event would fail to retract the periscope automatically and close the door behind it to keep out the heat. They would also not be in a position to respond to a special switch which is thrown automatically when the G forces of re-entry reach .05 G, at which time other automatic sequences start for various events involved in the landing maneuver. All of this was supposed to be done automatically, but, for safety reasons, it all hinged on the jettisoning of the retro-pack. If the pack was not jettisoned automatically, I would activate these other functions as well. I was prepared to do all of this, of course, but it was not the way we had planned it; and since any deviation from the standard procedure always leaves a certain amount of room for doubt and suspense, I frankly hoped that we could make a normal descent. I was somewhat concerned, therefore, when the Texas Cap Com sent me the following transmission 17 minutes before I was due to land:

"This is Texas Cap Com, Friendship Seven," he said. "We are recommending that you leave the retro-package on through the entire re-entry. This means that you will have to override the .05 G switch which is expected to occur at 04:43:53. This also means that you will have to manually retract the scope. Do you read?"

"This is Friendship Seven," I said. "What is the reason for this? Do you have any reason? Over."

"Not at this time," the Cap Com answered. "This is the judgment of Cape Flight. . . . Cape Flight will give you the reasons for this action when you are in view."

Some 30 seconds later I came within range of the Control Center at the Cape and heard Al Shepard's voice over the radio.

"Recommend that you go to re-entry attitude and retract the scope manually at this time," Al said.

"Roger," I said. "Retracting scope manually." I reached down for the handle and began to pump the scope in. It came all the way, and the door closed tightly behind it.

"While you are doing that," Al said—and here I finally learned for certain what the problem was—"we are not sure whether or not your landing bag has deployed. We feel it is possible to re-enter with the retro-package on. We see no difficulty at this time in that type of re-entry. Over."

"Roger," I said. "Understand."

"Estimating .05 G at 04:44," Al added.

It was now 04:41, or 4 hours and 41 minutes after launch. In another few minutes, I would be in the middle of the hottest part of my ride. The automatic control system had been acting up again—drifting off center and then kicking itself back into line again—so I was now controlling almost completely by the manual stick. The fuel in the manual system was running low, however—the gauge read that I had only about 15 percent left in the tank. So I switched to fly-by-wire in order to draw on what fuel was left in the automatic system. I was still controlling manually, however, since this was the advantage that the fly-by-wire system provided. I used the manual stick; the nozzles that I activated and the fuel that I expended belonged to the automatic system.

During the final descent through the atmosphere, the blunt nose of the capsule had to be kept pointed so that the heatshield would hit the particles of the atmosphere first. If the capsule were not properly aligned, some of the intense heat could spill over the edge of the shield and flow back along the sides of the capsule, which are not nearly so well protected against the extreme temperatures building up during re-entry. In addition, the capsule might start to oscillate quite a bit as it was buffeted by the atmosphere. That is, it would sway back and forth. This could also let some of the heat impinge on the side of the capsule. As I have said before, it was not the kind of re-entry that we had hoped for. But we had included all of these eventualities in our training, and I was set. It was going to be an interesting few minutes, however.

As we started to heat up on re-entry, I could feel something let go on the blunt end of the capsule behind me. There was a considerable thump, and I felt sure it was the retro-pack breaking away. I made a transmission to Al Shepard to this effect, but he apparently did not hear me. By this time, the capsule was so hot that a barrier of ionization had built up around it and cut off all communications between me and the people on the ground. This was normal, and I had expected it to happen, but it left me more or less alone with my little problem.

Just 24 seconds before John Glenn made this transmission, Al Shepard had started to recommend to Glenn that he jettison the retro-pack as soon as the Gs built up to 1 or 1.5. Glenn did not receive the message, however. The communications blackout had already set in.

I saw one of the three metal straps that hold the retro-pack in place start to flap around loose in front of the window. Then I began to see a bright orange glow building up around the capsule. "A real fireball outside," I said into the microphone. The loose strap burned off at this point and dropped away. Just at that moment I could see big flaming chunks go flying by the window. Some of them were as big as 6 to 8 inches across. I could hear them bump against the capsule behind me before they took off, and I thought that the heatshield might be tearing apart. As it turned out later, these were parts of the retro-pack breaking up. It had not fallen away after all, and the heatshield itself was coming through in perfect shape. This was a bad moment. But I knew that if the worst was really happening it would all be over shortly and there was nothing I could do about it. So I kept on with what I had been doing—trying to keep the capsule under control—and sweated it out.

I knew that if the shield was falling apart, I would feel the heat pulse first at my back, and I waited for it. I kept on controlling the capsule. It was programed to do a slow, steady spin on its roll axis at the rate of 10 degrees per second. The purpose of this maneuver was to equalize the aerodynamic flow around the capsule and to keep it from exceeding the limits that we had estimated were maximum for re-entry. The automatic control system was normally supposed to handle this procedure but I kept control with the manual stick and did it myself. Pieces of flaming material were still flying past the window during this period, and the glow outside was still bright and orange. It lasted for only about a minute, but those few moments ticked off inside the capsule like days on a calendar. I still waited for the heat, and I made several attempts to contact the Control Center and keep them informed.

"Hello, Cape. Friendship Seven. Over. Hello, Cape, Friendship Seven. How do you receive? Over." There was no answer.

Down in the Control Center at this point, the men at the consoles were definitely worried. They were still tracking the capsule's descent on radar and they knew where it was and that it still seemed to be intact. But they were deeply concerned over the fate of the heatshield—and of John Glenn. They knew from previous tests that the temperature of the shield would be about 3000 degrees Fahrenheit. The temperature of the heat pulse which had built up around the capsule would stand at about 9500 degrees Fahrenheit—or slightly less than the temperature of the sun itself. The combination of this concern plus the absolute silence in their headsets was almost unbearable. The communications blackout lasted for 4 minutes and 20 seconds. Here, too, the seconds passed "like days on a calendar." Someone behind Commander Shepard's console said,

"Keep talking, Al." Shepard spoke once more into the micro-
phone anchored in front of his lips.

"Seven, this is Cape," he said. "How do you read? Over."

This time John Glenn heard the transmission. It was 4
hours, 47 minutes and 11 seconds after launch, with 7 minutes
and 45 seconds to go before Glenn's capsule was to hit the
water.

"Loud and clear," I said. "How me?"

Al's voice really sounded welcome when it finally came
through.

"Roger," Al said, cool as ever. "Reading you loud and clear.
How are you doing?"

"Oh, pretty good," I said.

The heat had never come. Instead, the high temperature
pulse began to simmer down and the glow gradually disappeared.
The Gs built up to a peak of about 8 now, but they were no
problem. Al informed me that they had worked out my impact
point in the recovery area and that I should be landing within
one mile of one of the destroyers.

"My condition is good," I said, "but that was a real fireball,
boy."

Twelve seconds after this transmission I reported that the
altimeter read 80,000 feet. Nineteen seconds later we were at
55,000 feet. The capsule was rocking and swaying quite a bit at
this point, and I was having trouble controlling it. We were almost completely out of fuel in both control systems by now.
But, even if I had had sufficient fuel, we were now so far into the
thick atmosphere that the control nozzles would not have had
much effect on the capsule's movement. I decided to deploy the
small drogue chute a few moments before it was due to come
out, and damp the oscillations that way. The capsule beat me to
it, however. I was just reaching for the switch to override the
automatic timer when the drogue chute broke out on its own.
I could feel the thud of the mortar which launched it. The
window was covered now with a thin layer of melted resin that
had streamed back from the heatshield. However, I could still
see the drogue open up at 30,000 feet. This was about 9000

feet higher than where we would normally break it out. The chute held, and the capsule began to settle down into a much smoother descent. The swaying was cut sharply. I had to pump the periscope out by hand since we had interrupted the automatic sequence. At about 20,000 feet, the snorkels opened up to let in outside air. At 10,600 feet, a barometric switch started the landing sequence. Through the periscope and the coated window, I saw a marvelous chain reaction set in. I watched the antenna canister—which housed the chute—detach. It dragged the main chute along behind it, still wrapped up inside its bag. When the shrouds of the chute had stretched out to their full length, the bag peeled off and left the chute, still in a reefed condition, trailing out like a long ribbon straight above me. Then, when the chute was partially full of air and had found its proper position, the reefing lines broke away and the huge orange and white canopy blossomed out, pulsed several times and was steady. I could feel the jolt in the cabin as we slowed. From the indications of the instruments we seemed to be dropping a few feet per second faster than I thought we should. But I studied the chute closely through the periscope and window, and it appeared to be in such perfect shape, with no rips or holes in it, that I decided not to use the reserve chute which was still packed away in the roof of the capsule and available if I needed it. It was a moment of solid satisfaction. As I told Al over the radio—with a real trace of relief and some excitement in my voice, I guess—it was a "beautiful chute." It was a wonderful sight to see that good chute open up.

I was descending now at the rate of 42 feet per second and had 5 minutes and 10 seconds left before impact. I contacted the destroyer *Noa*, which had the code name of "Steelhead," and told the skipper that my condition was good but that it was a little hot inside the capsule. He informed me that he had picked up on his radar the chaff which the main chute had kicked out and that he was heading in my direction. He estimated that it would take him about an hour to get on station.

I started to run down the checklist of landing procedures. I unfastened from my pants leg the plug which connected the biomedical sensors. I removed the blood-pressure equipment

from the suit, loosened the chest strap and got it free, un-
hooked the respiration sensor from my lip mike and stuffed it
inside my suit, disconnected the oxygen exhaust hose from the
helmet and unstowed the survival pack that I had to the left of
my couch and kept it handy in case of an emergency. Al Shepard got on the radio at this point to make sure that my landing-
bag light was on green so that it would deploy and take up the
shock of landing.

"That's affirmative," I said. "Landing bag is on green."

Then Al came on again to recommend that I remain in the
capsule unless I had "an overriding reason for getting out." He
knew that the destroyer was only about 6 miles from where I
would land and that instead of using helicopters to pick me up
as we had planned, I would have to be hoisted aboard by the
destroyer. It would be simpler in this case if I stayed shut up
inside so we would not take any chance on losing the capsule.
We had rehearsed this method of recovery as well as the heli-
copter method, so I was prepared for either one and I rogered
for his message. I kept up a running account now of my approach
to the water so that everyone on the network would know my
status.

"Friendship Seven," I said, 48 seconds before I hit. "Ready
for impact; almost down."

Fifteen seconds later: "Friendship Seven. Getting close.
Standing by."

Twenty seconds later: "Here we go."

Ten seconds after that: "Friendship Seven. Impact. Rescue
Aids is manual."

I pushed the button which started the flashing light on top of
the capsule and the automatic radio signals which would help
the recovery force home in on my position.

The capsule hit the ocean with a good solid bump, and went
far enough under water to submerge both the periscope and the
window. I could hear gurgling sounds almost immediately. After
it listed over to the right and then to the left, the capsule righted
itself and I could find no traces of any leaks. I undid the seat
strap now and the shoulder harness, disconnected my helmet and
put up my neck dam so I could not get water inside my suit

if I had to get into the ocean. I was sweating profusely and was very uncomfortable. I kept the suit fans going, but they did not help much. The snorkels in the capsule wall were pumping in outside air, but it was extremely humid outside and this did not help to cool me off one bit, either. I thought about removing the lid of the capsule and climbing on out. But I decided against it. I knew that any body movement would only generate more heat and make me even warmer. The thing to do was sit tight, stay motionless and try to keep as cool as possible.

"Steelhead" kept up a running commentary on how she was doing. First, she was 4 minutes away, then she slowed down and was 3 minutes away; then her engines were stopped and she was coming alongside. The capsule window was so clogged now with both resin and sea water that I could not see her. Strangely enough, however, the capsule bobbed around in the water until the periscope was pointing directly at the destroyer, and it kept her in view from then on. I could read her number—841— and I could see so many sailors in white uniforms standing on the deck that I asked the captain if he had anybody down below running the ship. He assured me he did. Then he drifted alongside very slowly until we gently bumped into each other.

Two sailors reached over with a shepherd's hook to snag the capsule, and moments later we were on deck. I started to crawl through the top to avoid blowing the side hatch and jiggling the instruments inside the capsule. I was still so uncomfortably hot, however, that I decided there was no point in going out the hard way. After warning the deck crew to stand clear, and receiving clearance that all of the men were out of the way, I hit the handle which blew the hatch. I got my only wound of the day doing it—two skinned knuckles on my right hand where the plunger snapped back into place after I reached back to hit it. Then I climbed out on deck. I was back with people again.